D0876556

Twenty-nine years on from his release from prison, Leaf Fielding has been a teacher in Spain and a philanthropist, setting up a home for orphans in Malawi. He now sells organic produce in the south of France where he lives.

To Live Outside the Law

A memoir

Leaf Fielding

To Steve —
with thanks!

"October Song" by Robin Williamson
© 1967 Warner-Tamerlane Publishing Corp. (BMI)
All rights administered by Warner/Chappell North America Ltd
All rights reserved

A complete catalogue record for this book can be obtained
from the British Library on request

The right of Leaf Fielding to be identified as the author of this work has been
asserted by him in accordance with the Copyright, Designs and Patents Act 1988

Copyright © 2011 Leaf Fielding

All rights reserved. No part of this book may be reproduced, stored in a retrieval
system or transmitted in any form or by any means, electronic, mechanical,
photocopying, recording or otherwise, without the prior permission of the
publisher.

First published in 2011 by Serpent's Tail,
an imprint of Profile Books Ltd
3A Exmouth House
Pine Street
London EC1R 0JH
website: www.serpentstail.com

ISBN 978 1 84668 796 9
eISBN 978 1 84765 761 9

Designed and typeset by sue@lambledesign.demon.co.uk
Printed and bound in Britain by Clays, Bungay, Suffolk

10 9 8 7 6 5 4 3 2 1

Mixed Sources
Product group from well-managed
forests and other controlled sources
www.fsc.org Cert no. TT-COC-002227
© 1996 Forest Stewardship Council

FSC

The paper this book is printed on is certified by the
© 1996 Forest Stewardship Council A.C. (FSC).
It is ancient-forest friendly. The printer holds FSC
chain of custody SGS-COC-2061

I dedicate this book to Sue,
my fiercest critic
and principal supporter

Anybody who sets out to turn the world upside down has no right to complain if he gets caught in its gears.

Frederik Pohl and C. M. Kornbluth, *The Space Merchants*

Contents

1   *Operation Julie*

26 March 1977

I WOKE WITH A START. The light of a torch lanced the darkness and settled on my face. I raised my hand to shield my eyes and was pinned to the bed by an octopus, hands everywhere.

'Got him!' a voice yelled triumphantly.

'Give us some fucking light! Let's have a look at what we've caught.'

The light came on. Through the spread fingers over my face, I could see I was being held down by several men.

'What are you doing?' This was my worst nightmare come true. I tried to turn my head to see what was happening to Mary, but my hair was gripped tightly and I couldn't move an inch. 'Let go!' I yelled.

'Shut up, cunt,' someone hissed in my ear. 'Right then, lads. Let's be having him.'

They hauled me from the bed and stood me on my feet. Only two were holding me now. The other three stood in front of me, bristling. One of them had drawn a gun. Mary was hiding below the duvet. A grim-looking woman stood at her side of the bed. The stink of sweat and adrenalin hung heavy in the air. The guy on the left, a big unshaven bruiser in a red sweater and jeans, stared hard at me. Triumph and loathing struggled for the upper hand in his expression. Van Gogh's *Sunflowers* peeked incongruously over his shoulder. Without taking his eyes from mine, red sweater barked, 'Get him his fucking pants and take him below!'

My arms were released so I could take the Y-fronts that were thrust at me. When I'd put them on, I was grabbed and frogmarched out of the room and down the stairs.

We were in Mid-Wales, spending the weekend with our friends, Russ and Jan. A dozen men in sweaters and jeans were engaged in ransacking their house. Several uniformed police stood around watching. A scruffy longhair with a gun guarded the door. I was pushed in front of an older man in a sheepskin coat who stood apart. He cautioned me and asked if I had anything to say.

I stood, fur-tongued and thick-headed. It was dark outside. I looked at the clock on the mantelpiece. Just after five. We'd gone to bed three hours before, full of curry and wine. My head was pounding. I felt as though I might throw up at any moment. Suddenly I desperately needed a shit.

'I've got to go to the toilet.'

'All right.' The boss turned to my escort. 'Watch him! Don't let him close the door. Don't take your eyes off him for one moment.'

I lingered on the pan, trying to get my broken brain to work. Three days ago I'd laid a hundred and twelve thousand hits of LSD on Russ. He was supposed to be passing it straight on. Had he moved it all? Were we stuffed or might we have a chance to get clear?

'Hurry up! There's another one here needs the crapper.'

I washed my hands and splashed cold water on my face, trying to wake myself up. Please let this be a nightmare, I implored the god of events. But it wasn't a dream, it had the stink of reality. As I left the toilet, Russ stumbled in. He looked as bad as I felt. I was handed my clothes and glasses and sent to join Mary, who was dressed, sitting on the sofa and looking at the floor.

'I'm so sorry, honey,' I said, pulling on my trousers.

'Shut up!' my guard shouted. 'No talking.'

Mary's long blonde hair was falling over her face, hiding her expression. I sat down and took her hand. Soon we were joined by Russ and Jan. Two uniformed police were detailed to watch us.

'What's going on, Megan?' Jan asked the policewoman.

'I can't say, Jan,' Megan replied, in a strong Welsh accent. 'Sorry love, but we're under instructions. You're not allowed to talk.'

The searchers were swarming all over the house, emptying drawers and cupboards, dismantling anything that came apart. The absence of speech was eerie. Everything was being put into tagged plastic bags. My heart sank as I watched them methodically gut Russ's home.

'What are you doing?' Jan shouted across to the man in the sheepskin coat. She was close to hysteria. 'You can't treat us like this! I'm expecting a baby…'

While Megan and the constable were trying to calm Jan down, I whispered to Russ.

'You clean?'

He nodded.

'Good. Say nothing. We'll be fine.'

'Hey!' the armed hippie on the door screamed at our guards. 'Stop those buggers talking. Keep them quiet or you'll be left out in the rain! Got it?'

'Yessir,' muttered the local bobby.

I sat on the sofa, my arm around Mary's shoulder, feeling worse by the minute. Attempting to ward off the sense of hopelessness that was washing over me was like trying to stop the tide. As the plain-clothes men systematically took apart Russ and Jan's home, I felt my life disintegrating. The police ignored us completely. 'We've got you,' their silence shouted. 'Now we're just collecting the evidence.'

Jan started to cry. Megan began weeping too. The police-woman's tears completely undermined me; I wanted to join in.

'Fielding!'

I looked up at the sound of my name. Two coppers led me to the kitchen. Red sweater put a handcuff on my left wrist and tightened it with a series of clicks. He attached the other end to his right hand.

'Come on. Let's go,' he said, tugging at the cuffs. Metal handcuffs cutting at the wrist bone; that's the feel of being a prisoner.

'What's going on?' I asked red sweater as we drove south towards Carmarthen. It was as if I hadn't spoken. I tried again. 'Where are we heading?'

Neither he nor the driver would reply to my questions. I gave up and looked out the window at the early signs of the spring – a spring I suddenly realised I was going to miss. The thought stung like acid thrown in my face. My eyes were smarting, but I didn't want them to see me cry.

In silence we crossed the Severn Bridge and headed east down the M4. I looked sightlessly out of the window while a crowd of questions assailed my mind. How long would they hold Mary for? What could I possibly say the next time I saw her? When would that be? Then I began worrying about how Russ was going to cope with the questioning. And how would I manage? Why had I been taken off alone? Had they got any of the others? I clung to the hope that they hadn't.

It hit me that this was going to be a terrible blow to my dad. Though retired from the army, he was still working in Whitehall. I'd embarrassed him several times before, but nothing to compare with this. He thought my wild hippy days were in the past, now that I'd settled down with a lovely girl. I had a respectable livelihood running a health-food business and spent my spare time in the garden with my vegetables, chickens and bees. That was all true, but it was only part of it.

The fact was I'd been so affected by my first LSD trip that it had altered the whole course of my existence. I'd been turning people on to acid for ten years.

The driver took the Swindon exit and pulled up outside the police station. My tenants, a blameless young couple who rented the flat above my wholefoods shop, were leaving the building. Why on earth were they here? I was able to delay my departure from the car so I emerged just as they passed.

'What happened?' I asked.

They didn't have a chance to reply; the moment I spoke the two policemen ran me inside. At the desk, I was booked by a sergeant. He added my name to the list of cell occupants on the blackboard. I recognised Henry and Brian immediately. The flickering flame of hope I'd been nursing was blown out. They'd got us.

'Give me your glasses and belt,' the sergeant said.

'What? Why?' I asked.

'Stop you trying to kill yourself with them.'

The cell door slammed shut behind me. My connection to the rest of the world was instantly severed. I was alone, in the hands of my enemies. Until now I'd been trying to convince myself that I was somehow going to slide out of this situation, but in a cell it's almost impossible to think positively.

The brightly lit cube was small enough for me to see well, even without my specs. The walls were glossy and bare. There was a toilet, a concrete bed and nothing else. A small window, made of glass bricks, admitted a dim underwater light. I stood on the bed and put my face to the glass. I couldn't see anything clearly.

The air was rank with the sour smell of fear. Was that me? I sniffed my armpit. I stank. Smelling my body made me aware of the cell's ghosts, all the frightened people who'd been locked up in this cramped space. Needing to move, I walked three paces up, turned, took three paces back, turned... After a while I sat on the bed. Before long I was lying down, crying helplessly. I cried for Mary and for my friends in the adjoining cells, but mostly I cried for myself. What a mess. What a horrible bloody mess!

Eventually I cried myself out and lay, clothed in the rags of despair, dreading the interrogation that must be coming. The leaden minutes sank out of sight, one by one. Finally, the key turned and the door opened. I clenched my fists and stood to face my questioners.

'Come and sign for your property,' the copper told me.

I followed him into the corridor.

'Say nothing!' came a shout from another of the cells. I recognised Henry's voice.

Back in the cell, I tried to read the novel I'd picked up from the desk, but I couldn't concentrate. My mind kept looping round and round the approaching ordeal. I couldn't stop thinking how helpless I was.

We'd known all along about the possible consequences of our actions. Brian, Henry and I had talked about what to do if we were ever arrested. All that theorising seemed irrelevant now that the police had us at their mercy. They could do anything they wanted. My stomach turned when the door burst open. It was only my lunch on a tray. I had no appetite. An hour later, the door opened again. They'd come for me.

I had no idea what was going to happen, but expected the worst. The two men led me upstairs. 'Upstairs is good,' the shrunken, but not entirely silent, hope-for-the-best part of my mind noted. 'Beatings take place in the basement.'

'Movie cliché,' a darker corner replied. 'Nothing to do with reality. Who are these guys anyway?'

They looked like bedraggled acid freaks at the end of a long festival, but they weren't. They were undercover cops. They took me to a stripped-down office with a desk, three chairs, a filing cabinet and a calendar on the wall.

I was offered a seat and a cigarette and accepted both. Round one to the police. They introduced themselves: Detective Sergeant Pritchard and Detective Constable Bentley – Martyn and Steve. Unshaven and untidy, they looked more like hippies than I did. They sat behind the desk and looked at me for a while.

'I think you know why you're here.' Pritchard broke the silence. He was stocky, cocky, had long greasy blond hair and the look of a fairground tough.

'Where's my wife?' I asked. My voice came out firm and clear, suggesting a strength that wasn't there.

'We're holding her in police custody, pending further enquiries.'

'She's not involved in anything,' I said. 'You can let her go.'

'Oh yeah? What is it that she's not involved with?' Pritchard stroked his beard and smiled.

I'd resolved not to say anything at all, but I had to get Mary out of the firing line.

'The hash on the mantelpiece was mine. It's nothing to do with her. She doesn't smoke.'

'Listen, Leaf,' Pritchard said, 'the hash is neither here nor there. You're in a lot more trouble than possession of a bit of dope. You've got big problems, man… big problems.' He looked at me with something akin to sympathy. 'How did you get into such a fix?'

I'd been asking myself the same question.

'I probably know more about you than your parents do,' he continued. 'You've been under observation for months. You haven't gone anywhere, met anyone or made a phone call without my knowledge.'

Surely he was bluffing. I hadn't said anything on the phone, had I? What about my last visit to the stash near Fleet and the helicopter that had hung interminably in the sky? I'd told myself it was the traffic police, monitoring the M3. Had they been watching me? How much did they know?

Pritchard picked up a bulging folder and slammed it down on the desk. 'That's your personal file, Leaf. You're nicked. There's no way you're going to wriggle out of this. We know you occupy a key position in the gang. The only thing we need to establish is just how important you are. Are you a prime mover or are you one of their tools?'

'I haven't a clue what you're on about! What gang? What tools?'

'Look, you're not doing yourself any favours, fooling around like this. Anyway, that's enough for the moment. We've been up for thirty-six hours and we need to sleep.' He rose to his feet. 'You and I will have a proper chat tomorrow. I think you'll be ready to cooperate… if you've got any sense, that is. Tonight I want you to think about three special letters. You know the ones I mean.' He leant forward, until his nose was virtually touching mine, and spat the letters in my face. 'L… S… D!'

I've bedded down in all kinds of strange and uncomfortable places in my time, but that first night in the police cells was one of the most miserable of my entire life. Doors slammed, boots clumped up and down the corridor, voices shouted. At intervals the spy-hole in my cell door opened and an eye looked in at me. I got no sleep, but lay on the concrete bed with my thoughts ricocheting round the walls.

Had they really been watching us for months, or was Pritchard just saying that to demoralise me? The more I thought about it, the more ominous it seemed. Russ's house had been swarming with coppers, others would have been at Brian's and Henry's. They'd even gone to my shop and arrested my tenants. That more than anything convinced me of the size of the operation they must have mounted against us. It looked like we'd had it.

So, if there was no escape, then surely the best course was to admit my guilt. But if I kept my mouth shut, maybe I'd get off... Where was the evidence against me? Why hadn't I thought to ask for a solicitor? How much did the police really know? Were they going to get heavy? How well would I handle it? I spent all night raising questions I couldn't possibly answer. I wondered where Mary was and hoped she was OK. I missed her terribly.

Morning came with a jangling of keys and a copper holding a mug of tea and a plate of greasy eggs. He put my breakfast on the floor and slammed the cell door shut. Hearing Brian's distinctive Brummie accent in the corridor, I put my ear to the door and listened to my old friend being led away. I paced up and down, then lay on the bed, then began pacing again. I was dying for a fag, dying for it all to be over.

Hours slowly bled to death, one after another. When the cell door finally opened, I braced myself for round two with my inquisitors.

'Exercise!' A uniformed copper stood in the doorway.

Exercise was a handcuffed walk in the underground car park. Lit by dull yellow spotlights, stained concrete columns bulged under the enormous weight of the police station above. Our footsteps echoed hollowly. Water dripped from low ceilings and splashed into black pools.

'Quite a criminal mastermind then, aren't you?' the copper said, breaking into my sad thoughts about the life I'd just left.

'What?'

'Oh yeah. You're all famous now. The BBC extended the news by fifteen minutes last night for you lot. Operation Julie – that's what they're calling it. Eight hundred police officers involved and over a hundred people arrested. It's the biggest drugs operation ever, in fact I think it may be the biggest ever criminal operation.'

He spoke as though he were just a simpleton making conversation, but I felt he was trying to undermine me before the next round of questioning. I acted as if I hadn't heard him. We walked on in silence until he said, 'OK, that's enough.'

As we left, Pritchard appeared from behind a column. He took the other end of the cuffs and led me upstairs.

Pritchard and Bentley were in clean clothes, freshly washed and shaved. Somehow it made them seem less menacing. Yesterday Pritchard had done the talking. Now, working as a double act, they told me about our conspiracy. A few of the things they said were wide of the mark but most of it was depressingly accurate. How did they know so much? We must have been under observation, as they'd claimed yesterday. Or someone had been talking.

'So, you can see we're not bluffing. We do know the score. Now, are you going to come clean?' Pritchard looked at me enquiringly.

'I think you must have me confused with someone else. I don't have the first idea what you're on about.'

'Listen, Leaf,' he warned me, 'please don't fuck us about. It's not going to help you at all. There's no question about your involvement. None. We know everything about the whole chain. I won't pretend we've got every tiny detail, but the few gaps are being filled in fast. Everybody's talking. You're one of the few grey areas. My guv'nor is convinced you're in it up to your neck. Steve and I think maybe they were using you. We want to give you the chance to tell it for yourself. Things will go a lot better for you if you play ball. If you don't... well, you're going to look like one of the ringleaders.'

I inspected my feet and said nothing.

'Don't be a mug,' he urged. 'You think I'm feeding you a line and doing the same to the others to turn you against each other?'

Of course I did. I'd watched loads of cops and robbers movies. He gave me a hard stare which I returned.

'You really don't believe me, do you? What a mug! Stay there. I'll be right back. I'm going to show you what your friend Russ has to say about you.' He stood, came round the desk, whispered in my ear, 'Just you wait!' and left the room.

Bentley gave me a cigarette and a light. He stuck his long legs on the desk, leant back, blew out a long plume of smoke and said, 'I've been in your shop a couple of times. As a customer. Cool place, good vibe. Nice business you've got there.'

'I want to see a solicitor,' I announced, remembering at last.

'Relax,' he replied. 'This is all off the record. We can say what we like. It doesn't count unless there are two officers present. Yeah, if only you'd stuck to your health foods, Leaf.'

I'd been thinking that on the exercise walk. Into the lengthening silence, Bentley said, 'A few months ago, I was in a room with a bunch of heads. Smashed out of our skulls on good Afghani. Listening to the Floyd. All sitting on mattresses on the floor. A few joints were going round. You know the scene…'

I nodded. I knew.

'Well, as I passed a joint to my neighbour, burning bits of dope fell on to his sweater. Brushing them off, he spilled tea over the chick sitting next to him. Scalded, she jerked away and banged into the record player, making the needle skid across the album. A guy on the other side of the room leapt to his feet to rescue the record, but slipped on a rug, hit the light and broke the bulb…'

The chaos snowballed until the whole room was in an uproar. Bentley told the story well. It was difficult not to laugh.

'Then, just as things were settling down,' he continued, 'the door opened—'

Pritchard burst back in. 'You won't believe this,' he said. 'I was going to bring you Russ's statement… but he's still writing it! Ten pages so far and a lot of it is about you.'

'Look, I'm not saying anything until I've spoken to a solicitor.'

'As you like.' He sounded disappointed, as if I'd let him down somehow. 'You've had it, you know. You're only hurting yourself by not holding your hands up. Refusal to cooperate doesn't go down well at sentencing time. Anyway, that'll do for the present. Take him down, Steve.'

As I was leaving, he added, 'Next time I'll show you what Russ said about you. By the way, I've spoken to your wife. We're satisfied she's not involved in your acid ring and we let her go home.'

~ ~ ~ ~ ~

They called me again in the evening. Pritchard had some papers in front of him; Russ's statement, he claimed. He went through it, sheet by sheet, skimming quickly through the early part, speaking word for word when he came to sections that concerned me. I listened in appalled silence as he read out Russ's account of how we met and the things we'd done together. The closing part of the statement described our final handover. It included the words: 'last Tuesday I went to stay at Leaf's house in Binfield Heath. The following morning I received a hundred and twelve thousand microdots from him.'

A hundred and twelve thousand wasn't a figure to be plucked from the air. Russ had definitely been talking. With dumb misery, I ignored Pritchard's exhortations to cough and clung to my hopeless silence as the pair of them fired questions at me.

Back in the cell, I kept thinking about Russ. I'd liked and admired the guy for years. He had a quip for every occasion and he'd stayed cool when we'd been in a tight spot in Morocco. What had they done to him? Had they convinced him his child would be born in prison unless he cooperated? Poor Russ. Frightened as I was, I knew I had to stick to the code of my youth: never grass up your mates. Never. Being up to your nostrils in shit is bad enough; it's worse if you open your mouth.

'Russ is blaming everything on you,' Pritchard began, the next morning. 'If you don't give your side of the story, you're going to look like his controller.'

'I want to make a phone call. I want a solicitor,' I said.

'No calls. You'll get a solicitor in due course. OK, you don't want to make a statement, but while you're here you may as well help us get down your antecedents for the court – or are you going to refuse to cooperate on that too?'

I agreed to talk about my previous history and gave them a highly censored version. They then talked about their pasts. Both of them had worked undercover for long periods and they knew a lot about the drug scene. Another of Bentley's dope stories got me laughing. My guard was slipping. For the last fifty-odd hours I'd been alone with my fevered thoughts. I had no one to talk to but these guys.

The interrogations blurred one into another. Pritchard and Bentley kept telling me the others were piling all the blame on to me and that I had to set the record straight for my own protection. Being escorted up for another session, I bumped into Brian on his way down. When we drew level on the stairs, he muttered, 'They got us in the lab. We're fucked. I've admitted it. Say what you like about me. It doesn't matter.'

Upstairs, Pritchard said that if I confessed my guilt I'd probably get off with a short sentence. If I maintained the pretence of being innocent and was found guilty, as I inevitably would be, I'd be in prison until I was an old man.

I had no more resistance and made a statement admitting supplying LSD.

The following day we were all remanded in custody at Swindon Magistrate's Court. At the hearing I met the solicitor Mary had engaged for me. He confirmed what the copper had said in the car park: that on the night of

Operation Julie, eight hundred police had participated in raids on eighty-seven homes. Over a hundred people had been arrested.

During the hearing, which took place amid considerable confusion, I had a chance to speak to some of my co-conspirators. Most had made statements. Only big Henry had said nothing.

At the next interrogation, Pritchard pressed me for more information. 'We want details,' he said, slamming his fist on the table. 'Names, dates, places... and stashes.'

I refused to talk about anyone else, but I did agree to hand over the trips I'd left at Eric's collection point. They were going to find them anyway. At the remand hearing, Eric had said he'd told the police about his pick-up arrangements and offered to show them the cache. He thought it was empty. The fact that it wasn't was down to me.

Pritchard took me to Fleet in a police car. We were followed by a vanload of police officers. I showed him where to park, then led the group through the woods to the cache. Several of the policemen were armed. They fanned out among the trees to guard against a rescue attempt.

Their precautions were surreal. Who did they think was going to come and save me – the acid army? The police may have watched us for a while, but they didn't have a clue who we really were. They'd come tooled up to take out the peace and love brigade. We didn't have a gun between us. We were the last of the hippy activists, non-violent revolutionaries trying to transform the world through chemical enlightenment.

Shivering, I took my free hand from my pocket and pointed to the spot where the tabs lay hidden. The container was unearthed with great excitement. I was forgotten in the general jubilation and stood, handcuffed to my minder, with the horrible feeling that this was only going to make things much worse.

Pritchard came over with the container. 'There's a hundred thousand here, right?'

'Mmm,' I nodded.

'Yes!' he yelled, punching the air. 'It's the world record! Fellas, we've got the world record!'

The Operation Julie officers threw their hats in the air and capered around in a ring, stirring up the fallen leaves and cheering.

It began to rain, lightly at first, then with a persistence that suggested it would rain for a long time. Cold, wet and handcuffed, I stood there wondering how the bizarre course of my life had led me into this god-almighty mess.

2 The Abbey

1956

BOYS WERE CRYING in the junior dormitory on that first night in boarding school. At mid-morning break the next day, we were let out before the other classes. Uncomfortable in our scratchy new uniforms, we clustered around the milk crates like ducklings, talking among ourselves and looking around nervously. Another form noisily burst out of the school and headed towards us. Suddenly I was ringed by four bigger boys.

'How old are you, kid?'

'Nearly eight.'

'What's the matter with his ears?'

'Ugly little bugger, isn't he?' The speaker flicked my earlobe. It was Bully Johnson. I'd been told about him at breakfast.

'Stop it!' I glared at my tormenters.

'Don't tell me what to do, you little runt! I'll fight you. Take off your jacket,' Bully Johnson shouted, ripping his off.

I couldn't move until he hit me on the nose and jerked

me out of my paralysis. Stung, I flew at him and got him on the ground. He soon turned me and pinned me to the gravel. I was choking on the blood pouring from my nose and the fight was over.

I lost the battle but won acceptance and even a certain respect for flooring Johnson. Boys who failed their initiation test were tormented until they were able to persuade their parents to take them away. Violence was part of life at the Abbey School.

A couple of days after the fight, the headmaster caught me using the front stairs and told me to wait outside his study after class. His door finally opened; the smell of dead tobacco crept out. With an orange-stained finger, the head beckoned me inside. I stood shivering in the book-lined room while he tested different canes from the rack, flexing them and practising his swing. He was smiling as he said, 'Right, Fielding. The caning is not over until I tell you to stand up. You then say "Thank you, Sir" and leave. Now, bend over that chair.' He stubbed out his fag and pointed to a dining chair in the middle of the study. 'Grip the rungs under the seat and hold on.'

I was aware of him positioning himself, measuring the distance between us. My heart was thudding against my ribs. There was an intake of breath, a swish of air and my arse exploded in pain. Involuntarily, I stood.

'Bend over, damn you!'

I bent and the next stroke followed immediately, biting into my stinging behind and bringing tears to my eyes. I had to chew my lip not to cry out. He hit me four times. It hurt abominably. I was trying not to blubber as I left his study.

The bloodhounds were waiting in the corridor.

'How many strokes?'

'Has he drawn blood?'

A dozen boys escorted me to the toilets to have a look.

'No, you aren't bleeding. He was going easy on you.' Disappointed, the crowd drifted away.

Alone, with my pants around my ankles, I let the tears fall. It wasn't fair! We'd been allowed to use those stairs on the first day. I was pulling up my shorts when my brother Roger appeared.

'You all right?' he asked.

My bottom was on fire, but I nodded and wiped my nose.

'Well done,' he said, punching me on my shoulder. 'Listen, Nigs, you must stand up for yourself here, you know. I'm the only new boy in our class and everyone wants to fight me. I can't do your scrapping for you as well. Listen, I'm afraid we can't play together any more. Boys in our class never associate with the juniors. I'm sorry. You understand, don't you?'

'Yes,' I answered miserably.

'Buck up, then. It's your birthday next week! Think of all the presents you might get.'

I doubted if I'd last another week. Roger squeezed my forearm and whispered, 'Listen, if ever you're feeling worse off than the others, remember this – we've got to be at boarding school because of our special family circumstances. Everyone else is here because their parents sent them away.'

The school round was marked by bells calling reveille, meals, lessons, breaks, games, post, tuck, homework, prayers, assembly and church. Everything happened at its appointed time. Our education and our basic physical needs were catered for, but our regimented life lacked any kind of warmth or kindness.

At the end of term, we took the bus to Nanna Fielding's in Ipswich. Daddy had a few days leave from his regiment and joined us for Christmas. Our sister Judy came up from Auntie Con and Uncle Bob's in Somerset. She brought up the presents she'd been given for her fifth birthday. It was wonderful for us to be together but, for the second time, the vast absence of our mummy overshadowed Christmas. I'm sure the others were remembering her too, though nobody brought up the subject.

Instead Roger and I told Daddy about our new school. There were already some things we couldn't possibly say. As all boarders must, we had partitioned our minds, so we could switch back and forth between two completely separate realities.

Daddy was busy with the army and couldn't make it for the school Speech Day. Aunt Joan and Uncle Norman Ballard, who lived near Woodbridge, came in his stead.

'What does that say, Nigs?' Uncle Norman asked, pointing at the blackboard in my classroom. I screwed up my eyes, but had to go closer to read it.

'The Abbey welcomes—'

'I thought so! You're short-sighted. Don't worry. We'll fix you up with an eye test.'

My glasses didn't arrive until the last week of term. Those final days inched past amid mounting fever. Even the staff got caught up in the delirium of the approaching long holidays. The great thing about The Abbey, I came to see in those strangely luminescent moments that closed the school calendar, was that it made us all the same – in term-time we were all without families.

Finally the holidays arrived. My brother and I packed our little suitcases for the seaside.

We slept in a dowdy bed and breakfast in Felixstowe. Roger and I had one room. Nanna shared the other with little Judy. Our daytime base was Nanna's spick and span beach hut. Three huts down were our cousins, the Ballards. Several times in the last year we'd visited Aunt Joan and Uncle Norman's. I loved those precious days, when we could enter the charmed circle of their family life. The twins, Annie and Judy, were two years older than me, Peter some months younger. In Felixstowe we were Roger's little team. We swam, played and roamed all day, along the beach, up the cliff and in the abandoned pillboxes of Brackenbury Fort, but mostly we searched for treasure.

The tarry breakwaters of Felixstowe were hung with thick ribbons of bladderwrack. I had to be careful, as I clambered from bay to slippery bay, not to lose my new specs in the North Sea. At the base of the breakwater posts were pink bits of shell, crabs' claws and brittle starfish. All the time our eyes were scanning the ever-shifting boundary between land and sea. The restless water dragged the pebbles from under our feet as we looked for the chunks of Baltic amber that were sometimes washed up on this coast.

~~~~~

All too soon it was time to take the dismal bus-ride to Woodbridge. Roger and I picked up our cases and began our return journey into hell. With half an hour to metamorphise from children back into boarders, we didn't say much to each other on the bus. We were busy putting our armour on, steeling ourselves. Then we got off the bus and walked up the long hill to The Abbey. My suitcase was pulling my arm out of its socket.

The Abbey boarders were all as hard as oak, or trying to be. World War Two wasn't long past and the ethos in the school was fiercely militaristic and nationalistic. Hundreds of war comics circulated, most of our play involved war games and when we weren't racing around outside shooting each other, we were indoors making model tanks, battleships and warplanes.

Behind the fighting front, I lived my interior life. Here I spun out long stories with impossibly happy endings: I would become the youngest cricketer to play for England... My mother would return as a national heroine after her long secret assignment behind the Iron Curtain...

I would have died rather than admit these reveries to anyone. There were other feelings too that I couldn't talk about: the sense of immanence when, looking at the sky one crisp winter's night, I saw the heavens – really saw them – for the very first time. I still had a childish belief in Bible stories and my skin felt the beat of angels' wings in the services and carols that brought the Christmas term to an end.

Wise men and shepherds, the Iron Age, Romulus and Remus, Shrove Tuesday, long division, George and the dragon, dead legs and Chinese burns, silly mid off and a five-card trick... I was nine and trying to keep abreast of it all.

For five years Roger and I went to Ipswich in the holidays. Nanna was our rock, but she had very strict, old-fashioned ideas about what children are and aren't permitted to do – and we were too young for almost everything.

When the weather was fine, we were allowed to roam Broomhill Park. On rainy or cold days we played endless games of cards, or else read the children's classics Daddy had had when he was a boy. Roger and I may have been in a terraced house in Ipswich, but we were living amid clansmen, knights, legionnaires and pirates. Reading was my joy.

Holidays kept hurrying to an end. We shuttled between the school and Nanna's. Judy sometimes came up from Auntie Con's. Daddy called in when he could, which wasn't often. His rare visits to Ipswich were times of meltdown intensity for us, desperate attempts to fuse our splintered family over a weekend or a Sunday afternoon.

One summer we had a wonderful fortnight with Daddy and the Ballards on the beach at Felixstowe. Then he was promoted to Major and posted to Hong Kong to command a battery of artillery. We saw him twice in the next three years.

3　Built on sand

IN SEPTEMBER 1960, aged eleven, I moved up from the Abbey to Woodbridge School, changing from short to long trousers, but staying in the same grey uniform.

'The most important thing you'll learn here...' housemaster Basher Lewis told us new boys, in front of the house's loaded trophy cabinet, 'is team spirit. On your own, you're nothing. As part of a Queen's team, you'll be invincible.'

We all had to go out and cheer each time Queen's was playing. Every team member was required to give his all for the glory of the house. Basher was always there, limping along the touchline, waving his walking stick, outshouting the other housemasters, roaring his boys home. Our small house won almost every cup in sight. Other houses might value creativity or academic prowess, but in Queen's the ability to kick, hit or catch a ball was prized above all else.

In our first year, we were shielded from the full blast of boarding-house life among the big boys. That changed the following year, in the Remove.

Boys in the Remove did all the menial tasks required to keep the boarding houses running. We cleaned the common rooms and changing rooms, kept the fires alight and acted as orderlies, bell ringers and prefects' fags.

A fag was a servant whose duties included polishing boots, ironing shirts, making toast and tea and keeping his prefect's study clean. I wasn't called on at first, but had to step in to look after a prefect called Murdoch when his fag fell ill.

Murdoch was an absolute bastard. I could see exactly why his parents had sent him away to boarding school; I'd have done the same. Murdoch greased his hair and spent a lot of time combing it and practising his sneer in the mirror on the back of the study door.

I opened the door too quickly one day and banged his elbow.

'Sorry, Murdoch.'

'You little shit!' he squeaked, 'oh my God.' He nursed his injured elbow then suddenly screamed, 'Out, get out!' and drove me from the room with kicks and slaps around the head. Five minutes later he sent for me.

'I don't like the way you do things, Fielding,' he drawled. 'And I don't like your attitude. I'm going to teach you a lesson.'

I didn't like the sound of that. Prefects were allowed to beat the smaller boys with a slipper or gym shoe. Murdoch enjoyed it so much he put a slab of lead in his plimsoll. He beat more boys than anyone else, and he always watched when other prefects were slippering someone.

There were endless numbers of trivial things you could be punished for in the school, especially if you were untidy and absent-minded, as I was. In the following weeks, Murdoch found a whole series of reasons to beat me.

I got a break from persecution after Daddy sent news from Hong Kong that he was getting married at the end of his Far East tour. Roger and I were given permission to attend his winter wedding on the Isle of Man. Judy was there already when we arrived at Nanna's in Ipswich. We'd seen so little of her over the years that we had become more like cousins than siblings.

'Isn't it fantastic,' I said excitedly. 'We're going to be a proper family again!'

'No one can replace our mother.'

Roger's response was a bomb that went straight through the bottom of the fragile boat I'd built to keep myself afloat.

How could I have forgotten? How could I possibly have forgotten my mother?

'Who's going to help me with breakfast?' Daddy asked, flourishing the frying pan.

'Me, me!' My cry came slightly behind my brother's.

'Well, now that Roger's nine, he can help with the frying.' Daddy handed the big pan to my brother who sagged under its weight. 'You're in charge of bacon and black pudding. I'm counting on you. Now, what about you, Nigs – how old are you?'

'Nearly seven,' I replied crossly. He knew how old I was!

'Six and a half.'

'I'm not, Roger! I was six and a half ages ago.'

'That's enough.' Daddy held up his hand. 'Nigs, you can stir the beans and watch the coffee. Can you manage that?'

'Of course.'

Daddy had two frying pans full of eggs, tomatoes, mushrooms and fried bread. The kitchen filled with the smell of cooking. When everything was ready, he carried a tray upstairs for Mummy's Saturday treat, breakfast in bed. After we'd eaten our massive meal in the kitchen, Roger and I went upstairs to bring down Mummy's empty tray.

'Can we come back up to read, Mummy?' I asked. She usually let us.

'Yes, when you've helped Daddy clear up.'

She'd taught me to read before I went to school. My favourite time of all was when I was curled up in bed next to her, my head leaning into her side, her arm around my shoulder, while we slipped into the magic forest of words. This was the new world she'd given me. There was real life where you run around doing things, and there was this separate kingdom of writing with giant stories rolling out of little books.

After supper we had time for a game of hide-and-seek before bed. Mummy's count receded as I tiptoed upstairs. Where could I hide? Roger had already bagged the bedroom. I crept into the airing cupboard. Hearing her on the stairs, I had to bite my lip not to give myself away by making a noise. Mummy came to the door of the cupboard.

'Anyone in there?' she asked.

'No,' I replied, realising as I spoke that I'd been tricked.

She swung open the door, swept me into her arms and covered my face with kisses. 'Right,' she laughed, tickling me as we headed towards the bedroom, 'I wonder where your brother's hiding…'

Not long afterwards, we were in the living room with the baby sitter, waiting for our parents to return. They'd been ages. When the bell went, I beat my brother to the door. Uncle Bob and Auntie Con stood on the threshold.

'Where are Mummy and Daddy?' I asked.

'Oh, boys,' Auntie Con said in a strange voice.

Thinking it was a game, I ran outside, expecting to find Mummy hiding behind the holly tree. She wasn't there. I ran all the way round the house. When I came back to the front, Con was hugging Judy and crying all over her.

Something was terribly wrong.

Uncle Bob squatted down in front of Roger and me. His thick glasses made his eyes look enormous. With a heavy hand he gripped my upper arm. 'You must be brave boys now. There's been a car accident. Your Daddy's in hospital. Mummy has gone to Jesus.'

'No, it's not true. It's not true!' I screamed and hit out at him. But my crying and thumping didn't bring her back, nor did praying to God, pleading with him, or banging my head against the fireplace. Nothing I could do would bring her back. She was gone forever. I punched the floor with my fists. No! It just couldn't be true.

Grandparents, aunts and uncles came and went, trailing clouds of misery. Auntie Con stayed on to look after us. Weeks later, Daddy arrived home with his head in bandages and the awful smell of whisky on his breath.

~~~~~

After the death of my mother, when I was six, I retreated into myself. The early realisation that life is built on sand, that nothing is solid, changed me for all time.

We were kept away from the funeral. This enabled some part of me to deny her death. I clung to the slim hope that there were mysterious grown-up reasons why she'd had to go away and we couldn't be told. I sat in the bay of Nanna's front window, on the lookout. I didn't like to interrupt my vigil for fear of missing her. I wanted to be waiting in the window when she returned, so she would know that I, at least, hadn't given up.

It feels like I spent years in that bay window. I could be diverted, but I'd be scoured by guilt whenever I caught myself having a good time. What kind of boy could laugh and play when his mummy was missing? After a time I couldn't bring her face into my mind's eye and realised I was even losing the memory of her.

These recollections of my mother were looping round in my thirteen-year-old head as we flew to the Isle of Man for our father's marriage to a woman we'd never met.

'Golly, look at that!'

Roger nudged me. Glad of the distraction, I leant over him to peer through the little window at the dinky cars on ribbons of road. I thought I'd better lay my claim now.

'Bags I the window seat on the way back.'

It was the first flight for all four of us. I could tell by Nanna's thin lips that she wasn't happy. When the aircraft dipped its wing as it came in to land on the island, Judy was sick.

Daddy met us off the plane and drove us to our hotel.

Everyone was busy with wedding preparations and we were in the way wherever we went. We met Daddy's bride-to-be amid a crisis over bridesmaids' dresses. Katie wasn't at all what I'd been expecting. I'd envisaged someone warm and kindly, but she looked like an armour-plated school matron, short and stocky with a large bosom and the hint of a moustache.

'Oh, I've heard so much about you. How lovely to meet you finally,' she exclaimed in a voice full of false notes. 'I've brought you presents.'

I unwrapped mine. It was a metal beer mug with a glass bottom and a dragon engraved on the side.

'Gosh, thanks,' I said, echoing the others' words.

'Well, aren't you going to give her a kiss?' Daddy said a little testily, waving us forward.

'Sorry, yes, of course.' When it was my turn I kissed the proffered cheek. Her make-up tasted disgusting. Though desperate to wipe my lips clean, I knew it would be bad form and forced myself to be still. I couldn't think of anything to say and nor could anyone else. We stood there awkwardly, with fake smiles plastered on our faces, until Daddy said, 'Well, can't hang about. Must get on. Lots to organise.'

'Now you see what I mean,' Roger said when we were back in our hotel room and I was washing my lips to rid myself of the vile cosmetic taste.

On the morning of the wedding, Roger and I squeezed into starched shirts. We knotted ties, donned suits and brylcreemed our hair. Nanna and Judy came out of their room in their best dresses. Off we went to the kirk for the ceremony, Nanna complaining all the way that her feet were killing her. After the speeches, Daddy and Katie left in a flurry of confetti. My brother and I went back to school.

Murdoch had a new torture for me. He gave me two weeks of changes for having dirty shoes. Four times a day, I had to report to him in a succession of outfits: army uniform, games kit, Sunday suit and PE kit. With each change of clothing, he would inspect me. If I wasn't immaculate, he'd send me back to put it right.

'Those boots are filthy, you worm. Go away and make them shine.'

Changes used up all my available time and made it impossible for me to function properly in house or school. In the mid-morning break I'd run full-pelt to Queen's. With frantic haste, I'd start changing. If I passed all the inspections, I'd just about make it in time to my next class. But if I was sent back I'd be late and wouldn't have had time to sort out the correct books. Punishments began to pile up, a five-hundred-word essay, a detention, a hundred lines: 'I must be on time for class and I must bring all my books.'

But I didn't have a moment to do any lines or essays. A hundred lines not handed in on time became two hundred; two hundred not done meant a caning. Getting caught doing lines during evening prep meant a slippering.

On the last day of my fortnight of changes, Murdoch surprised me doing lines in the toilet after lights out. He gave me another week. I was being run ragged. After my tormentor persuaded another prefect to join in the fun, I had three or four punishments on the go at any one time and was being beaten two or three times a week. I was swimming in a sea of pain, barely keeping my head above the waves.

Disillusionment was setting in. Fuck team spirit – and fuck the system that could let this sadism flourish. I didn't know what I could do about my situation or how I could stop the persecution. I was smouldering with helpless resentment.

At Easter, we took the train to our new home, a married officers' quarters on an army estate on the edge of Bushey. Judy was there already, looking rather woebegone. We gathered in the living room.

'Now we're all together,' Dad began, 'we'd better make it clear how this household operates. My job is to bring in the money to support the family. Your mother's job is to run the house. At home you'll do as she tells you.'

It was an ominous start.

'Why is she so horrible?' Judy asked us, the first time we were alone together. 'I can't do anything right.'

'Judy!' Katie's imperious voice rang through the house. 'Come here, girl, and clear up this mess.'

'I don't care whether you like me or not,' Katie snapped, the first time we clashed, 'but you will respect and obey me.'

She was a formidable woman with a will of steel. A newcomer to the world of service life, Katie went straight on the offensive, lording it over everyone she didn't have to defer to. That included the wives of junior officers and our family.

Roger and I were still awake at the end of the first dinner party they gave. After the final guests left with cheery good-nights, Katie closed the door and tore straight into Dad.

'How dare you!' she screamed. 'How bloody dare you!'

'What's the matter?'

'I don't have to put up with this.' Her voice turned to ice. 'I'll go home to the island. Then what would you do, eh? What would you say to your precious friends?'

'What are you talking about? What have I done?'

'You contradicted me in front of the Eastmans, that's what. I felt a complete idiot.' She'd worked herself into a spitting, foot-stamping fury. 'And don't think I didn't see you making eyes at that Anderson woman. It was disgusting the way you were carrying on.'

'Wait a minute. You've got it wrong.'

'There you are, contradicting me again. Everyone saw what was going on.'

'My love, the Andersons are old friends. It's a game we play. Nothing's going on. I promise you.'

'Don't "my love" me, John Fielding! I won't have it and that's that. You try it on again and I'll pack my bags and go. Don't think I won't!'

If only she had. Social occasions are an important part of an army officer's life. After every single one, Katie would go mental and accuse Dad of belittling her in front of their subordinates, of flirting or getting drunk and making a fool of himself in any number of ways. After several fearsome rows, he seemed to accept there was no winning. She was prepared to go to extremes of rage from which he shrank. To our dismay, he capitulated. Katie came to direct the course of family life.

Roger and I had certain chores to do but we were able to get away from the house for much of the day. There was no such escape for Judy, who was endlessly criticised for the interminable work she was made to do. The worst of it was that Dad wouldn't intervene.

'Your mother's in charge of the house,' was all he'd say when we appealed to him.

'She's not our mother,' we muttered.

In November, Katie gave birth to a daughter, Susan. Judy had more work added to her load, helping with nappies and washing, taking the baby for walks in the pram and babysitting. We knew it wasn't Susi's fault, but we felt angry about the difference between her pampered life and the labours of her Cinderella sister.

Roger and I ricocheted between the brutal boarding school and a home that was under enemy occupation. My only consolation was that Murdoch had left Woodbridge. He was gone forever. There was nothing else to feel good about. Almost everything in this bleak life was either compulsory or forbidden.

One visiting Sunday, in need of refuge, I rang the Ballards. 'Hello, Aunt Joan. It's Nigel. I wondered if I might come over for the day.'

'Of course, Nigs. Always glad to see you.' There was a weariness in my aunt's voice. I saw, for the first time, that I was something of a burden to my kindly relatives.

I took the bus to Wickham Market, then began the long walk to their home in Easton. It was a beautiful February day, cold but clear. The bare trees were silhouetted against the pale winter sky. I realised that I was entirely on my own – a strange sensation. At first it felt odd, but after a while I began to enjoy it. My eye was caught by a single leaf, hanging from a tree. It alone had somehow clung on since the autumn. Under my gaze it detached itself, twisted to the ground and landed at my feet.

I was inexplicably moved. Something important had happened. But for me, this moment would have passed unnoticed. I was fifteen and going through many changes.

I'd stopped drinking from the team-spirit bottle. When I wasn't on my own, I was likely to be hanging out with the rebels from the other houses, smoking cigarettes and talking sedition.

While I was rebelling, my brother was conforming. At the start of our schooldays we'd been almost everything to each other, but our paths had long been diverging. In '64, Roger left school and joined the army.

I passed my O levels and became a sixth-former – the only one in our house who wasn't a prefect. The new housemaster said he couldn't rely on me. Quite right. I had no wish to help a regime I'd come to loathe. I didn't want my crack of the whip, my opportunity to make life hell for some poor kid from the Remove. The cycle of violence has to be broken somewhere.

With none of the prefect's tasks to perform, I had lots of free time, but little idea of what to do. Soon I was going to be a new-bug all over again, starting at the bottom of the job treadmill. It all seemed so unutterably depressing that I tried not to think about it and I spent my time listening to the pirate station, Radio Caroline, or going across to the school hall to watch my form mate Brinsley Schwartz and his pal Nick Lowe rehearse for the upcoming concert of their rock 'n' roll band, The Democrats.

When I wasn't studying or listening to music I was devouring books like a starving man. A good read could lift me away from the grim reality of school and transport me to another world. I hustled alongside Jack Kerouac in *The Dharma Bums*. George Orwell put me among the down and outs then magic-carpeted me to Catalonia and filled me with respect for the anarchists, whose fight for liberty perfectly expressed my longing to have some kind of say in my life. After discovering Orwell, I read everything I could find about the Spanish Civil War and started thinking more about politics. I understood that I'd turned against the authoritarian stamp of empire. My blood now raced with subversive foreign thoughts of liberty and equality.

In my final year at Woodbridge, I was mostly left to my own devices. The new housemaster wanted to isolate me so that my disaffection didn't infect the junior boys. But I wasn't trying to stir up a revolt, I just didn't want to be fucked over any more.

Although I was counting the days until I could leave, I had no idea what to do after school other than go to university. On my application form, to say something different, I added fascism to the list of my more conventional interests.

I was called for an interview at Reading. The panel consisted of two Indians and a white guy.

'Tell us about your interest in fascism,' one of my interviewers said. 'You regard yourself as a fascist, perhaps?'

'Absolutely not,' I replied. 'Fascism is one of the great evils in the world. The defeat of the Axis in the war doesn't mean the end of the problem, because the seeds of fascism lie within every society.'

I tried not to sound too rehearsed. I meant what I said, which helped. The atmosphere in the room lightened considerably. We talked about the dictatorships in Spain and Portugal, we discussed Orwell then moved on to literature in general. At the end, they asked me to wait outside, then called me back in almost immediately.

'We're going to offer you a place here, subject to your grades,' the chairman began. 'I have to say that meeting you has been a considerable surprise to us – in view of the information we had about you.'

'I'm sorry?'

'Your school report was the worst I've ever seen. In fact, your housemaster made you sound so appalling that we were curious to see you.'

4   *Summer in the sixties*

IN THE SUMMER OF 1966, life was full of promise. The whole country was on a high after England's victory in the World Cup and I was delirious with the knowledge that I never had to go to school again.

Along with a thousand other first-year students, I arrived at Reading University a week before the start of term. We had seven days to get our bearings, register for our courses and enrol in the societies and clubs that interested us.

At the inaugural meeting of the anarchist group, the members argued interminably about whether they should obey the university rule that societies take proper minutes of their meetings. I caught the eye of another fresher at the back of the room and lifted my eyes to the ceiling in despair. He laughed. We left together and walked along Redlands Road, scuffing up the brown and gold leaves that carpeted the pavement.

'Name's Jack,' he said. He was a long-haired northerner, small and quick, with the bright eyes of a blackbird.

'Hi Jack. I'm Nigel. What did you make of the anarchist group?'

'Fuh!' he replied scornfully, 'Middle-class wankers! Real libertarians wouldn't care tuppence what the university thought.'

Over egg and chips in the university buttery, Jack told me about himself. He too was in revolt against the stifling authority of his childhood. His father was a miner from Nottingham, a doctrinaire communist who slavishly toed the party line. Stroking his goatee beard, Jack spoke passionately of the early anarchist writers, Bakunin and Kropotkin, of the First International, the history of the labour movement and its betrayal by the communists. I was spellbound. I'd never met a communist, let alone a communist's anarchist son. Jack had never known anyone who'd been at boarding school. Fascinated by each other, we hung out together, unburdening ourselves of the horrors of our childhoods and talking politics, ideas, girls and music.

We cemented our friendship by listening to *Blonde on Blonde* in a darkened room, for hours on end, day after day, week upon week. Dylan's spare songs painted vast interior landscapes that illuminated the shadowy caverns of my youth and haunt me still.

My student grant for the first year, calculated according to my father's income, was a hundred and fifty quid. Dad was supposed to make it up to three hundred and forty pounds, the full grant. I buttonholed him in the Christmas holidays.

'Dad. I need a hundred pounds for the next term.'

'Didn't I tell you often enough?' he said exasperatedly. 'I've told you a thousand times that I'd look after you until you were eighteen, then you'd be on your own. You're eighteen, Nigel. Your finances are your problem from now on, not mine.'

'What? You're not serious… How am I supposed to live?'

'I bloody well am serious. What you live on is your problem. If you're short of money, you'd better find yourself a part-time job.'

Horrified, unable to think of anything to say, I stormed out of his study. I was in my room, digesting the news, when Katie came in without knocking. Her head was tilted back and slightly to one side, a sure sign she was spoiling for a fight.

'What do you call this?' she snapped, throwing a wet towel at my feet.

'Might it be a towel?'

'Don't get clever with me, Nigel Fielding!'

'Ah, you prefer me to be stupid.'

'You think you're so smart, but you'll trip yourself up, you young fool. I will not have my bathroom left in such a state—' The swelling growl in Katie's voice warned of the approach of one of her berserker rages. But I didn't care any more. I'd had enough.

'Don't worry about your fucking bathroom. I won't be using it again. I'm off.'

All but broke, I returned to Reading. To save money, I quit my digs in the Caversham Road and went halves on a bedsit in Westcroft, a large country house where Jack had a flat. I shared the bedsit with a Jamaican student.

Errol was the first black guy I'd ever had a conversation

with. My new best friend was a miner's son… university was showing me what a limited environment I'd grown up in.

Errol was sharp and sardonic. He took his politics studies seriously and worked long hours in the library. In the evenings, before we turned the lights out, we lay on our beds and talked.

'What are you going to do after uni?' he asked me one night.

'Dunno… travel around, have a look at the world before I decide.'

'Me, I have a plan. I have ambitions. My aim is to return to Jamaica with a good degree that will get me a well-paid job in Kingston. I will take an interest in local affairs, enter politics, become a member of Parliament and work hard for my constituents. Then we will see…'

'Errol, that is so fucking bourgeois! I can hardly believe you said that. You're a clever guy—'

'Stop it!' he fired back angrily. 'You don't have an idea in your head but you dare to judge my ambition. You young white rebels are so predictable it's pathetic. After your state-subsidised protest you'll wake up to financial reality, get a job and take full advantage of a global economic system that's set up for the First World to plunder the planet's resources.'

'The what?'

'The First World, the developed countries – America and Western Europe. You live off the backs of the world's poor.'

'I don't. That's not me you're talking about, Errol. I'm not part of that system.'

'You will be. Wait and see.'

'You're wrong, Errol. I won't. Not me.' Though my words were firm, I was on the back foot, unsure of myself, wondering, 'Will I? Will that really happen to me?'

After I'd paid the term's rent for the bedsit, I was left with two pounds. I could still eat for a while – sixpence would get me a lunchtime plate of chips from the university buttery or a couple of thick peanut butter sandwiches from the tea ladies in St David's hall – but I had to do something quickly or I'd be penniless.

St David's wasn't a hall of residence. It was the umbrella for the students who lived in digs in the town. Next door to the Students' Union bar, St David's consisted of a reading room, two common rooms and a kitchen. At the far end of the smoky Junior Common Room a group of freshers had a late-evening three-card brag school. I took a deep breath and joined in.

Flash Andy was dealing that first hand, fag in mouth. He twisted his head to the side and squinted to keep the cigarette smoke out of his eyes. Andy was handsome and brash. Full of restless energy, he commented on everything.

'And a third ace to go with my other two,' he said, dealing himself the last card. He put a penny in the centre of the table. 'I'm in.'

After we'd all ante'd up, he said to man on his left, 'Over to you, Rod.'

Rod and Andy were the stalwarts of the brag school. Other members might come and go, but they were there, night after night. Dressed in black, Rod was stillness to Andy's incessant movement, quiet to his friend's light chatter. Without looking at his cards he whispered, 'Penny blind,' and placed a coin in the centre.

'With you,' I said, putting my penny next to his.

'Thruppence open,' Blond Jim, the chess wizard, ventured.

'You can't raise a blind man.' Andy slapped the other newcomer down. 'Tuppence is the bet if you've looked at your cards.'

'Tuppence then.'

'Stack.' Barry threw his cards in. Andy followed suit.

'Sixpence blind,' Rod breathed inexorably.

'With you.' I threw a silver coin into the pot. I knew I daren't follow another blind bet without looking at my cards.

A commotion at the other end of the Common Room made us turn our heads.

'Nothing,' Andy said dismissively. 'It's just the rugby buggers thumping each other. Look at them, the oafs. Anyway,' he added to Jim, who'd been hesitating, 'a shilling if you want to go.'

'OK, a shilling.' Jim didn't look happy.

Rod peeked at his cards and threw them across the table with a muttered oath. The bet lay with me.

'Sixpence blind.' I smiled at Jim. I felt I had him on the run.

'Are you mad?' he wailed. 'You don't even know what you've got.'

'I won't need much to beat you.' I looked at him and waited.

He thought for too long, then threw his cards in. I'd won one and ninepence and I didn't even know what my cards were. I stacked them without looking. It was a great start and I was still ahead at the end of the session.

The brag school didn't get going until after the bar closed. The other players had had a few drinks and were playing for fun, with money they could spare. I was sober. I was there in order to make enough to eat and was taking it very seriously, even though I laughed and joked along with the others.

I'd been playing cards for as long as I could remember. Roger and I had learnt from Grandpop Davies in Wales when I was five and we'd been cutting and dealing ever since. There was no shuffle in brag, so I counted the cards, remembered what had gone, and kept in my head a fair mental picture of the shape of the ever-revolving pack. Just doing that would have given me an edge over my carefree gambling friends, but I was also concentrating on reading the behaviour of each of them, their tell-tale mannerisms when trying to hide a strong hand, or the little giveaway movements they made when bragging.

I had bad days, but not as often as my good ones. I was usually ahead at the end of the night. I got my grubstake up to a fiver, then to a healthy twenty pounds. After one disastrous all-night session my reserve plummeted to thirty bob. But I clawed my way back. I was living on my wits and keeping myself afloat. At last I was beholden to no one. I got up when I wanted and did whatever I felt like doing. For the first time since I'd been a little boy, I had that fine stretchy feeling that life was good.

At Easter Jack and I joined the Aldermaston March. Most weekends we hitch-hiked around southern England, going to picket American airbases and protest against nuclear bombs. More often than not, we'd go home after our action, but occasionally, if we'd travelled a long way, we'd find someone to put us up.

There was always someone. A powerful feeling of solidarity existed among the few who felt strongly enough to take to the streets in the cause of peace. Often there would be a dozen of us at the crash-pad. We'd talk into the small hours, smoking cigarettes and drinking black coffee while we sorted out the world's problems.

Demonstrating at the weekends and playing cards until three or four in the morning meant I wasn't keeping up with my studies. I made special efforts to follow the philosophy course, which fascinated me, but I let the other subjects slide. For the first time in my life I had freedom and it had gone to my head. I'd squandered too much time protesting and having fun, I realised, as the first university exams approached.

I sailed through philosophy but failed my other two subjects. That meant if I didn't pass all three on the re-sit, I'd be kicked out.

In the early summer of 1967, there were extraordinary stories in the media about the hippies in San Francisco. Lurid newspaper articles claimed pop stars in London were getting high on hashish and marijuana. The Beatles' new album, *Sergeant Pepper's Lonely Hearts Club Band*, apparently contained references to mind-bending substances like LSD, the most powerful drug of them all.

I'd never seen any drugs. None of my friends had either. Wild rumours circulated around the campus, but we were never able to track them to their source. The harder it became to discover what all the fuss was about, the more Jack and I longed to find out.

A couple of second-year students and two guys from town lived above us, in the attic flat at Westcroft. In June, we saw them playing around in the garden, being really stupid but having lots of fun. We guessed they had to be high on something. Figuring that this was our best chance yet, Jack and I dared each other up the stairs. In the end we went together. Jack spoke up when the door opened a crack.

'Hi Tom, how are you?'

'What is it?'

'Well, we were wondering, er…' he cleared his throat and started again. 'Do you know where we could get a bit of hash?'

Silence.

'You know, the resin,' I added, to show we knew what we were talking about.

The door opened wide. Lenny stood at Tom's side. What he lacked in height, Lenny made up for in aggressiveness.

'What do they want?' he asked Tom, looking at us with distaste, as if we were peddling doorstep religion.

'They want to score some charge.' To us John said, 'Can't help you, I'm afraid.'

'No, we haven't got any.' Lenny grinned broadly.

What to say next? I was hovering, wondering how we could extricate ourselves without looking like prats, when Tom added casually, 'I do have some LSD… but I suppose that'd be too strong for you.'

'No, it wouldn't,' I said without thinking.

'Not at all.' Jack added his denial to mine. 'We'd like to try some.'

We were invited inside where we agreed to swap my new Hendrix album for two trips. Tom handed us a sugar cube each. Jack and I gave each other a little 'Why not?' look and ate them on the spot.

It started with a loose, sloppy feeling in my stomach and a humming, tingling sensation all over. I felt I was growing larger. Jack was staring in amazement at a grape he'd been peeling. He looked up. Our eyes met and locked.

'This is it!'

'Did you think that or did I?' Jack's grin was pulsing, radiating great waves of energy.

'We shared,' I replied. It was difficult to talk because my tongue was as big as my mouth and too big for its boots. Laughter seemed the only way forward.

Waist-deep in mirth, we stumbled outside. The world, waking up from its sleeping-beauty slumber, was as conscious of me as I was of it. Life sparkled and twinkled from every flower and leaf, every insect and tree. The energy of the universe was pouring through us. I could see it all in microscopic detail, but it was coming at me so fast there was no time to even think.

Staggered by the immensity of life, we lurched down the lane and collapsed in a meadow. For an aeon, speechless and unable to move, I could do no more than sit on the ground, propped against a tree, with a ringside seat in the cosmic dance. Jack sat beside me, my co-pilot. We were flying the planet round the sun. At telepathically linked intervals, we looked at each other with glowing eyes.

I soared through time and space, pondering the big questions of life, but unable to retain any coherent thought

processes. Patterns unfolded in my eyes and thoughts
flew through my brain like flocks of birds. I'd merged with
creation. I looked at Jack looking at me. He had too. No
longer individuals, we'd become part of everything.

The doors of perception were cleansed. I could see the
infinity that William Blake had glimpsed. I thought of trying
to explain this idea to Jack, but it was far too complicated
to even begin, ridiculous to consider it.

'What are you laughing at?' he asked.

'All of it. Wow! This is unbelievable.'

'Yeah. Too much.'

He was right. I was bombarded with awareness of everything at once: his vast presence, the little itch on my toe,
a plane passing overhead, the way the sunlight splashed
off the beech leaves, the stolid ant that was traversing my
jeans, wind ripples in the young wheat, sweat on the bridge
of my specs, birdsong in the hedgerow, the smell of the
blossom, the gurgling noises emanating from my stomach
and anything else within the reach of my wildly overper-
forming senses.

'Correct,' I said gravely, 'it's far too much.'

By the time we stopped laughing, we were both on our
feet. He pointed to the lane. 'Deepest Berkshire.'

I was a human archetype, making every journey of exploration that every man has ever made for as long as we've
been walking the earth. I watched myself moving forward,
assessing danger, looking for opportunity, alert to the possibility of treasure. With an instant change of perspective, I
saw myself leaning out of my narrow window of consciousness and scanning the wide horizons, observing the very
processes of existence unfolding. It struck me that my life,
my taken-for-granted life, is a gift, a scarcely imaginable

gift, one to be spent as freely as possible.

'Look!' Unable to say more, I pointed at a spider's web, stretched between two branches.

'Oh, wow!' Jack peered at this marvel. 'Too much.'

The erratic passage of a butterfly moved me to tears of happiness. All creation was lit with its own inner light, everything – even me. I was as marvellous, in my own way, as anything else. I too was a miracle of being, not just a prat. Of course I was that as well.

My stomach, slopping around in the liquid region between my mind and my feet, illustrated perfectly the kind of person I was: there was nothing solid at the centre of me. Half the time I didn't even know what my opinions were. I just followed the lead of people I admired and pretended to share their ideas and tastes. I was a sham. I'd taken this acid – without a clue about what I was letting myself in for – in order not to look like an idiot in front of someone who could see right through me.

The sad truth, I had to admit, was that I was a complete waste of space.

I trudged home, reflecting on my uselessness, and put myself out with the rubbish. It was the only place for the likes of me. As I climbed into the dustbin I was laughing so much that I got helplessly stuck. I'd cracked it. After what I'd seen today I didn't have to worry about holding the right opinions any more. I was past all that stuff. What a relief!

I'd been an idiot, but I knew I'd been struggling along, doing the best I could. My heart swelled with compassion for the damaged boy I'd been and I began to cry. As I remembered those black days, all the loneliness and pain that I'd bottled up after my mother's death came gurgling out.

And then, for the first time in years, her face appeared in my mind's eye. She was laughing in the kitchen of Grandpop Davies' house in Rhyl. In an instant that whole happy summer swept over me. Aunts in light summer dresses chattering and giggling while they made great piles of sandwiches in the kitchen. Roger and I, with our cousins, tearing in and out of the house, up and down the stairs, pursued by cries to look after the little ones. Parties in gardens, on the beach or up in the hills. The perfect summer of ginger beer, cakes and laughter was over in a moment, then my mummy was waving goodbye and blowing me kisses.

The light was fading when I came back to myself. I was still by the bin in the back yard. I straightened my bowed spine. A weight had gone from me; somehow I'd had a chance to say a proper goodbye to my mother. This LSD was unbelievable. Not only could it enable you to see the broad sweep of life, it could help you look within and understand things about yourself you'd never known before. 'This is the most important day of your life,' I told myself.

Much older and wiser, I climbed the stairs and opened the door. Purple waves of sound rolled over me and Hendrix was inside my head, asking, 'Are you experienced, not necessarily stoned, but out of your mind?'

Yes. Absolutely.

The world had suddenly switched from black and white to colour. I'd seen that all creation is a shimmering dance of energy. At the highest level, we are one.

'Where can we get some more of this?' Jack and I were afire with our trip and talked about it for days. He too had experienced a sense of oneness with nature, life as energy and worlds in grains of sand as well as the sensory overload, distortion of time and space and hallucinatory after-images. Our lives had been turned on their heads and we were a great deal better for it, we agreed. Our friends ought to try this miraculous stuff. Everyone should.

We got Tom to introduce us to his contact and bought an eye-dropper bottle with fifty hits of acid. One drop on a sugar cube was one trip. We started handing laced cubes around to our friends. When we ran out, we got another bottle. Not everyone wanted to try it, but virtually all those who did took to it with the same breathless enthusiasm as us and wanted to turn on their friends too. In scores of such psychedelic distribution centres throughout the land, the magic circle of trippers grew day by day.

The light of joy was in our eyes; we'd stumbled across the elixir of life, the substance that was going to transform humanity!

5 The Julie mob

ON APRIL FOOLS' DAY, after a week in police custody, the thirty remaining Operation Julie suspects were handcuffed and bundled into a large coach, stiff with coppers. I only knew a few of the prisoners: Henry and Brian who ran our organisation, Russ and Eric, the guys I supplied, Smiles who was Russ's main man, and a couple more. Who were all the others? There were some attempts at talk during the loading of the coach, but once we were underway most people fell silent.

At the centre of a large convoy of police cars and motor-cyclists, we travelled westward down the motorway. I gazed hungrily at the passing countryside. How many years before I smelt wood smoke again?

The two women were dropped off at Pucklechurch Prison, near Bath; we men were taken on to Bristol. The coach drove into the nick and the great doors of Horfield Prison were closed and barred behind us.

Among our number were two doctors, two chemists, a teacher, an author, a musician... I don't think Bristol nick had ever seen anything quite like the Julie mob. Surrounded by dozens of warders, we were escorted to reception where we were split up, six to a cell, and uncuffed. I rubbed my wrists and looked across the room at Russ.

'Hey, Leaf,' he said ingratiatingly, 'you're good at crosswords. What about this clue? Postman with a heavy load…' He looked at me expectantly like a spaniel.

I couldn't bring myself to talk to him.

'How many letters?' Eric leaned forward to ask.

'Fucking hundreds!'

They laughed together. The two young Bristolians in the room with us laughed too. They'd been loudly cursing their bad luck at being admitted to prison at the same time as our lot.

'This is going to take all fucking day, Spider,' the big one had moaned. Now he boasted he was starting his third stint in Horfield and would probably pull a three or a four this time for GBH. Joe knew the score and took delight in telling us rookies all the details.

'They measure your weight and height and check you for scars and birthmarks and shit. Next they want your address, date of birth and all that crap. Everything in your pockets gets written down in a book and put in your property box, with your clothes. After you've stripped, there's a de-lousing shower. It smells fucking horrible, don't it, Spider?'

'Yeah, fucking horrible.' Joe's sidekick wore a crazed look and a tattooed dotted line round his neck with the words CUT HEAR. Spider had teeth problems and sprayed the air as he spoke. I hoped I wasn't going to be in a cell with him.

After handing over my clothes, I took the stinking shower, dried myself with a sandpaper towel, stood in a line and was eventually issued with remand clothes: white pants and vest, a blue and white striped shirt, scratchy brown trousers, a brown jacket, grey socks and black shoes. When everyone was dressed, some forty-odd screws made a cordon round us and shepherded us to our new quarters.

D Wing, the remand wing, was a huge brick Victorian building, long and cavernous, four stories high, full of echoes. Cells lined both sides. It was hot and stuffy and smelt of drains and floor polish. Our arrival drew the attention of a group of prisoners with mops and buckets. They nudged each other and nodded in our direction.

'Nit-o. It's the Julie mob,' one of them muttered as we passed.

While we hung around outside the screws' office, waiting to be allocated cells, the cleaning orderlies drifted in our direction and sifted in around us, talking behind cupped hands or muttering without moving their lips.

'Hi. Name's Sid. Get you anything you want. Talk later.'

After a few minutes of waiting and milling around, we were allocated cells and issued with bedding, plastic cutlery and a plastic pint mug. Clutching our gear, we climbed the metal stairs to the top landing. The south side had been cleared for us. The cells were seven feet by eleven. Originally designed for one inhabitant, they now held three. On the left of the door were two bunk beds, on the right a single. I was in a cell with Eric and Andy. I'd known Eric for years, but I'd never met Andy, our replacement chemist. Henry and Brian had kept the lab separate from the rest of the organisation.

We drew lots for the three beds. Andy got the top bunk and I won the single.

At first I was just glad to be out of the clutches of the police, I think we all were. No more interrogations. Here we could at last talk to each other, find out how bad things were, look for crumbs of comfort. Mostly we looked in vain. We'd been comprehensively bust and all the major conspirators were facing long prison sentences. Statements made to the police had torn great rents in the fabric of trust, woven through years of friendship. We were all wondering who might try to climb out of the shit by treading on the heads of old friends. I was lying on my bed, stewing in my thoughts when the cell door was unlocked and flung open.

'Fielding. Visit. Get a fucking move on then!'

I tucked my shirt in and ran my hands through my hair as the screw escorted me across the yard to the visiting area. It had to be Mary. Swallowing convulsively, I sat at a little square table and waited. Then she was walking towards me, arms held out. I rose to my feet. We hugged. I pressed myself against the warmth of her body and clung on. She smelt wonderful. I didn't want to let go and have to look into her eyes.

'I thought you stopped all that ages ago,' she said flatly when we separated and sat down.

'I did,' I replied miserably. 'But I started again a couple of years back. You were always away on a flight or jet-lagged at home. You never noticed. I'm sorry, honey. I'm so sorry you were dragged into all this. How was it with the police? Were they OK?'

She nodded.

'What about your family?'

'They're not pleased with you.'

'No, of course not. But how are they with you?'

'Oh, Leaf…' she collapsed into my arms across the corner of the table. It was an uncomfortably twisted position for us both. We sat back when the visiting-room orderly came over and asked if we wanted tea. Not having any money, I had to wait for Mary to reply, 'Yes, please. Two teas, no sugar.'

'Did you know the shop was raided?' she asked, leaning forward and putting her elbows on the table.

'Yes.' I leant forward too, so our heads were almost touching. 'I saw our tenants leaving Swindon police station. Are they OK?'

'They were shaken up, of course, but they're fine now. It's in the past for them…'

We sat in silence while I absorbed the implicit message. I was grateful for the arrival of the tea. On the point of explaining what needed to be done in the shop, I was rendered dumb by the smack-in-the-face realisation that I could say what I liked but I couldn't help any more. Mary was going to have to deal with everything on her own from now on. Our life together was over – for years at least.

'Everyone's been brilliant, especially Martin. He and Lou have kept me going.' Martin and I were partners in the health-food business. Mary bravely plugged on in the face of my numbed silence. 'Mart said to tell you the shop will be fine, but we've put the restaurant plan on hold. I'm doing your work now. Mostly I'm bagging up out back, but sometimes I have to serve in the shop. It's so weird. I feel all the customers are looking at me, wondering if I was in on it. The whole country's talking about Operation

Julie. Everyone knows in the village. I haven't got a clue what to say to any of them... Oh God, I shouldn't go on about my problems when you're the one who's in the worst trouble.' She looked at me seriously. 'Are you OK? Are you managing?'

'Yeah.' I managed to stop there. I was sure that if I said another word I'd break down.

'Are you really?' She gazed at me with loving concern.

The visit had been relatively easy until she looked at me that way. Right then I'd have given anything, anything at all, just to be left alone to live happily forever with my lovely Mary – but it was too late for that. I'd blown it.

'Leaf, are you listening? I said visitors can bring you things while you're on remand. Tell me what you're allowed to have and I'll make sure you get it. Mart's coming to see you the day after tomorrow...'

The prison day started at 7 a.m. with a clanging bell and a screw unlocking the cells, screaming: 'Slop out! Slop out!'

We had a brief opportunity to empty our chamber pots, use the toilets, wash, shave and take fresh water to the cell. Fifty of us competing to use two toilets, two urinals and three sinks in the few minutes before breakfast.

For all meals we clattered down the four flights of metal stairs, had the food dolloped on to a metal tray and went back up to our cells to eat. We were banged up twenty-three hours a day, sometimes twenty-four.

If it wasn't raining, there'd be an hour of exercise in the morning. The small exercise yard was bounded by cell-blocks and a high mesh fence, topped with rolls of razor-wire. Beyond the wire, across a passage patrolled by Alsatians and screws, the old brick prison walls shut off our view of the world. We walked round and round in circles.

On exercise we didn't hang out with our cellmates. Other than in the meal queue, this was our only time to talk to other people. At first I walked round with my old pal Brian, then I had a spell doing the rounds with his partner Henry. After that I struck up a friendship with the original chemist, Richard Kemp. Richard was tall and gaunt. He had a limp but I still had to walk fast to keep up with him.

Richard was a man after my own heart. We talked long and excitedly in one-hour bursts. He too had wanted to turn the world on and he'd gone a long way towards achieving his aim by producing kilos of acid, enough for tens of millions of trips. In the course of his syntheses, he'd accidently discovered a way of shortening the complicated process of turning the raw ingredients, ergotamine tartrate or ergotamine maleate, into LSD. This short cut yielded the purest acid the world had ever seen, purer even than the stuff made by the Sandoz laboratories in Switzerland, the place where Albert Hofmann accidently discovered the properties of LSD25, on 19 April 1943.

He told me all this one day while we loped round the yard and ended by saying, 'And look where our idealism got us.' His despondently waving arm took in the prison walls, D Wing and the punishment block.

'Well, we're not the first people to be persecuted for what we believe in,' I replied, 'and I don't suppose for a moment we'll be the last. We'll be exonerated in the future, don't you think?'

'Maybe. But that doesn't help us now.'

The bell brought another exercise period to an end.

~~~~~

Andy, Eric and I were obliged to spend virtually all our time together. We listened to the radio Mary had brought me, we read, wrote, talked, played cards or lay on our beds thinking about the lives we'd lost or the future we faced.

I was lucky in my draw of cellmates. Eric was a great guy to be with, ever cheerful in the face of adversity. If competent authorities filed him, he'd go in the salt-of-the-earth category. Short, jovial, inclining to fat, Eric's receding hair was the length of the dirty-blond stubble on his face. When deep in thought, he had the habit of restlessly rubbing his hand across the breadth of his half-beard.

Before the bust, Eric had run The Last Resort, a fashionable cocktail bar in London. He was full of stories and ideas to keep us entertained. We studied Arabic together on the radio and set up a theoretical betting syndicate, based on a system he'd heard about, where we put a tenner on the second favourite in the first race. If we won, we stopped – a few quid in front. If we didn't, we doubled the stake for the second race and doubled it again and again – moving on to subsequent days if necessary – until we won.

The make-believe cash rolled in. Soon we were forty thousand quid to the good and dreaming of the real money we'd make after our release. Our winnings kept mounting until we were five hundred thousand pounds ahead. Then we hit a bad patch and lost race after race at meeting after meeting, until all our gains were wiped out and we were having to pay millions on each bet.

'It's a bit like the acid game,' Eric said, as we folded the imaginary syndicate. 'You think you're doing really well

and you've got it sussed, then you suddenly lose everything
– and you realise it was all a stupid idea.'

Andy, with his high-domed forehead and abstracted air,
had only been in the nick a few days before he was being
called 'the Professor' by cons and screws alike. Andy was
Everyman from the Tarot pack, walking along with his head
in the clouds, full of fascinating ideas, just on the point of
stepping over a cliff. His knowledge was encyclopaedic. He
introduced me to the Albigensian heresy.

'I've never heard of it,' I said doubtfully, 'and I studied
European history.'

'It's not in the textbooks,' he explained. 'The Catholic
Church and the French state conspired to keep the lid on
it for hundreds of years. The Church was very corrupt in
the thirteenth century and a lot of people in Languedoc had
turned to the religion of the Cathars – also called Albigen-
sians because they were strong in the town of Albi. Pope
Innocent III launched a crusade against them. This was the
opportunity the northern French nobility had been waiting
for. With papal blessing, their crusader army destroyed the
independent county of Languedoc, city by city, in a whole
series of massacres. That's how Paris extended its rule to
the Mediterranean.'

'Wow! How do you know all that?'

Andy ignored Eric's question. He hadn't finished. 'The
popes squashed the gnostics too. Their error was that they
called God direct, they didn't need priests to phone on their
behalf. If their ideas had caught on, the Catholic hierarchy
would've been made redundant. So the gnostics had to
go…'

Andy was a well-spring of information. Dip your bucket in his pool of knowledge and up might come answers to drench you. Breaking a long silence, one endless afternoon, he smacked his lips and said, 'Did Brian or Henry ever tell you about the time I lost a hundred and fifty thousand trips?'

'No,' I replied. 'What happened?'

Andy jumped down to the floor and sat on the end of my bunk. He leaned forward with a conspiratorial air. He enjoyed telling stories and used hands, voice and movement to enhance his words.

'Well, synthesising acid is a long and tiring business. Spaces you right out too. At the end of the session, I lay down for a moment and the next thing I knew it was 3 a.m. That wouldn't have mattered except I hadn't put the flask of acid in the fridge.'

He pushed his blond forelock out of his eyes and smoothed his hair down. 'I ran upstairs, grabbed the flask and was about to open the fridge when I thought I'd better check the temperature. So I put a thermometer in the flask…' He paused dramatically and looked at each of us in turn with a you-won't-believe-this expression on his face. 'I've always been a bit clumsy. The thermometer slipped from my fingers and went straight through the bottom of the glass flask. The acid all poured out, over me and onto the carpet.' Andy's laugh was deep and dirty. It sounded strange, emerging from the lips of a man who looked like he should be wearing a gown in a lecture room.

'Were you OK?' I asked.

'Sure.' He pushed the errant forelock back again. 'I took off my clothes, rolled them up in the carpet and put them in a big plastic bag. Then I had a shower. I was fine. After the bust, I warned the police about the carpet, but I bet they get tripped out when they move it.' He laughed again. 'They probably don't have any real idea of just how concentrated acid is. One gram is enough for five thousand trips.'

A dozen of the Julie prisoners had nothing at all to do with acid, but were Welsh hash importers, swept up in the great police dragnet. They began to be released on bail at the weekly remand hearings in front of a magistrate in Swindon.

Getting us to and from the magistrate's court was a massive pseudo-military operation, repeated each week. We were taken from our cells to the central courtyard. The coach came in from the gate compound only after we'd been handcuffed in pairs. We boarded it, along with a score of screws. Handcuffed inside the coach, at the centre of a convoy of several police cars and half a dozen motorbikes, we were escorted through the streets. The police had all their sirens wailing and lights flashing as if they were taking the President to meet the Queen.

None of the main acid conspirators were released at these remand hearings. The police opposed bail, saying that we still had a lot of LSD stashed away. That was true enough, but they added spurious stories about connections with the IRA and the Baader-Meinhof gang, and hinted at plans to spike the water supply of Birmingham. These tall tales helped justify the massive police escorts and the armed marksmen around the court. They also helped raise the profile of the Julie squad and obscure the embarrassing fact that – though they'd watched us for years while we made and distributed millions of LSD tablets – they had signally failed to find the bulk of our acid.

At the third remand hearing I learnt that they'd mishandled some of the acid they had found. While I was waiting for the hearing to begin, a police officer opened the door of the holding cell and leaned against the door jamb. He was middle-aged and overweight.

'That acid of yours…' he paused awhile.

'Yes,' I replied warily. Though most of the Operation Julie officers hadn't expressed any personal opinion on LSD, a couple of them had told us we were evil. I waited to hear what this one had to say.

'I was one of the guys sent to dismantle the Seymour Road lab. Did you hear about that?'

'Yes, I heard. Welcome to the club. How was your trip?'

'Well, strange stuff that acid of yours. I was in the bath when I felt the first effects. It was like the water had folded around me, I can't really explain. Then I saw the picture. Wow!'

'What picture?'

'On the wall of the bathroom. Typical poncy rubbish, I'd thought. Van Gogh. I was looking at it and I suddenly got it. That sun was really burning in the sky, you could feel it beating down on the cornfield, hammering everything flat…' He paused, seemingly embarrassed by the enthusiasm in his voice. 'Oh, I didn't say, the name's Wally.'

'Hi Wally. I'm Leaf. So what happened after the picture?'

'Well, I heard my mates, Andy and Dave, laughing downstairs, so I went and joined them. We fooled around for a while. Everything we said seemed hilarious. We knew we weren't normal but we'd planned to go to the pub so we went. At the bar, Dave thought his beer mug was so heavy he couldn't lift it. Andy poured his pint straight down his throat in one go then kept saying "I can't believe I did that".'

Wally looked at me sheepishly with his big soft eyes. 'I was staring at the patterns in the foam as it slid down the inside of my glass. I don't think I've ever seen anything so amazing in my life.'

Noise in the corridor brought our conversation to an abrupt halt. It continued after the end of the hearing. Wally discovered his hearing was abnormally acute. If he focused, he could hear what the people in each group in the pub were saying. He could tell, just by the way the group sat and the manner in which each individual spoke and listened, how they interacted with each other and what their relationships were. He saw envy in a gesture, love at a glance.

'I had no right to know so much,' Wally said, almost indignantly. 'Then I suddenly realised I was in an illegal state of mind and almost panicked at the thought I'd be arrested. Then I remembered it was OK, because I was a policeman.'

He began laughing. I had to join in.

'Might see you here next week,' he said as he left.

I saw him a few more times. He carried on his story, telling me how they'd had a wonderful walk from the pub, awestruck as the spangled night revealed real beauty in the strangest places. They strode spongy pavements in time and in tune with one another, pointing out marvels and miracles as they headed back to the house of dreams. Indoors, a moment's shared doubt caused them to phone the police station and turn themselves in. They were taken to Kingston Hospital.

'Bummer,' I sympathised.

'Oh, yes. Big mistake. Harsh lights, questions, examinations. It wasn't pleasant. Not at all. It put the other two right off. But me, I can't help thinking back to the first part, before the hospital.'

Whenever he could, Wally hung around the door of my cell in Swindon police station, before and after the magistrate's hearings.

'Funny thing about that acid of yours…' he'd begin and then he'd get more and more excited, describing the hidden treasures behind the secret door he'd found, when he'd suddenly remember his uniform and his role as my jailer and the words would falter, he'd cough and say, 'Course, it's not my line at all. I'd never do it again. No. Gin's my poison. That's what I'm comfortable with. And it's not against the law.'

'But gin was against the law in the States, during Prohibition, Wally. It still is in some parts of the world. The drug laws are just the product of the place you live in and the time you were born. LSD was legal in Britain until 1966.'

'Yeah. Funny thing about that acid of yours…' Wally was itching to talk about his trip, but this wasn't a subject he could easily bring up in the police canteen; I was his only confidant. I grew to like Wally and looked forward to our meetings. Here was a policeman with whom I had some strong common ground. I was sad when our talks came to an end at the final remand hearing at the end of June, when the Julie mob was committed for trial.

As prisoners must, we fell into the routine of the days. After exercise we'd wait to see if we had the lifeline of a letter, something to lift us out of the swamp of our thoughts. After lunch we'd lie on our beds, hoping to be called for a visit. You could have one per day, twenty minutes long. Your visitors were allowed to bring in a meal and a bottle of beer or half a bottle of wine. More important than the goodies was the fresh air they brought in from outside and the feeling they gave you that you hadn't been forgotten, casually rubbed out of existence.

Mary managed to get down to Bristol a couple of times most weeks. These visits were tearing occasions. It was wonderful to see her but the sound, the smell and the touch of her, and then their absence when the short visit was over, made prison almost unbearable. She looked tired but she was showing courage and resilience. Her strength made me feel both good and bad. I was proud of her for the way she was dealing with an awful situation, but the weak part of me was dismayed that she seemed to be managing fine without me – she didn't need me any more. Maybe she did and was putting on a brave face for the visits. I know I was.

She coordinated my other visitors so that they didn't clash. Mart, my business partner, often came to see me, as did many of my mates from Reading. After a few weeks, my old pal Scooter started visiting me. Scooter and I had done various deals in the past and he feared the police were waiting to grab him. Once he'd learnt he was in the clear he came to see me and returned frequently, usually bringing me a bit of dope, which I'd stash in my mouth.

Sometimes getting high made me achingly aware of my predicament. Usually it enabled us to have a laugh together, or helped me float off into the airy spaces of my mind. With one of us on guard by the door, we'd take it in turns to stand at the window with the spliff and blow the smoke outside. Smashed out of my skull one evening on good Nepalese, listening to *Carmina Burana* on Radio Three, I let the half-smoked joint slip from my fingers. It fell to the exercise yard, four floors below. The following day, I was first out on exercise and spotted the jay immediately. It was close to the feet of one of the supervising screws. After a few circuits of the yard, I got Brian to distract the warder by asking him a question. At the same time I knelt down, next to the joint, ostensibly to tie my shoelace. My fingers were poised to move towards the stub when the observant screw said, 'What, swooping already, Fielding?'

Swoopers are one of the lowest forms of prison life.

'Not me,' I replied, standing and kicking the joint into a drain.

Even with such fine companions as I had, the days snailed past on mucus trails. Slowly, those days began adding up to weeks, then months. The heating went off. Summer arrived. Out in the world, Virginia Wade won Wimbledon and the Queen celebrated her silver jubilee. There were no street parties in Horfield nick.

The night is a bad time in prison, only the days are worse. Sleep never came easily. I lay for hours in the dark, counting my losses and worrying about what was to come. When I eventually dropped off, I roamed free in my dreams and surfaced in captivity. There is no more depressing start to a day. Getting through each one was like swallowing a hedgehog. On the bad-hedgehog days, when the spikes were facing the wrong way, the prison metronome ticked metric time: a hundred seconds a minute, a hundred minutes to the hour, a hundred hours per day.

Week after endless week I lay on my bed, trying to set myself free by reliving the extraordinary series of adventures that had followed my first LSD trip, back in the days when I'd thought myself invulnerable.

6   *A leaf in God's forest*

THE FIRST UNIVERSITY EXAM resits came up over the event horizon then receded into the ever more distant past. I didn't turn up. That way, I told myself, I was dropping out rather than being thrown out. I had a few twinges about my education ending on a note of failure, but I reminded myself I was doing something far more important than trying to get a degree. I was on a mission to save the planet by raising the human race to a higher level of consciousness.

I weighed the shimmering, fragile beauty of the world against our growing destructive power and I worried. I could understand how we'd become as we were – our nature had been shaped by the constant struggle to survive and we were still haunted by the fears and suspicions that had dominated our forebears' lives.

But our technological ability had outgrown our wisdom. The world was now divided into two hostile camps, each threatening the other with annihilation. Something had gone seriously wrong with the great human adventure.

Unless we could sort it out, we were for the chop.

Protesting about the bad state of affairs had little effect. People had to see for themselves what was going on. With acid there was a good chance that they would. I had, and I wasn't alone. In the summer of '67, hundreds of thousands of high-spirited trippers were optimistic that mankind was on the point of taking the next step up the evolutionary ladder.

The qualities that had enabled *Homo sapiens* to manipulate his environment had also placed him on the brink of destruction. To survive, we needed to transform ourselves into *Homo tolerans*. LSD was the tool that could help us to see a way back from the brink, by enabling us to appreciate that fundamentally we are all one – while giving us the confidence to celebrate our diversity and our differences.

What fun, being on a mission to save the world. What an adventure! Having tripped over the philosopher's stone, it was our pleasant duty to turn everyone else on. As an outward manifestation of our kaleidoscopic appreciation of our existence, we discarded the drab straitjacket clothes of the straights. We wore colourful outfits that flowed and waved in the wind. Our hair grew unchecked. We adorned ourselves with beads and bells and flowers and we danced.

Acid freaks had no trouble recognising each other and it wasn't just the clothes and the hair. Trippers had an aura visible to other acid heads. A group apart, we psychonauts were the only exclusive club who welcomed anyone who wanted to join.

There wasn't a blueprint for the alternative society, it was a rainbow alliance, all colours welcome. As more and more people turned on to psychedelic drugs, tuned into the changing times and dropped out of the old way of thinking, I believed, those dinosaurs clinging to the past would become an irrelevant minority, a curiosity like Chelsea pensioners.

I danced through those grasshopper days of the summer of love, at parties, be-ins and concerts. In the autumn the acid ran out. Living in the moment, I hadn't thought to store up anything for winter. A few weeks after my nineteenth birthday, broke and desperate, I did what many teenagers do when things turn bleak. I swallowed my pride and rang to ask my father if I could return home.

'As long as you pay your way,' he replied gruffly.

Military men's dwellings change every couple of years, their real home is the army. My father's house was now in Strangways, a row of officers' quarters on the edge of Larkhill Camp in Wiltshire. The only hippy in the place, a splash of colour amid the khaki, I stood out at Larkhill and was something of an embarrassment to my Dad, the head of tactics at the School of Artillery.

In the daytime I worked as a petrol pump attendant in the garage on the camp. In the evenings I painted or read in my attic bedroom. Sometimes, when there was a moon, I walked across the fields to Stonehenge and had the place to myself. Life in Larkhill had its moments, but I got a lot of flak at mealtimes.

The generation gap was a growing chasm. You had to shout to be heard on the far side. Dad thought I'd gone completely to pieces and bluntly told me so. I rounded on him for being prepared to kill to order. Our meals were artillery duels where we pounded each other from our entrenched positions.

'Why you… you're a communist, that's what you are!' Katie exclaimed one blighted dinner, in the dead ground between Christmas and New Year.

'Not at all. I'm an anarchist! The two could hardly be more different.'

'That's enough!' Dad snapped. 'Anarchist, my foot! You don't know what you're talking about. Not another word.' He was bursting to say more. Eventually he could contain himself no longer. 'You can't spend your life serving petrol to gunners,' he snapped. 'What do you think you're playing at? I tightened my belt for years to pay for your education. You've got to get yourself a proper job.'

I was badgered into applying to the Civil Service. At my interview in Bristol everything appeared to be going smoothly until one of the interview panel asked what I thought of the Torrey Canyon, the supertanker that had gone down off the Scilly Isles. Its oil slicks had tarred and feathered miles of the Cornish coast.

'An absolute disgrace. Utterly criminal!' I replied with feeling.

'I hardly think criminal is the right word. It was an unfortunate accident—'

'No, I don't agree,' I cut him short. 'The sea's a dangerous place. Transporting vast amounts of oil around in giant tankers is criminally irresponsible.'

'I say. Come on now,' another board member joined in. 'Economies of scale mean we have to have big tankers. It's so much cheaper—'

'Except it's not cheaper at all when you've got to spend millions cleaning up. And no amount of money can buy back the lives of all those birds!' I didn't care that I was interrupting, I felt strongly about this. I'd read *Silent Spring* and knew the damage that the industrial society was inflicting on the world.

'Greed allows these atrocities to happen,' I lectured them. 'Our greed may kill us in the end. If the human race is to have a future, we've got to clean up our act. Are you too stupid to see that?'

'Look here, young man—'

'You listen to me—'

'How dare you!'

'Mind your language—'

They all tried to talk at once and fell silent together. It was a good time to leave. At the door I turned and shouted, 'You straights haven't got a fucking clue, have you? Intelligent creatures don't shit in their own nest!'

That was my last attempt to join the suits. I packed my bag and returned to Westcroft. Spring was coming. I could earn some money in Reading and then go travelling.

Nigels were never the heroes in the girls' magazines my sister Judy used to read. The few who featured always turned out to be cads who ended up getting dunked in a lake or tipped into a heap of dung behind the stables. Nigels in books were cheats and cowards, they weren't inspired artistic types or even good honest chaps. I'd never liked my handle, and its diminutives, Nigs and Nige, were even worse. Until I tripped I'd assumed I was stuck with the name. Now I realised that I could call myself anything I liked.

I thought about it for a while and decided to name myself Leaf. There were a number of reasons why it was right: it was a kind of play on my surname, I was a nature boy, smoked marijuana, was a big fan of Tolkien... and in *The Prophet*, Kahlil Gibran wrote, 'You are a breath in God's sphere, a leaf in God's forest...'

I was a leaf in God's forest – that was exactly how I felt. I'd go wherever the wind took me. A travelling feeling had been growing within. I'd been exploring my mind, now it was time to stretch my legs, have a look around and see what was going on in the world.

I wanted to experience that feeling of being completely in the present, not dwelling on the unchangeable past or wrapped up in the illusion of an imagined future. The way I saw it, Leary, Alpert, Ginsberg, Kesey and the other diarists of the new psychedelic era, were pretty much saying the same things as William Blake – that the essence of experience lay in the naked moment. I'd seen that myself while tripping. Comforts and routines were blankets and blinkers that stopped you appreciating the miracle of your life. I wanted to break the chains of habit that locked my being. By going on the road, I found a way to make every day totally different.

In the summer of 1968, while I was hovering on the verge of my first solo journey, Chicago police armed with clubs tore into anti-Vietnam War demonstrators at the Democratic convention. They beat the shit out of them for daring to exercise their right to dissent. The world was no longer the loving place it had seemed a year before.

France too was in uproar, convulsed by *Les Evénements de mai*, an enormous anti-governmental revolt. Radical students took over public buildings in the centre of Paris. Car workers occupied their factories. Ten million union members were out on strike. President de Gaulle left the country. In his absence the government was paralysed and seemed close to collapse.

But that wasn't why I travelled to France. I went because it was the first stop on the way to anywhere. In August I hitched to Dover with a small rucksack on my back containing a change of clothes, wash bag, sewing kit and a map. My sleeping bag was rolled on top of the rucksack, my cooking gear dangled from it. My head was full of Bob Dylan's hobo songs, an invisible Japhy Ryder strode alongside me. I had six quid in my pocket. A one-way ticket to Calais cost two pounds ten shillings. If I kept enough cash for the return fare, I had a quid to spend. Even in 1968 this wasn't a lot.

I stood at the rail of the ferry watching England grow smaller. My first solo trip abroad! Mostly I felt very excited but there were moments when I could have pissed myself with terror. I've always pushed myself beyond my comfort zone. There's something in my essentially cowardly frame which won't allow me to be ruled by my fears. Perhaps it was because I grew up with a big brother and tried to act beyond my years in an effort to earn his approval.

Maybe going on the road on my own became possible after the acid insight that I could do anything I had the courage to attempt.

On deck I fell into conversation with a couple of guys. I told them my name was Leaf; it sounded strange in my mouth but they accepted it without question. My two new friends were postgraduates from Oxford, on their way to the Rhineland, happy to give me a lift. They dropped me at Châlons sur Marne. I walked to the southern side of town and stuck up my thumb. Paris, my projected first stop, already lay far behind me. I was now making for the Mediterranean, my true destination – a sea that had glittered in my imagination since I was a boy.

A ride with a farmer in a van left me in the upper Marne valley as dusk approached. Leaving the road, I walked towards the river and found a good place to camp. I filled my saucepan with water, made a fire and brewed tea to have with my supper of bread and cheese.

Yawning, I unrolled my sleeping bag on a thick bed of sweet chestnut leaves. I was exhausted. What a day! I was somewhere in northeast France. The stars twinkled through the canopy of leaves.

'The time of my life,' I said to myself before realising there was no need to keep quiet. 'This is the life,' I called to the trees. 'This is my life,' I sang to the stars.

The hairs on my arms prickled when I realised it was the first night I'd ever been entirely on my own. Nobody knew where I was. For a while I listened to the sounds of the night – the wind, running water, an owl. Then I lay on my back and revelled in my solitude; there was nothing in the world but the trees, the heavens and me. When I was too tired to carry on watching for shooting stars, I took off my glasses, put them in my shoe and turned on my side.

I woke to the unmistakable sound of digging. But it was hardly light. What was going on? I scrabbled around for my specs, put them on and cautiously raised my head. A Citroën 2CV was parked some forty yards away, on a track by the river. The back was open. Alongside the car, a beefy man was digging. With a chill, I realised I was witnessing a murderer disposing of his victim's body. If he saw me, he'd kill me too. A seven-stone weakling, I'd be no match for him in a fight.

I started to edge out of the sleeping bag then froze, horrified by the loud rustling noise I was making. Too frightened to move, I lay on my back staring at the sky. Why had I come on this stupid adventure? Why hadn't I got a gardener's job with the council in Reading and lived to a ripe old age, instead of being battered to death on the banks of the River Marne?

The digging stopped. I nerved myself to sneak another look. The man was lifting half-filled sacks into the back of the car. Not a murderer, just a leaf-mould thief.

On the bus to the southern outskirts of Dijon, I got talking with a flashing-eyed, dark-haired girl. Saying she wanted to practise her English, Sylvie invited me to her parents' farm at Nuits St Georges. Wanting to see more of her, I accepted. We sat outside, with her father and friends, at a long table, eating cheese and fruit and drinking wine, when an old man burst into the courtyard.

'The Russians are attacking!' he yelled. 'Get the radio.'

We clustered around the radio while Sylvie's dad tried to tune in a news station. Eventually a solemn voice emerged through the crackling:

'…and Russian tanks are on the streets of Prague. As yet there is no news of President Dubcek…'

Prague was just a few hours' drive from where I sat. Dark clouds covered my journey south. A couple of days later, breasting a hill, I caught my first sight of the improbable blue of the Mediterranean. But where were the ruined temples, the vestal virgins and pomegranates of my imagination? The Côte d'Azur was all Vespas, ice creams, sunglasses and impossibly beautiful people wearing next to nothing.

At first I felt very self-conscious among the beach-brownies, but once I'd lost my British whites I relaxed and began to enjoy myself. For a month I hitched up and down the Riviera, living off the leftovers from the street markets and the generosity of bakers.

Penniless, I struck inland, heading northwest. There were orchards by the roadside, fields full of melons. I called in at village bakeries to enquire if they had any of yesterday's bread. I asked for work at farms I passed and was fed. Everywhere I met with friendliness and open hospitality – except for one place where the farmer turned his dogs on me.

I walked for two weeks, eating from the fields, roasting corn-cobs for my supper, sleeping under the stars. The weather held good. Day after day I ambled along the minor roads of Provence, zig-zagging towards the Rhône Valley. At Orange I reached the main road and held up my thumb to the northbound traffic. Nobody stopped for the sunburnt starveling at the side of the road. I guess I looked a sight.

That night I slept in a big drainage pipe. In the morning I was ravenous. I walked across a couple of fields to a vineyard and stuffed myself with unripe grapes. That day brought no ride, only stomach cramps. The night gave no sleep. I had to keep wriggling out of the pipe to go squat in the bushes. In the morning I yelled insults at the vehicles hurtling by. I could hardly believe it when a car finally stopped.

The two young Germans in the VW Beetle practised their English for a while then got into a furious Teutonic argument. The dispute lasted all the way to Paris. We travelled north at a hundred miles an hour while the passenger punched, slapped and abused the driver. In fear of my life, half-crazy with hunger, I hunched in the back, chain-smoking their cigarettes.

My first time in Paris. I headed for the Left Bank and soon found myself in a smoke-filled bar in the Rue de la Huchette. Someone gave me a glass of red wine. I handed round the cigarettes I'd liberated from the Germans. In the corner, a guitarist strummed and threw out clumps of words. Beside me, a black-clad poet drank and read from his work. He topped up my glass and introduced himself as Laurent. In a quiet moment, full of wine and bonhomie, I made a small contribution to the proceedings.

'Paris has been an example to the world in the past,' I began haltingly. 'Once again, this great city shows that the spirit of freedom—'

The doors burst open and several people ran in.

'The cops!'

'The CRS!'

'We're trapped!'

Panic swept through the bar. I grabbed my bag and went outside. Lines of helmeted police blocked both ends of the short street. They beat their batons on round shields and swept forward, clubbing anyone who impeded their advance. Everyone on the street ran into the café. The police stormed in and began catching people and dragging them off. By keeping still I remained invisible, until a fleeing student cannoned into me and knocked me into the path of two policemen. They grabbed me, hustled me outside and threw me into a *panier à salade*, a black police van. Laurent the poet landed on top of me. More people were tossed in after us before the van set off, siren wailing, barrelling south down the Boulevard St Michel.

At the police station, we were manhandled into a large wire cage already full of students. More vanloads of captives were squeezed in after us. Laurent was next to me, jammed up against the wire.

'Can I have some water?' he asked the policeman standing by the cage.

'Communist toad!' screamed the gendarme and poked the poet in the face with his truncheon.

Laurent reeled back, blood pouring from his nose. 'Help me,' he cried weakly as he collapsed. I grabbed him under the arms – he was as light as a meringue – and eased him to the floor.

'Bastards.'

'Pigs.'

The angry cries of my fellows in the cage provoked an assault by a dozen infuriated policemen. For a mad minute they lashed the arms and heads of anyone within the range of their fury, taking their revenge on the generation that had seemed, for a giddy moment, to be on the point of sending the old guard packing.

7 *Bail*

'**WHAT DO YOU RECKON** on your chances?' Eric asked me.

'Close to zero,' I said.

We'd been committed for trial after our twelfth weekly remand hearing. This left us just one final opportunity to apply for bail, before a judge in chambers. My application was due to be heard in Bristol in October. But my lawyer had told me that I had only the slimmest possibility of getting a result.

'No, it's just a game,' I continued. 'A waste of time – but that's the point, isn't it, to waste some time. It gave me something to think about and hope for, but now I just want to get it out of the way, same as I want to get everything out of the way – the trial, the stretch, the lot.'

I'd increasingly come to use prison slang. We all had to some extent or other. Partly protective colouration, but mostly because it was the common coin.

'I keep thinking that tomorrow night I could be at home with Mary. And the fact that it isn't going to happen doesn't stop me from driving myself crazy thinking about it. Being locked up is sending me nuts. We're designed for a life on the move, our ancestors were nomads for thousands and thousands of years. We're built to walk. That's partly why we're fucked up in this cell, we're not getting the exercise we need.'

'There's other reasons why we're fucked,' Eric laughed.

I tried not to think about those and to get my head into the space I'd been in 1968 when I was nineteen.

The rough handling from the police in Paris hadn't put me off life on the road. I wanted to return to roaming in the spring, but first I was going to save up some money. Back in Reading, I got a job as a gift-wrapper in Heelas department store and moved into a dingy basement bedsit in Caversham.

One autumn afternoon a bearded beatnik in a trench coat materialised at my workstation. He stood in front of me, smiling faintly, clicking his fingers. 'You Leaf?' he asked.

I nodded.

'Hi. I'm the Electric Eel.' He grinned as he held out his hand. 'Don't say anything about my name and I won't say anything about yours.' He whipped off his shades to reveal twinkling hazel eyes. 'I hear you're going overland to India… I'm headed that way myself… maybe looking for a travelling partner…'

That evening, at my place, I gave the Eel the makings for a joint, put the Velvet Underground on the turntable and made a pot of tea.

'I'll be your mirror, reflect what you are…'

Nico's disembodied voice filled the low-ceilinged room. She faded into the background as the Eel got into his stride.

'Know who I dig, man? Bert Jansch.' He was sitting cross-legged on the floor, flawlessly rolling a large conical spliff. He paused to lick the gummed strip. 'That cat has got it. If I could play half as well as Jansch, I'd die happy.' He lit the joint and asked, 'What about you, man? Who turns you on?'

'Dylan, of course…' I puffed on the joint and considered. A roomful of names jostled to be voiced: 'Lennon, Huxley, Ginsberg, Hendrix, Leary, Kerouac—'

'*On the Road*, man. I know exactly what you mean!' The Eel whipped the joint from me and took a toke. 'We'll go on the road together, Leaf. We have the spirit for it.'

'Pass the things over.' While I stuck skins together the Eel carried on talking.

'My last trip east, I ran out of money on the Turkish–Iranian border. The middle of winter, it was. Stupid really. People go missing in Eastern Turkey… dangerous place.' His tone was casual as he rattled on in staccato bursts, telling me extraordinary stories of desperate journeys through icy wastelands and burning deserts, of villains outsmarted and beauties bedded. A glutton for embellishment, the Eel knew how to tell a tale and I lapped up his words. He was a couple of years older than me and had the irresistible allure of a seasoned traveller. All the time he was talking, he was on the move, nodding his head, drumming lightly with his fingers, scratching his beard, playing the spoons, tapping his feet. The Eel was never entirely still, even in his sleep he twitched a lot.

He was carrying a canvas satchel the next time I saw

him. His travelling gear was even more compact than mine. 'I need somewhere to stay,' he said bluntly and moved in.

The Eel didn't have any money, but he hardly cost me anything. He shoplifted most of what he needed from the supermarket round the corner and made it look easy.

'I've had enough of this,' he moaned, when thick October clouds blanketed Reading and the year was racing towards winter. 'I want to be somewhere warm for Christmas. I've got a good chunk of money due. Tax rebate. Did I tell you?'

'Only a dozen times.'

'I'm off as soon as that money comes through. You're coming too, aren't you?'

In November '68, I quit my job at Heelas, picked up my pay and left the bedsit. The Eel and I went to Bracknell to collect his rebate, but there was a hold-up, he had to wait another week. To pass the time, we hitched down to the West Country. Walking into Bristol, the Eel paused to look at a poster.

'Hey, The Who! I wouldn't mind seeing them.'

'We need to keep our money for the journey to the east,' I said.

'I wasn't talking about paying,' he replied scornfully.

'What are you thinking of doing, then?'

'Dunno. I'll figure something.'

We went down to suss out the venue in the late afternoon. 'This is our way in,' the Eel said, pointing at a door at the rear. 'We'll get some scran and come back here to eat it while we wait for the road crew to turn up. When they go in, we tag on behind. Once we're in, the trick is to look like you belong. Grab a bit of spare kit if you can. Nobody questions anyone who's carrying equipment.'

It worked a treat. We stood watching from the side of the stage while the band thundered towards their climax. I was leaning on a tripod, the Eel clutching a case. We could have picked up some groupies after the show if we'd had anywhere decent to take them. In the small hours we broke into a derelict house that we'd reconnoitred during the day. I stashed my wages under a loose floorboard, unrolled my sleeping bag on the floor beside the Eel's and went to sleep with the music still pounding in my ears.

In the morning, we went out for an egg, chips and beans breakfast. When we returned to the derry, my money was gone. We kept looking, but it was gone.

'Well, we need to eat, so we're going to have to beg.' The Eel gave me a challenging look. 'I'll show you how.'

He sauntered up a busy street in the town centre. The first people he spoke to brushed him off, then he hooked someone, then another. He returned with eyes shining and a shilling and a sixpence in his hand. He gave me a bit of coaching and set me off down the road. We'd agreed to meet in half an hour.

I didn't see how I could approach a perfect stranger and ask for money. I had to try though. I saw someone who fitted the Eel's ideal profile: a middle-aged prosperous male. He was even smiling. I rehearsed my words as we approached each other. Then he was past and I hadn't said anything. The same thing happened the next time I tried. I just couldn't do it. I wandered around unhappily until shortly before our deadline. Rush hour was over and there weren't many people around. When I said I hadn't got anything the Eel would be bound to ask if I'd asked anyone.

I was about to fail an important test, simply for want of nerve. In desperation I stopped the next passer-by.

'Excuse me…'

He was a young, well-dressed black guy. He stopped, looked at me and asked, 'You OK?'

'Yes, fine. Er, I mean, no. Actually, I haven't got any money and I'm hungry.'

'Are you hungry? Really?'

I nodded, too ashamed to say more. He fished a handful of coins from his pocket and gave me one. It was a half-crown.

'Have a good supper,' he said, with a broad smile.

'I only got another sixpence,' the Eel grumbled. 'How about you?' He didn't sound expectant.

'Half a crown,' I said as casually as I could. 'So we've got four and six altogether.' I flipped the coin in the air.

'Heads!' The Eel grabbed the spinning disc and hugged me. 'Come on. There's a fish and chip shop round the corner.'

The Eel's money had arrived when we returned to Bracknell, but by the time we'd celebrated in Reading and he'd paid off a couple of debts, we had only twenty-five quid with which to conquer the East.

In late November we hitched to Folkestone and made a night crossing to Boulogne. Northern France was as cold and wet as England. The Frenchmen of our generation were mostly lying low after the pasting they'd received in the summer. In Paris, the Left Bank seemed mostly to be inhabited by foreigners. The Eel and I fell in with a Frank Zappa lookalike called Alvin who was studying at the Sorbonne and had a place near the Odéon. We dumped our bags on the floor of his tiny flat and went out in search of some action.

Alvin showed us where to score and helped us smoke the dope we bought. It was expensive. Paris was very expensive. In a few days our money was nearly gone. Begging helped stretch it a little further and then we were broke again.

Shouldering our packs, we walked south along the Boulevard Saint Michel. When we got to the Périphérique we started to hitch. We walked all day with thumbs held out, jauntily at first, drooping as the day wore on. We kept moving because we couldn't find a good spot to hitch and because the knifing December wind made it too cold to hang around. Finally we found the perfect spot for hitching, a place where a driver would have time to see us and somewhere to pull in. But by then the evening crowd had thinned right out. The few vehicles that went by weren't stopping.

'We'll stay here for a bit,' I suggested. I was knackered after walking all day. 'Give ourselves the best chance of them stopping.'

'OK.'

Standing still made me realise how hungry I was. Nothing since breakfast. We paced up and down, stamping our feet, banging our hands together. Big soft flakes of snow began falling. All around were huge warehouses. There was nowhere to get under cover. It had stopped being funny long ago. There were virtually no cars now. We stomped back and forth and I grew numb, mechanically trudging up and down, feeling colder and colder.

Hitching in France wasn't easy. Was it because we were a pair of scruffy longhairs, or was it because the French are a bunch of bastards? We argued the toss for many a long hour at the roadside that winter. Finally a car stopped. The shaven-headed driver leaned across and opened the passenger window. Instead of the usual question, 'Où allez-vous?' – where are you going?' he asked. 'Have you got any money?'

I had to do all the talking, for the Eel didn't speak or understand French. 'No, we haven't,' I replied, discounting the few francs that remained to us.

'You're not French,' he said. 'Where are you from?'

'England.'

'Get in then. I can't hang about all day.' He looked around anxiously. Once we were speeding south he went on. 'Where are you headed?'

'South.'

'You say you don't have any money… Well, I haven't either. We can't go much further without putting some petrol in this heap.'

'We've got ten francs,' I admitted.

'I've got five,' he said. 'That will get us some way. After that we'll just have to see.'

From the back seat, the Eel observed, 'This car's been nicked. It's been hot-wired. I'll tell you something else – only criminals have their heads shaved in France. This guy's just been released or else he's on the run. Ask him if he's got anything to eat.'

After spending our money on petrol, our driver spoke. 'Either we dump the car when the gas is gone or we steal some. I know how to do it. Are you up for it?'

'Sure.'

It was a slow process, which involved disconnecting the fuel pipe of a 2CV and working a lever to pump petrol, squirt by squirt, into our bottle. We did this half a dozen times through the night.

Our journey progressed and we began to relax more with our French partner-in-crime. Stories of cars they'd hot-wired passed between the driver and the Eel through me.

'Tell him I was in Borstal,' the Eel demanded.

'I've been inside too,' the driver laughed. 'In fact I woke up in prison this morning…'

We reached Valence just before dawn. Delivery trucks were dropping off perishable foods outside the local shops.

'Time for breakfast. Get out here,' the driver said, pulling up outside a grocery store. 'I'll drive round the block and pick you up in two minutes. When you see me coming, grab some milk and fruit from the doorstep, jump in the car and we're away. Hey, you'd better take your packs. You never know – the cops might pick me up round the corner—'

I was telling the story to Andy and Eric when the lights in the cell went off with a click.

'Oh shit! Well, goodnight.'

The goodnights came back. We'd agreed early on in our imprisonment that we had plenty of time for chat in the day; we'd be silent after lights out. The idea was sound, but right now I wanted to go on telling my story and not think about what might happen at tomorrow's hearing.

The following afternoon I was called for a legal meeting. Tony Bradshaw, my solicitor's clerk, looked serious as we shook hands.

'You know I told you not to expect anything from this hearing,' he said solemnly.

'Sure,' I replied, readying myself for the bad news.

'Well, that shows how much I know, because you've been given bail and your wife has raised the thirty thousand pounds surety. You're free to go home!'

'What?'

'Extraordinary thing. The public prosecutor missed his train from London and wasn't there for the start of the hearing. The judge was clearly irritated. He instructed the senior police officer to present the Crown's objections to bail. Greenslade over-egged his case, the way he'd done with the magistrates, and we caught him out in a couple of factual errors. The judge saw no reason not to grant bail.'

He held out his hand. Dazed, I took it. The feel of his flesh made his words real. I was free to go. That evening, I was let out of the small door set into the prison gate.

If being locked up was a slow death, being on bail was active torture. I was too emotionally fragile to voice my thoughts, but I was sure Mary and I were experiencing the death throes of our marriage. After six months apart, we were different people. She'd had a tough time, under constant pressure: working in the shop, trying to cope with the demands of the house, garden, cat, chickens, bills, bees, trips to Bristol, criticism from her family... she was worn out. While she'd been run off her feet, I'd lain on my bed for half a year, my thought-snakes endlessly eating their own tails.

We might have got over our difficulties had I been back to stay, but we both knew that this was a break in a much longer separation. I'd be going back to prison soon and there was nothing I could do about it. Friends had put up the surety for my bail and they'd lose their money if I went on the run. The knowledge that I'd have to go back inside was a shackle that filled my heart with a cold black fog.

Everyone knows that some blokes are led around by their pricks. Unexpectedly at liberty, I regarded my single male friends with cold eyes, helpless anger eating my insides. Which one of them would be first to make a move for my wife once I was locked up again?

I knew the police had me under observation and assumed my phone was tapped too. Not wanting to lead the cops to my friends' houses, I mostly stayed at home when I wasn't working, and I worked as long and hard as I could. There was a lot to do because I'd returned in the middle of a bread strike and Reading Wholefoods was the only retailer in town with a continuing supply of brown flour. I spent the days in the storeroom, weighing up bags of wholemeal and granary. At home I chopped wood for the coming winter and tidied the garden. Whenever I stopped to think, I'd feel myself sinking into the quicksands of despair.

This life was so fundamentally miserable, it was almost a relief when my bail was revoked at a special hearing the DPP called in November and I was returned to prison.

8 Electric Eel to Florence

'I TELL YOU WHAT,' I said to Andy and Eric, when we were back in the cell together. 'I never thought I'd be glad to be inside, but all the time I was on bail I couldn't help thinking that my sentence was just hanging over me. I wasn't getting through it, as you've been, Andy. Now I'm back where I was six weeks ago, but fucked up by some of the most miserable days of my life.'

'Yeah, being out on bail was real weird.' Eric mused. He and several more of the Julie mob had been bailed in the wake of my release. 'Well, at least those strange days are over,' he continued, laughing ruefully. 'Now we've only got prison to deal with.'

Silence fell. I hadn't even needed a day to realise I'd been totally wrong about bail. Awful as it had been, festering in a cell was definitely worse.

Reliving my madcap days on the road with the Eel was far preferable to picking through the details of my predicament. I cupped my hands behind my head and cast my mind back to the end of '68.

~~~~~

In Valence, we had our first stab at being pavement artists. With the coins I'd hidden from the petrol fund we bought a set of chalks. The Eel began, doing a lightning sketch of a yacht racing through heavy seas, heeling over in a strong wind. The light was right, the picture had real movement and life. It was an accomplished work, done in a few minutes.

'I didn't know you were an artist.' Once again, the Eel had astonished me.

'I'm not. I learnt how to draw the yacht at school. It's the only thing I can do. The rest is up to you.'

I started with a girl's face, a long-haired blonde. She was pretty, but somehow insipid – as my portraits usually are. Then I carefully wrote out our message. *Nous sommes étudiants Anglais, en tour dans la belle France. Merci.*

The Eel scattered our remaining centimes around my words as ground-bait for our fish. 'Nobody likes to be the first,' he told me, 'but everyone loves to join in something that's going well. Notice how people don't go in an empty restaurant and walk straight past a market stall if there's nobody there? But if a woman's checking out the goods, they stop to see what she's looking at. I've often thought about hiring myself out as a fake customer. I'm sure it would work. The trouble is I'd have to smarten up to pull it off.'

To give myself something to do, I embellished the text by wrapping it in a vine. Once I'd done that I had to jump up and down and move around to get my circulation going. The Eel kept warm by switching between the spoons and harmonica. I set to work on a rural landscape.

A few coins rained down, then a few more. A guy with a guitar walked by. The Eel snagged him and borrowed the guitar for just one number. He played *Angie*, the tune Bert Jansch had made famous. In spite of cold fingers, he did it beautifully. Several people gathered round and more drifted in. At the end there was applause and money. A small pavement party got under way. The owner of the guitar offered to put us up for the night.

We made more money from the drawings as we continued down the Rhône Valley. Life as a pavement artist was grand – as long as the weather stayed good. People stopped to look, to talk and to try out their English. They often ended by giving us a meal or a bed.

'This is nothing,' the Eel said. 'Wait 'til we get to Italy. The Italians are really generous. We'll make so much money we'll have to start saving!'

At Orange, we left the N7 and trekked up into the wilds of Drôme. Our destination was a rural hippy commune, where there was a girl the Eel wanted to fuck. We found the hilltop commune at the end of a long day's hike. It was deserted, except for an old lady half mad with loneliness. The youngsters had all split to Paris for the winter. She was the last villager, she said. While we supped on our bread and cheese and her beans and greens she told me the same few sentences over and over again.

'Laurence is a good girl. She's kind. I don't like Marc. He's mean to me when the others aren't around. When I was a girl this village was full of children. Where have they all gone? Laurence is a good girl. She's kind…'

In the morning we wound down the hill and retraced

our steps along the valley floor. Wherever we walked there was no escaping the Mistral, the biting wind that blows down from the Alps. We spent a miserable night lying in a shallow ditch, the only way we could get ourselves out of the wind. The next day we straggled into Avignon. As soon as we warmed up in a bar, we began to itch. We'd picked up lice from the old lady. I went in search of a shampoo that would rid us of them. We washed our hair and clothes in the icy waters of the public fountains. We probably would have frozen had we not been taken in by a young English teacher. After a day resting at his place, the Eel came up with a new plan.

'India's still thousands of miles away,' he said. 'It'll be cold all the way. Italy is great, but after that the going really gets tough.'

He reminded me of some of the hardships he'd endured last winter on the India trail. He laid it on so thick that I was ready to agree when he suggested:

'Let's go down to Morocco – spend the winter getting stoned in the sun.'

We reached Perpignan during a bitterly cold spell in mid-December and spent the first two nights in La Terre, a cellar that had been converted into an art gallery. The place was damp and smelt of mushrooms; it had a deep chill that slowly crept into our bones.

The arty people who ran La Terre were divided about whether we were international members of the alternative society or just a pair of dossers. To prove our credentials, we took part in one of their happenings. The Eel played the spoons, while I recited Stanley Unwin's lines from the

Small Faces album, *Ogden's Nut Gone Flake*. Très surreal.

On our third night in town, we were glad to unroll our sleeping bags on the living-room floor of an Algerian teenager we'd met while doing our drawings. Ahmed lived with his mother in a high-rise flat with no furniture. Poor though they were, their hospitality was immense. They housed us for a week and shared their food with us.

Each morning we went to town, found a pitch and began our routine with the chalks. At first we made enough to eat but, as the days went by, our takings shrank. We were fast exhausting Perpignan's fund of goodwill. On two successive days we packed our bags, said goodbye to Ahmed and his mum, walked out to the south of town and held up our thumbs under the road sign that said Spain. But nobody stopped to give the longhairs a lift and at dusk we straggled back to Ahmed's. The second time this happened, we realised we were stuck in Perpignan.

A couple of days before Christmas, another pair of drifters floated into town: two young Swiss–German lads on the run from military service. Nice kids who'd recently left home, neither of them had a clue about life on the road. They hadn't sorted out anywhere to stay, they didn't even have sleeping bags and would have died of cold had the Eel not taken pity on them. Hustling on their behalf, he got them installed in the art cellar.

On Christmas morning, the four of us agreed to do a tour of the town's restaurants, where we would offer our services as washers-up in return for the leftovers of the previous evening's *Reveillon* feast. I had to do the talking because the Eel still couldn't string together two words of French and the Swiss boys were too embarrassed to open their mouths.

The town was dead, the restaurants shut. When our banging and ringing did raise a reply, we were confronted by an irritated restaurateur who sent us on our hungry way, with insults ringing round our ears.

My spirits were sinking. The Eel had to use his powers of persuasion to cajole me into ringing the bell of the most expensive restaurant in town.

'OK,' I agreed, 'but this is definitely the last one. No more.'

An attractive middle-aged blonde opened the door. 'I'm afraid I can't help at the moment,' she said in reply to my query. 'My chef has the keys to the kitchen and he won't be here until later. Why don't you come back this evening?'

The windswept streets were devoid of people; there was no point in working the pavement. Christmas day felt as empty as our stomachs. The Eel and I took the long walk back to Ahmed's flat.

In the evening, the Eel put on his coat and said it was time to check out the restaurant.

'What's the point of walking all the way back into town?' I moaned. 'Can't you see she was just giving us the brush-off?'

'We might as well try,' he persisted. 'What else have we got to do?'

There was no answer to that. After meeting up with the Swiss lads we presented ourselves at the service entrance to the restaurant. The smiling owner opened the door. In an ivory blouse, pencil skirt and pearls, she looked stunning.

'Welcome. Welcome. Please come in.'

We followed her into the warm kitchen, where she introduced us to the chef. My mouth immediately began watering at the rich mix of cooking smells that filled the

air. We drew a few looks from the seated diners when the
lady and the chef led us through the main restaurant to
a small banqueting room. A table was set for six. We all
sat down. A bottle of champagne helped loosen our frozen
tongues. Laughter broke out and rolled round and round
the table. Waiters bustled in laden with plates full of food.
Course followed divine course: pastries stuffed with wild
mushrooms, prawns grilled with garlic, wafer thin slices of
beef, duck in a thick sauce, sweet melon, a gigot of lamb,
sorbets, cheeses... With each dish came a new bottle of
wine and a flurry of toasts.

'To peace and understanding...'

'To the kindest and most beautiful lady in Perpignan, no,
in the whole of France... Tell her that, Leaf.'

'To the best chef there is...'

'To the only decent restaurateur in town. To the pearl
among the swines...'

At the end, one of the Swiss boys rose unsteadily to
his feet, held his glass high and carefully said, 'I drink the
good health of the kind lady who has given us a happy
Christmas.'

On Boxing Day the police came to the Algerians' flat.
Warned that they were climbing the stairs, we grabbed our
bags and scooted up to the roof where we hid until they'd
gone. They were checking out stolen cars, Ahmed told us. It
was time to move on. After another cold night in the fungal
La Terre, we woke coughing. We had to find somewhere
else to sleep before the day was out.

Chilled to the bone, we went at dawn to the Café des
Anglais to have a drink and warm up. The Eel spent our last

centimes on a cup of a hot chocolate. I went to wash in hot water in the toilet. Afterwards I joined my pal at our table. His turn in the loo. Good man, he'd left exactly half a cupful of chocolate. I had a sip and forced myself to wait before I had another. A waiter came over to see what I wanted.

'Thanks, I'm fine for the moment.' I said. 'Maybe a glass of water.'

As soon as the proprietor realised that I wasn't buying a drink, he came over to remonstrate. I gulped the chocolate just before his waiters grabbed me and threw me out into the street. My pal was ejected moments later.

'Bastards. They're going to regret this,' the Eel swore as we walked off up the street.

We cased the café that afternoon. The Eel said that breaking in would be a piece of piss. All he needed was a good lever. At the ironmonger's, while I made enquiries of the shopkeeper, the Eel nicked the heftiest screwdriver in the place.

That night we slept in the emergency fall-back we'd spotted a few days before. In the park in the centre of town there was an exhibition of African village life, complete with a thatched hut and a life-size carving of a woman cooking over a fire. At the end of the day we slipped inside the hut, bedded down and went to sleep.

My shoulder was being shaken. Torchlight dazzled my eyes. The cloudy waters of sleep suddenly drained away and I saw I'd been captured.

We were hauled down to the police station, thrown into cells and left to our thoughts. When the day shift came on duty they fingerprinted us, took our mug shots, front and profile, and then invited us to explain the massive screwdriver, the torches and masking tape in our rucksacks.

Burglars' equipment, they claimed. We said nothing; we'd done nothing. In the evening, they let us go.

After being registered by the cops, I assumed the robbery was off. Not so. The Eel explained things to me.

'We'll starve if we stay here, but we're stuck unless we can get some money. This is what we do. We hit the café at three in the morning then take the five o'clock train to the Spanish border.'

Deep in shadow, we watched the Café des Anglais from across the street. The last car went by at 2 a.m. After that it was quiet. The minutes silently unwound.

'How much do you think there'll be in the till?' I whispered, when I couldn't bear the silence any more.

'They can't have gone to the bank since Christmas Eve. It could be hundreds of pounds. Come on then. Let's do it.' The Eel grinned at me.

I felt very nervous but somehow lightheaded, almost elated.

We stole across the road and shifted one of the outdoor tables into position by the big plate-glass window. Above it was a line of ventilation windows. The small, swivelling panes were held top and bottom by a pair of aluminium clips. While I kept watch, the Eel set to work with the screwdriver. He had the first pane out in no time. The next one wasn't so easy, but it came. Soon he'd cleared a space big enough to slither through. He walked round to the door, unlocked it and bowed me in.

The till only held the float – coins and small-denomination notes. We cleaned it out and helped ourselves to a bottle of brandy and a couple of cartons of cigarettes.

Before leaving, the Eel peeled off a glove. In an insane act of bravado, he ceremoniously placed his fingerprints on the till, carefully rolling each finger, to provide a perfect print, exactly the way the police had done a few hours before.

'You're fucking nuts,' I breathed, as we ghosted towards our rendezvous with the Swiss kids.

'Stop worrying.' The Eel punched me on the shoulder and cackled. He was on a high. 'We'll be out of the country before anyone is awake. I'd love to see their faces when they dust the till for prints. It's a great big V-sign. Fuck off, fuzz.'

We sorted out the money in La Terre. The notes and the silver came to seventy quid, more money than we'd had at any time since we'd met. We gave the copper to the Swiss boys. At least they wouldn't starve for a while.

During the interminable wait at the railway station I began to shake uncontrollably. Then I realised what a stupid mistake we were about to make.

'Listen, man,' I told the Eel, 'if we go to Spain we'll have to come back through France. And we'll get bust, because you put your prints on the till. Listen. There's a train to Marseilles at six. Let's go there and carry on to Italy.'

'No. We've got to get out of here as quick as possible. The cops could arrive at any moment.'

It was our first real argument. It continued, in hushed tones, until the train pulled in. The Eel got on board, I wouldn't leave the platform. He argued Spain, I insisted on Italy. As the train was about to pull out, the Eel climbed down. He spent the next hour pacing and muttering, 'The fuzz'll come. They're bound to come. I'm a fool. Why didn't I just go on my own?'

He laughed out loud when the Marseilles train pulled

in. We changed up our silver in the port and took another train to Genoa. At the bottom of the steps of the cathedral, our drawings made so much money that the Eel decided to treat himself to a watch. The Italians were as generous as my pal had promised.

By New Year's Eve, we were in the port of La Spezia. A street of restaurants by the harbour seemed a good place to set up our pitch. A knot of merchant seamen rolled up soon after. They were shouting-drunk and at first I thought they meant trouble. But the Eel matched their *cazzos* and *stronzos* and they laughed and shook hands and showered our drawings with fistfuls of change. Some of them stayed on to chat and try out their Americanisms. Before long they'd invited us to see in the new year with them.

We celebrated with our new friends in a dockside restaurant. I woke up in the same seat I'd occupied the night before, with a raging toothache to accompany my hangover. A slug of brandy helped dull both pains. We wound our way to the sailors' boat for a new year's lunch that lasted until dusk. When we lurched on to the quayside and waved goodbye, we'd agreed with the first mate to sign on as deckhands for a three-week triangular trip: Tangier, Montevideo and back to La Spezia. We needed to do something – most of our money had just evaporated on fares and meals and booze.

In the morning, the port authority torpedoed our plans by refusing to issue the necessary permits. So we went to Pisa and drew our pictures by the base of the leaning tower. Two raven-haired beauties stopped to look at our drawings and stayed to practise their English and chat us up. Mine was called Francesca. They invited us to join them for dinner that evening.

We ate pasta at long benches in a packed student refectory. There was a big conference on at the university and the place was heaving.

'We're off to Florence tomorrow.' I had to shout to be heard above the din.

'No kidding? We're from Florence,' Francesca yelled back. 'Listen, have you got somewhere to stay? No? Stay in our flat, if you like. We'll be back on Sunday.'

'OK, great.'

She gave me the keys and the address, then leaned against my shoulder, enveloping me in her musky perfume. One impassioned speaker after another climbed on to the tables and harangued the baying crowd.

'Fucking Maoists, man,' the Eel bellowed in my free ear.

After the girls went up to get closer to the orators, we slipped away.

The next day we got a ride straight to Florence. Maoists they might have been, but the girls had an imperial flat. After being used to sleeping on floors and sitting on cold stone steps, it was wonderful to luxuriate in a hot bath, sleep on a mattress and lounge around in large leather armchairs. There wasn't anything in the larder though. Hunger drove us on to the streets in the morning.

Every time we got down on our knees and started to draw, the police moved us on. Until now we hadn't even noticed the cops in Italy, but in Florence they wouldn't let us use any of the wide pavements or the piazzas in the wealthy areas.

'Go to the Ponte Vecchio,' they all said, as they moved us along.

'It's no good on the bridge,' the Eel grumbled as we made our way down to the river. It was bitingly cold in the street. The puddles were rimmed with ice. The smell of fresh bread from the bakeries we passed was making my stomach weep. I was tempted to go in and ask for old bread, the way I'd done in Provence, but the long queues of smart city people deterred me.

In medieval times the Ponte Vecchio had been the shop-lined meat market. The butchers used to throw their waste off the bridge and the River Arno would carry it away. Now the shops were filled with jewellery, clothes and souvenirs. We made for the centre of the bridge, where there was an open space. The pavement was made of small hexagonal tiles a hand-span wide. It was hopeless for our drawings. The Eel started on his yacht but quickly scrubbed it and wouldn't start again.

I did what I could, but it wasn't much use; my blonde looked like a cubist corpse. Our message wasn't easy to decipher. Hardly anyone was stopping to try, or giving us any money.

'That cunt over there is bloody well laughing at us,' the Eel snarled. Cold and hungry, neither of us was in the best of tempers. I looked in the direction of the Eel's nod. A young Paul Newman was grinning at us. In other circumstances I might have smiled back, but it's difficult to find your predicament amusing when your stomach is growling.

The cool-hand kid strolled over. 'Pretty hopeless, hey?' he laughed and defused the Eel's imminent explosion by adding, 'You cats care to join me in some coffee and cakes or something?'

In the warmth of the bar, our mood mellowed. This kid was fun. After a good breakfast, life seems almost bearable. While we'd been eating, our seventeen-year-old companion, John, had been telling us about himself. He was from New Jersey. His parents had sent him to the American school in Florence so that he could appreciate his roots and perfect his Italian. From the way he talked, he was clearly a head.

'Know where we can score a little hash?' I asked at the end of our long breakfast. Not that we had enough money for more than a smoke.

''Fraid not,' he replied, 'but I'll be happy to turn you on. Shall we go to my place?'

John Amati lived in an attic flat in the Via Ghibbelina, just off the Piazza Santa Croce. He took snapshots of us, sitting on his tiny balcony, looking out over the red-tiled roofs of the city and getting high on Lebanese Gold. The day slipped away, right in front of our eyes.

In the evening we took John to see our pad, knowing that he'd be astounded to find two hippy vagrants staying in such plush surroundings. The next day, Francesca and her friend returned. They were angry that their flat wasn't as immaculate as they'd left it. We were scornful of the gap between their egalitarian rhetoric and their luxurious lifestyle. Our reunion turned into a row. We left.

At John's invitation, we squeezed ourselves into the second room of his small pad. He was excellent company. Our friendship grew while his chunk of Lebanese shrank. Over three days it went from an Oxo cube to a pea and then it was gone.

That night, my new-year toothache returned. At first light, the Eel got John to write in Italian on a card, 'I am an English student. I have toothache. I need money for a dentist.'

I set off towards Michelangelo's *David*, clutching my card. It worked beautifully. The streets were full of people on their way to work. Many of them read my plea and gave generously. I was getting notes as well as coins; everyone knows dentists aren't cheap. In half an hour I'd collected more than we'd hope to make in a whole day with the chalks. In spite of the easy money, I wasn't happy. I'm not good at handling pain, I get irritable and can easily fall into a mood where nothing is right. I handed my card to another suit.

'I am a dentist,' the man said, pocketing my card. 'Come with me.'

I looked again. There was a person inside the suit, a short, neat guy with slicked-back hair and a pencil moustache.

'Come with me,' he repeated. 'I will treat you without charge.'

The Eel was delighted with the results his card had produced. 'You do realise, don't you…' he was buzzing, hopped up on his latest success, 'we never need be hungry again! Man, we can use this whenever it rains.'

'No, we can't,' I countered. My tongue couldn't stop exploring the strange new gap in my mouth. 'Look how quickly I ran into a dentist.'

The Eel walked over to me and quietly hissed: 'We've got to make some bread, man. We've smoked all John's dope. It's our turn to score.'

'We've got bread,' I whispered back. 'I made eight thousand lira before I met the dentist.'

'Don't worry about scoring,' John intervened. 'Just give me a hand shifting my bed.'

I helped him drag the heavy bed away from the wall. Kneeling down, he used a screwdriver to lever up one of the floorboards. From the space underneath, he pulled out a white plaque and threw it at the Eel. He tossed another to me. It was larger than my hand. The Eel was examining the first missile when the third hit him in the chest. Then we were laughing and whooping and hurling around two-hundred-gram plaques of Lebanese Gold. John ripped the cotton cover off one of them and smashed it into large chunks with a hammer. He threw one at each of us.

'Get rolling!'

The previous spring, John had gone to the Lebanon for the Easter holidays, intending to have a stoned week and return with an ounce that he could eke out through the term. Hash was scarce in Italy and he hadn't had a smoke since his arrival from the States. In his hotel in Beirut, he met another American who was also there to score. This guy had lost his nerve and was frightened to leave the building. John volunteered to score for him.

John Amati inspired confidence. He looked straight at you with his shining blue eyes and you just knew you could trust him. He went up to Baalbek with enough money to get eight kilos for his freaked-out compatriot. Instead of scoring in town he went into the hills, bought directly from a farmer and got twice the amount for the money. He gave his countryman eight kilos and returned safely to Florence with another eight.

He turned a few friends on and let some of them have a gram or two, but the school authorities got a whiff of what was going on so he stopped smoking with anyone else. He'd been sitting on his stash for nine months, getting out of his skull on his own. We were the first dopers he'd come across in all that time. John was broke, but he was too paranoid to raise money by selling to any of the school kids.

'No problem,' said the Eel. 'Leaf and I can sell some of your hash to my friends in Rome.'

We agreed a fifty-fifty split. For our first trip we took a two-hundred-gram plaque and hitched down to the capital on a bright winter's day. The Eel was in particularly high spirits. He was returning to his favourite city, going to see old friends. Grinning non-stop, he handed Rome to me like an opened oyster.

We slept the first night in an empty railway carriage, parked up in a siding by the main station. In the morning went to see a couple of the Eel's artist friends, Enzo and Gina, and stayed in their large crumbling flat in Trastevere. Our arrival cheered them up no end. There had been no dope at all in Rome for weeks. There weren't many smokers either in 1969; even though we had the only hash in town, it took a week to sell the plaque at the going rate of a thousand lira a gram.

Once we'd knocked out a few grams to Enzo's circle of friends, we bought needle-nose pliers, a small hammer, copper wire and beads and began to make jewellery. Stoned out of our minds, we spent the mornings in one of the eternal city's piazzas. We'd find a good spot and lay out our wares on a blanket. Every now and then one of us would go off to do a furtive dope deal in some dark back-alley or derelict square full of broken Roman columns and spitting feral cats.

We lunched in little working men's restaurants, where the tables were bare and the pasta came with a fiasco of Frascati. In the afternoons, sitting in the sunshine on the Spanish Steps, our jewellery spread in front of us, we worked at turning copper wire into elaborate looped necklaces and earrings. Brightened by beads, they sold well. The Eel offered to halve the price of an ornate necklace for one coquettish beauty. She hung around for quite a while, making her choice and giggling at the Eel's compliments and suggestions. Her name was Paula, she revealed.

'What a peach!' the Eel shook his head ruefully after she'd gone. He whipped out the pair of dessert spoons he kept in his back pocket and began to play. He was a virtuoso of the spoons, using every part of his body to produce the most extraordinary sounds and rhythms. His performance drew a small crowd. At the end of it, while the applause was still ringing, I muttered in his ear, 'She's back.'

Hands on hips, Paula stood watching us and smiling. Her long coat was unbuttoned, revealing her generous figure. Her blonde friend in the Afghan coat looked thin beside her. They stayed after the crowd dispersed. We talked for a while then packed up our goods and took them to a bar.

In the evenings we hung out in Trastevere, smoking with our new girls. I wasn't making too much progress. Anna was there in support of her friend, she wasn't very interested in me. I could hear and see, if I chose, the extrovert Eel making out with Paula on the other mattress.

When we sold the last of the Leb, we went back to Florence and relaxed for a few days before returning to the capital with two plaques to sell. On our third or fourth trip to Rome we heard that the police were looking for two English dope-dealers. We didn't wait to find out any more, but lit out for Florence. Paula came with us.

~~~~~

One February morning, I was woken by the introduction to 'Astronomy Domine', the opening track of Pink Floyd's *Saucerful of Secrets*. I opened my eyes. There was a new cassette player by my head. The Eel was bursting with excitement. He stopped the music.

'Thought you might like some sounds,' he said, trying to act offhand.

'Where did that come from?'

His grin grew until it filled his face. He'd gone out earlier with Paula. While she talked to the shop assistant, he'd nicked the player and the Floyd cassette.

'Piece of piss.' The Eel was nonchalant.

At the end of the tape, John turned the cassette over. We listened to both sides twice then agreed we needed more music. It was cold outside; we wrapped up well and headed into town. At the music shop, we filched half a dozen cassettes while John and Paula kept the staff occupied. On the way home, the Eel and I popped into a supermarket to pick up a couple of things for lunch. We bought some chocolate to add to the food we'd slid into our poacher's pockets. We'd paid and had just left when we were grabbed by a bunch of shop assistants and bundled back into the store. They searched us and found a tin of ham on me and a slab of cheese on the Eel. With shoves and threats, they pushed us into a small room and turned the key in the lock.

'We're calling the police!' one of them shouted through the door.

There was no way out of the storeroom. The Eel kicked a cardboard box to bits then sat down on the floor and looked at me.

'Whatever you do, don't mention the flat,' he said. 'We've got to agree on a story. We could say we were robbed in Naples, somewhere by the port. That's why we don't have any luggage. OK? We're just trying to get back to England. Right?'

'Got it.'

Silence fell as we considered what might be in store for us. Even the Eel looked a little shrunken.

We spent most of the day in the police cells. Finally they charged us with shoplifting and delivered us to Florence prison. I'd walked past its ancient grey walls only the day before.

We were taken in through a small door, set within a much larger one, and led across a courtyard. Shadowy figures were performing arcane tasks in the far corner of a large echoing stone hall. The police took us to a massive wooden desk and handed us over to the screws.

'Name?' The reception officer asked the Eel.

He gave his details. I followed suit. Then we had to undress and put on a shapeless, colourless prison uniform. The Eel was led away by two screws. He half turned and called over his shoulder, 'Good luck.'

I was taken up stone stairs, round corners, along stone corridors, up and down more steps until I'd totally lost all sense of direction. At the end of the walk I was thrust into a stone cell. The door banged shut behind me. The cell was small and clammy, the walls felt damp to the touch. Most of the floor space was taken up by a sagging bed. At its foot was a pisspot. Nothing clse. I climbed on the bed and stood on tiptoe to look out of the slit window – red tiled roofs under a flat grey sky. I got into bed with all my clothes on and pulled the two thin blankets up to my chin. They didn't smell too good, but that was the least of my worries. I felt very lonely and scared. What would the other prisoners do to me?

Supper came – watery spaghetti soup, bread and a mug of red wine. Soon after, the Judas-hole in the cell door snapped open. An eye looked at me. A voice said, 'Hey, fella! Whaddaya say? Howaya doing? Name's Salvatore – call me Sal.' The words were English, the accent New York.

There was an exchange in Italian outside, then the key turned in the lock and the door opened. A warder wandered off up the corridor, leaving me with the Yank.

'You didn't eat that shit?' he said, incredulous, pointing at my bowl on the floor. 'Nobody touches that garbage. You can have food sent in.'

I told him the Naples story, saying I had no money.

'Don't worry,' he assured me. 'We'll get you something. You're among friends. Hey, it's a real pleasure to talk English! See ya tomorrow.' He shut the door behind him.

When my door was next unlocked, the con who took away my bowl slipped me a bag of pears and a bar of chocolate.

'From Sal,' he mouthed.

I was halfway through the chocolate before it occurred to me that Salvatore must be a mafioso. I was in his debt already. He was sure to want something in return.

I couldn't sleep that night. Looming in my mind was the impending trial. What did they do to shoplifters in Italy? What would Salvatore want from me? Would my father be informed where I was?

The morning brought an answer to one of the questions

that had kept me awake. What Salvatore wanted was conversation. He got my cell door opened, sat on the bed and talked and talked. Fed up with Italy and Italians, he was desperate to communicate in a 'civilised' language.

Salvatore had been on remand for nine months already and still didn't have a trial date. Some people had been waiting for over two years, he told me. When I expressed polite doubt, he dragged me off to meet a doper who'd been inside for eighteen months and still didn't know when his trial would be. It didn't matter, the longhair said. Sal translated. Possession of hash drew a mandatory two-year sentence and it was better to do your time on remand because you could have visitors bring you decent food and drink. Sal and the smoker chatted on while my dismay grew. I could be inside for years, just for nicking a fucking tin of ham.

'OK, lock-up! In your cells.' The screws were shouting. The clash of hobnailed boots, the smash of doors slamming, each one louder than the one before, culminated in the crash as my door flew shut. It was the end of the prison day. I'd survived it and I'd be safe in my cell for the next few hours.

The temperature continued to drop. The slit of sky was full of tiny snowflakes. I huddled in bed, getting up to eat the pasta-soup meals or to talk to the inmates, like Salvatore, who had the run of the place. Time and snowflakes melted into slush. My mind was going that way too. The English section of the prison library consisted of seven Agatha Christie novels. I read them all, trying – and totally failing – to convince myself that I was on a weekend in an English country mansion and not a forgotten man in a medieval prison with stone walls five feet thick.

A couple of days later I was slipped a scrap of paper. It said 'HI LEEF IM OK HOPE UR2 CHIN UP. EEL.' Shortly afterwards, I was called for a visit. The Eel was sitting in a small room, facing a man across a desk. The guy looked up from the file he'd been studying. The Eel gave me a wink as I took the chair next to him.

'Nigel, isn't it? My name is Kidd, I'm the consular representative. Your American friend told us about you. I was just saying to Edward here how lucky it was for you that he did... Well, Nigel, it looks like you've got yourself in a bit of a mess. How are you getting on? Are you all right?'

'I'm fine, thanks,' I said and turned to the Eel. 'Got your note.'

'Cool. Did you know that—'

The consular official held up his hand and said, 'If you could just listen for a moment, please. We've managed to get you a hearing for the day after tomorrow. A lawyer's been appointed for you. I'm going to brief him after I leave here, so why don't you tell me what happened...?'

We changed back into our own clothes for the hearing. Screws and police led us into a large courtroom. Everyone stood as three robed figures emerged from a door on the far side. They sat down on the three gilt chairs at the focal point of the room. Everyone sat. After the coughing had died away, the nearest of the three men rose and intoned: 'Three weeks' jail and a fine of thirty thousand lira.' He sat and gazed up at the painted ceiling.

'That was quick,' I thought. 'So much for Italian justice.'

I spotted Paula and John in the public gallery. They

waved. I waved back. The furthest of the robes stood and began to speak. I soon realised I was listening to our defence council. He had a lot to say; it took the best part of an hour. Short and flashy, he strode around the courtroom declaiming and gesticulating. I'd been in Italy long enough to get the general drift. Paula reconstructed the opening of his speech later.

'Two young men, imbued with the spirit of enquiry, came to tour the historical sites of Italy. In their innocence they assumed a country with such a cultural heritage, such a splendid past, must contain noble, honest people. These English boys are not criminals but victims of a crime. Penniless after they'd been robbed in Naples, they began the long journey home.' Dramatic pause. 'What kind of people rob their guests?'

After dealing at some length with the shortcomings of Italian society, our man called one of the supermarket employees to the witness box. Step by step he took her through her statement, then he went for the jugular.

'But signora, if the English boys were at the cheese counter and you were at the till,' he purred, 'you couldn't possibly have seen them. This floor plan of the shop shows a large column in your line of sight.'

'I must have been by the fruit,' the rattled woman said.

Our lawyer pounced. 'Signora, you've just contradicted your sworn testimony.'

She burst into tears and fled the courtroom.

The charges were dismissed. We walked free. Paula flew into the Eel's arms. I gave John a big hug and thanked him for saving our bacon. Our celebration was cut short by three policemen, who took us back to the prison to be discharged. Afterwards, in the street, the biggest of the *carabinieri* grabbed the Eel and me by our jacket lapels, yanked us to within inches of his garlic-stinking face and snarled, 'We don't want you round here. Get out of town. If I see you bastards again, I'll find a reason to put you back in prison and keep you there for years.'

Paula came with us to England. We rented a flat by the canal in central Reading. Soon afterwards John Amati turned up. After getting a postcard with our address, the young nutter had put his remaining three kilos of hash in his suitcase, flown to Heathrow, strolled through customs and taken a taxi to our pad in King's Road.

I sold the dope for John. To move it quickly, I knocked it out at six quid an ounce – the going rate was eight. One day a lanky Brummie turned up, a guy with a small face framed by a mop of brown hair. He said his name was Brian and that I'd sold an ounce to a friend of his. His grin was so infectious you caught it and had to grin back. He was a fiend with money and haggled like a Turk, even though the hash was cheap. When he realised that nothing he could say would make me drop the price, he bought an ounce. The next day he returned for four more.

'I'll give you twenty quid.'

'The price is six quid an ounce, Brian, however much you buy.'

'Come on, man.' He counted out four fivers on the table. 'If you'll sell an ounce for six, surely you'll do four for twenty.'

'No.'

'Twenty-two?'

'Look, Brian. I've only got a certain amount to sell. It's

good and cheap and it'll go easily. It's six quid an ounce while it lasts.'

Brian knew a bargain when he saw one. He kept coming back for more. In the end he bought most of the hash.

John Amati and I decided to go east on the proceeds. The Eel wasn't coming, he was marrying pregnant Paula and staying in Reading. With a pang I realised how much I was going to miss my amazing road buddy, my very own Dean Moriarty.

9   *On a dirt road in Turkey*

THE OPERATION JULIE team had watched the labs for over a year while we made and distributed millions of tablets. When they'd finally swooped, they captured almost all the gang but, embarrassingly for them, they'd found very little LSD.

They knew so much about us. They even knew how much ergotamine tartrate and ergotamine maleate the two acid labs bought for their last production runs. From this they calculated there were fifteen million trips unaccounted for. In fact they exaggerated, as the police always did on drug busts. We only had half that.

But where was it?

Superintendent Greenslade and Inspector Lee, the officers in charge of Operation Julie, must have been desperate. A full year before the bust, they were in a position to close down both laboratories, effectively ending the production of LSD in Britain. Instead, they let their semi-autonomous operation run on and on, watching while we sold a million trips. The Julie cops were on to a good thing and clocking up loads of overtime by keeping us under continuous observation. They knew we had millions of tabs, but when they finally pounced, they couldn't find them. Greenslade and Lee must have known their careers would end ignominiously unless they could locate the stashed acid.

In November, however, they made a major break-through. With promises of preferential treatment, they persuaded one of Richard's lieutenants to go to work for them. The turncoat was able to worm out the location of Richard's stash. Greenslade's team dug up the concrete under the stove in his cottage and unearthed 1.2 kilos of pure LSD crystal, enough for six million trips. It was a massive triumph for the police, but they couldn't relax – they knew there were a lot more tabs that hadn't been accounted for.

The flurry of legal activity stirred up by the discovery of the crystal caused a delay in our impending trial and threw all kinds of information into the air.

Over the months on remand, I'd learnt the whole story of our conspiracy. Now, through Mike Mansfield and some of our other lawyers, we were able to piece together a picture of how it had unravelled.

The first LSD run had come together in 1969 as a result of the meeting of Dave Solomon, an American acid head living in Cambridge, and Richard Kemp, a chemistry student at Liverpool University. Richard's reaction to his first trip was like mine: he wanted to turn everyone else on – and he was a good enough chemist to do it. Using a university laboratory, the pair of them turned the base materials they'd acquired into five grams of brown sludge. Dubiously they tried a miniscule amount of the gloop and realised, with delight, that it worked. They'd made LSD!

Five grams was enough for twenty thousand full-strength trips. Dave got hold of several thousand empty capsules. He and Richard blended a gram with an inert excipient and started to fill the capsules with the mixture. Some of the caps were extremely powerful, others were so weak they were a waste of time. Amateur enthusiasts, they hadn't yet established a method for delivering a measureable dose. They didn't have any kind of organised distribution either and it took a while to sell the first gram.

They turned for help to Henry Todd, a Cambridge dealer. Henry in turn contacted my old pal Brian, who had great connections in the dope-dealing world. They began to set up a rudimentary distribution system.

In the meantime Richard and Dave had masses of LSD to turn all their friends on. Trippers floated in and out of Dave's house by Grantchester Meadows. One of them, Gerry Thomas, had been asked to look after a gram of Richard's acid. When Richard got it back, the gram had mysteriously shrunk. Light-fingered Gerry played no further part in the nascent acid ring. However, he knew all the principals involved. In time he saw them prospering.

Five years later, in '74, Gerry Thomas was arrested trying to smuggle kilos of hash into Canada. Desperate to avoid the heavy prison sentence he was facing, he offered to do a deal and identify the men who – he claimed – were making most of the world's acid. They were in Britain, he said. The Canadians contacted the British police to see if they were interested.

Scotland Yard ran a check on the names Thomas had given. They were all real people but none of them could be traced. That was rather suspicious. A task force was set up to locate these mysterious individuals and discover what they were up to. Eventually they were tracked down. Richard was in Wales. Henry and Brian were in London. They all went under observation. The police didn't yet know it, but they were watching two laboratories, two different organisations. The first acid team had split like an amoeba, both parts were functioning separately. In '73, there'd been a bust-up and Richard and Dave had stopped supplying Henry and Brian. Richard carried on making acid while he and Dave tried to put together a new distribution chain. Henry and Brian began the search for another chemist. By this time they'd solved the doseage problems and had a functioning distribution network.

A separate police investigation into LSD supplies had begun with the Thames Valley force. They sent out two undercover men, Pritchard and Bentley, with money to buy five hundred hits of acid at a pop festival. The dealer they scored from boasted he could get them thousands of trips, no problem, tens of thousands, if they wanted.

The dealer was put under observation and his phone was tapped. Everyone he met or spoke to was checked out. Once they'd found his supplier, he in turn went under the microscope. The Thames Valley police team methodically worked their way up the distribution chain.

The two police LSD operations were merged. At length, the chain gang followed the trail to Russ. He'd previously come to the notice of the police as a suspected hash dealer in London. In 1973, he'd been clocked returning from Morocco – with me. The police discovered we were still in regular contact. I too went under observation. An undercover team, disguised as a work crew, began to dig up the road near my house. When they saw Henry visit me, they knew that I was the connection between the lab and the dealers and that they had the whole chain.

Our trial was rescheduled for January. Once we'd chewed over every detail of every aspect of who had betrayed Richard and worried to death the topic of what effect the discovery of so much acid might have on the trial, Andy, Eric and I ran out of conversation and lay on our beds in silence, waiting for the year to end. God knows what the others were thinking about, but I was back being twenty and thirsty for travel and adventure.

In April '69, with an absolute fortune of five hundred pounds between us, raised from the sale of his Lebanese hash, John Amati and I set off on the overland route to India. We started out the easy way by taking a train to Florence. There we rented a partially converted farmhouse in the hills, ten kilometres south of the city.

The farm belonged to Lorenzo Sforza, the father of John's girlfriend, Susana. He was a squat, blue-chinned Italian-American lawyer who, Susana boasted, had worked for the East Coast mafia in the States. Lorenzo was broke, having sunk all his money into a swimming pool business which had gone under. With the water and electricity cut off, he'd retreated to his Florence flat, leaving his unfinished dream home to us at a rent of twenty-five dollars a week.

Each morning, we struggled up from the bottom of the hill carrying the day's water. After breakfast we went out into the garden to write. We set up a table and chairs in the peach orchard, among the irises, and spent the days smoking Lebanese and taking turns on John's typewriter to compose sections of our surreal book. At dusk the fireflies made a magical bridge between sun and moonlight. Nightingales sang all around us. After dark we'd light candles, get a fire going in the hearth to make our supper of pasta, tomato and parmesan with the creamy olive oil that came from Lorenzo's trees.

'So tell me about this ecology stuff you're studying,' I said one evening as we sat down to our dinner.

'Well, it's the study of the interactions between life forms in a living environment – an ecosystem. Scientists are coming to realise that everything is connected, every living thing plays its part in the life-support system that allows us all to flourish.'

'Except us, of course. We're not playing our part. Not when we put down DDT that ends up killing birds of prey.'

'That's right. Humans are the joker in the pack. We're changing balances that have been in existence for millennia, often with disastrous effect. Introducing rabbits into Australia, for example. This is a relatively new discipline so, as I see it, the challenge for the ecologists is to first master their science – learn about the way all life interacts – then convince our leaders that we must modify our behaviour to safeguard our planetary ecosystems. It's in our own interest.'

Everything is connected. I'd seen that on my first trip: it was reassuring to hear the scientists were saying the same thing. John was an extraordinary young man: vital, enquiring, inventive and good company. The weeks drifted by. We were having a great time until the owner turned up, angrily demanding the hundred dollars I owed him.

'But we don't owe anything. We're up-to-date,' John

replied. 'I've been paying Susana.'

'You have, sure,' rasped Lorenzo, 'but your limey buddy hasn't paid a cent.'

Our agreement had been clear. Suddenly Lorenzo was saying the rent was twenty-five bucks each.

'Gimme a hundred bucks,' he demanded.

'No way, man,' I said.

He brought the ensuing argument to a halt with a chopping motion of his hand.

'You pay what you owe… or else,' he growled menacingly, making a gun of his hand and pointing it at my forehead. Then he got into his car and roared off in a spray of gravel. John and I looked at each other wonderingly. We'd just had a glimpse into another world.

'I know where he keeps his gun,' John said.

'He's got a gun?' I was scared. I'd seen the look in Lorenzo's eyes when he was putting the squeeze on me.

'He sure has.'

We broke into his locked bedroom. The gun was in the drawer of the bedside table. It was loaded.

'Time to go,' murmured John, hefting the weapon.

'Actually, this is just what we needed to get us moving,' I said, attempting to sound unconcerned. 'We're supposed to be going to Asia, not arsing around in Tuscany.'

Rucksacks on our backs, we caught the bus into Florence, threw the little mafioso's shooter into the Arno and boarded a bus to Bologna. It made good sense to leave Florence without delay. After that it was obvious, at least to me, that we should hitch and not waste our money on fares. John went along with me at first, but he got easily dejected when we had to wait a long time between lifts or walk any distance.

'You're carrying far too much,' I pointed out, a touch irritably. 'You should never have brought the typewriter.'

'You wouldn't say that if you were a real writer.' He glared at me and clamped his jaw shut.

'So keep the Olivetti and chuck your other gear. Real travellers travel light.'

He didn't bother replying. For the rest of the day we scarcely spoke to each other. In Venice his normal good spirits returned.

'Let's get high and go and look at St Mark's Square,' he suggested. We smoked the last of our hash and careered out of our cheap hotel room. Laughing and joking, we wandered around the city, looking at the sights and repairing our broken bridges. But two days later, when it took an age to thumb to Trieste, John rebelled and said he wasn't hitching through Yugoslavia. He was going to take the train straight to Istanbul.

We changed in Belgrade, where I got him to cut off the hair I'd been growing since I left school, three years before. Hippies weren't welcome in Turkey, we'd heard. On board the train to Istanbul, we polished off our sandwiches and were hungry again by the time our carriage companions unpacked their hamper and ate. Taking pity on us, they invited us to share their food. The husband talked in stilted English.

'My name Hristo and this Irena,' he said. 'We live Sofia. Visit with we. Welcome guests.'

'Thank you, Hristo,' John replied, 'but we can't. We've only got transit visas. If the police catch us, they'll probably shoot us as spies or something.'

I didn't know if that was what would happen, but it seemed a reasonable supposition. Bulgaria was the most hardline of the communist satellite states, totally under the thumb of the Russians. The cold war had been a constant in my life. I'd grown up believing that only our toughness and unblinking vigilance prevented the communist hordes from overrunning the west and destroying democracy. Even though I'd grown out of my schoolboy attitudes, I was still frightened of the communists. Less than a year before, Russian tanks had been on the streets of Prague, crushing the Czechs' bid for independence.

It may have been bravado, Hristo's persistence or curiosity to get a glimpse of life behind the Iron Curtain, but it was probably his wife's beautiful eyes... I'm not sure why, but somehow we let ourselves be persuaded to get off the train in Sofia.

In the bright May sunshine, the Bulgarian capital looked very down at heel. The wide streets in the city centre were eerily quiet. People in shabby clothes walked, rode bikes or ambled along in bullock carts.

'No cars,' I said to John.

'Yeah,' he replied. 'Isn't it weird.'

Hristo and Irene's flat was halfway up a shoddy tenement block. The apartment was small and spare. It held the basics of life: a bed, a table and chairs, some kitchen gear and very little else. Our arrival caused a stir. Once we'd dumped our backpacks in the kitchen, we were introduced to the neighbours, who'd crowded into the open landing outside the flat.

'You first westerners they know,' Hristo told us.

Some thirty Bulgarians inspected us with lively curiosity. I smiled at the assembled crowd, a mix of all ages. They didn't look like fanatics with a burning ambition to destroy the western way of life, they looked like warm-hearted people. Everyone was smiling back at me. The little kids stared wide-eyed; everyone else wanted to shake our hands and ask if we knew The Beatles.

With Hristo as our guide, we wandered around the city. Our blue jeans flashed our foreignness to one and all. Everywhere we were met with good humour and enquiries about The Beatles. We had several meals in crowded workers' restaurants and each time someone at an adjoining table insisted on paying. The food was plain, beans or stew with bread or potatoes, and the restaurants were uniformly ugly. The only groceries for sale in the shops were giant jars of pickled gherkins. Everything seemed drab in this poor country except the personalities of the inhabitants, who were among the friendliest people I've ever met.

We had to be cautious anywhere near the city centre. When we heard a motor, we ducked out of sight. Cars meant Russians, bigwigs or police, and that could spell big trouble for us and for Hristo. Although hundreds of people must have known of our illegal presence in the city, no one denounced us.

After three days we slipped aboard the Istanbul train. My anxiety mounted towards panic levels as we approached the frontier with Turkey. Although the inhabitants of Sofia were like ordinary people everywhere, I was sure the border guards would be committed communists. Suspicious and thorough, they'd be certain to find out we'd stayed in the country without a permit. We could be locked up forever. Steeped in war literature since childhood, I couldn't stop myself thinking about the tortures they might use to make us confess we were spies.

Guilt was written all over my face as I handed my passport to the uniformed official. He glanced at me, looked at the photo and stamped me out of Bulgaria.

For months the Eel had filled my head with tales of Istanbul. Playing backgammon on the rooftops while smoking chillums and drinking tea from thistle-shaped glasses, gawping at the caskets of emeralds in San Sophia or at the ceilings of the Blue Mosque, haggling for puzzle-rings in the market, meeting travellers at Yenna's Restaurant, gorging in the pudding shops, looking across the Bosphorus to Üsküdar in Asia... I wanted to do all these things and more. Wired up for Istanbul, I was determined to hang out in the legendary Gulhane Hotel. John wanted to stay at the YMCA. He had the runs, he was tired out and more than a little fed up with me.

It takes a special sensibility to cruise through the forced intimacies, discomforts and uncertainties of travel. The Eel, with his constant buzzing energy, drove me nuts at the flat in Caversham. On the road he was the perfect companion. It was the reverse with John. He was a lovely, entertaining guy to hang out with, but travelling with him wasn't easy. Both of us were ready to go our separate ways.

Our money was evaporating fast. John laid claim to what remained of our fast diminishing communal pool of dollars.

'All this money came from my hash,' he said.

'But I sold it for you, man. We agreed an equal split... Well, fuck you!' I stormed off to the Gulhane. With my last few dollars I bought a big hunk of Afghani from a group of freaks heading west and started selling bits of it to newcomers from Europe. I'd found a way to stay alive. No one coming from Asia wanted to take their stash through the heavy Greek border controls; few travellers arriving from Europe wanted to score off the Turkish dealers – they had a reputation for informing on their customers. I knew that doing deals with the foreigners who flowed through the gateway between Europe and Asia was a stupidly dangerous game to be playing, but I had to do something.

It was 1969. This was the Turkey of *Midnight Express*, the bastinado and thirty-year drug sentences. The police had declared war on the hippies. At the Gulhane – which had been closed down after a bust and was only allowed to reopen under a new name, the Meri, the manager tipped us off when his informant told him there was going to be a drugs raid.

After a moment of intense paranoia, when doing a deal aboard a dinghy by the Golden Horn, I realised that I was completely out of my depth and decided to leave town. I went to visit Michelangelo, the first friend I'd made in Istanbul. He was now living on the island of Borgaz, in the sea of Marmara.

A Dutch traveller called Henki came with me. So did two American girls. Myla was jolly and sisterly. She usually followed the lead of her travelling companion, the petite and lovely Tyrell. Tyrell's light-brown hair curled into her chin like a pixie cap. A few days before, spaced out in the pudding shop, we'd given each other new names. She called me 'Greenland Tea'; I christened her 'Also Peaches'.

We disembarked at the quayside by the village and walked across the small arid island to an old Greek

Orthodox church. Beyond it was a goat path which zig-
zagged down a small cliff to a strip of beach. Our arrival
brought the hippy population of the beach up to a dozen.

Michelangelo had spent the previous harvest working
on a marijuana farm in Anatolia and had brought his wages,
a sack of pollen, to the island. The days went by in a warm
stoned haze, lazing on the rocks or the sand. When it got
too hot we swam. We caught fish on hand-held lines and
collected as many mussels as we wanted. There was a tap
at the church. All we needed from the outside world was
bread, lemons and candles. At night we made great fires
of driftwood, cooked and ate our seafood dinner, smoked
chillums, told stories and made music.

Each time the boat arrived it seemed to bring more
visitors. Our paradise was getting crowded. When I went
to the village for bread I thought the locals were growing
less friendly – or was I imagining things?

After a fortnight the weather changed. Clouds covered
the sun, then it began to rain. The girls and I decided to
have a few days in Istanbul. The ferry we were waiting to
board discharged half a dozen freaks.

'Hey, Leaf!'

It took me a second to recognise the guy standing in
front of me. I'd met him before, in Reading.

'Chris! Thought you were in India. What are you doing
here, man?'

'Heading home. Someone at the Gulhane said you were
here. Thought I'd check it out.'

'Look, we're off to town. We'll be back in a couple of
days. You staying?'

He nodded.

'Great. It's nice here. OK, catch you later.'

~ ~ ~ ~ ~

The next day, Dutch Henki turned up at Yenna's Restaurant, completely freaked. 'Big bust, man. Last night it was raining. Everyone was in the cave. There was a fire, music, drumming. I had a headache, so I went up to the little cave. I was sleeping, woken by shouting, lights. Lots of policemen. I kept very quiet. The bastards took everyone away.'

Myla, Tyrell and I nerved ourselves up to go to the police station, a fortress-like building at the top of a hill. There were four or five policemen hanging round the desk. They ogled the girls and scowled at me. The guy on the desk was the ugliest man I'd ever seen. 'Your friends are all fucked,' he said, laughing in our faces.

All we could do was alert various embassies and consulates. I took the ferry to the island to pick up my rucksack and sleeping bag, but the quay was policed and I wasn't allowed off the boat. The clothes I was wearing, my shoulder bag, my passport and a few dollars were all I had in the world.

Michelangelo turned up at the Gulhane. He'd been dumped at the Greek border along with most of the others and had come back for his pollen. Several people were still inside, he told us, including Chris, who'd been caught with hash in his rucksack and was facing a long sentence.

It hadn't really struck home until this point. Only the rain and a sudden stoned desire for rose jam and cream at the pudding shop had prompted us to go to Istanbul. Chris had gone to the island to see me. Had he not heard my name in the Gulhane and had it not rained... then he would be on his way home to England and I would be in his cell.

Twice in quick succession I'd been close to a long spell

in jail, in countries with savage prisons. I'd been dancing on the cliff tops. I had to stop before I fell. Enough adventures. I wanted to go home.

The girls were nearly as broke as I. Tyrell was having some money sent to Athens, so we headed there first. We started hitching on the outskirts of Istanbul and got a lift in the back of a lorry with a university professor and five of his students. They said they'd take us to Edirne, where Turkey, Greece and Bulgaria meet. Once we'd had dinner with them, in a roadside restaurant, the unease I'd been feeling died away. Though the vibe of the silent students was strange, we'd chatted with the professor in simple French and made friends after a fashion. A policeman arrived at the restaurant and came over to our table. There was an unmistakable sexual undertone to the conversation between the professor and the leching cop. I knew they thought all hippy girls were whores. But we were their guests at a meal; the Muslim law of hospitality meant that they were obliged to treat us honourably, I thought.

We continued our journey, rattling west in the back of the truck. After the sun went down we lay propped up against the girls' rucksacks, looking up at the large soft stars while we smoked the last of our hash. A huge full moon heaved itself into the eastern sky.

'We've had our ups and downs in this country, but at least our final memory of Turkey will be of this lovely night.'

No sooner had I said the words than we turned a corner and the going was suddenly bumpy. I sat up to see what was happening. The truck stopped behind the halted car of the professor. We'd left the road and were on a dirt track.

The students gathered round a back wheel of the car. Alarm bells were clanging in my head.

'Stay in the lorry!' I told the girls and jumped down to see what was going on. There was nothing wrong with the tyre. Hearing a scream, I ran round to the back of the truck, straight into the student who'd grabbed Myla. All three of us went sprawling. Four of these young Turks were scrawny, like me. The fifth was a very big boy. He lifted me off the ground, spun me round to face his friends and gripped my biceps in his huge hands. All my strength vanished. I was helpless while the other students took turns to kick and punch me.

'For the love of God,' I pleaded. 'Stop this. Please stop.'

The professor ran towards us. The moon gave enough illumination for me to see his twisted, snarling face. Silver moonlight flashed on the blade of the knife he held.

'Oh fuck,' I thought. 'This is it.' I looked my killer in the eye as he approached. He shouted at the giant and prodded him with the knife to make him let go. The students backed off under a tongue-lashing.

'I'm sorry,' he said to us. 'I'm sorry. It was a joke. Things got out of control. I'm very sorry.'

He herded his charges into the car and lorry. They drove off. I stood stunned in the track.

'You two OK?' I asked shakily. I'd just stared into the eyes of my death.

'Come on, move!' Tyrell hissed urgently. 'They might come back.'

Leaving the track, we crawled through a couple of maize fields, crossed a ditch and sat hidden in another stand of maize. The girls were in shock too. We didn't talk much. Just a few whispered queries and reassurances. I kept seeing the professor running towards me with the knife. I could see it all in slow motion, the professor soundlessly wading through the thick air, his face twisted into an evil mask, moonlight glinting off the knife he was going to kill me with. After a while, I began to ache from the blows I'd taken. We lay down, but sleep wouldn't come.

Lying in the maize, under that huge moon, trying to get the image of the professor's knife out of my mind, I realised that in any reasonable universe we'd have died tonight.

'Leaf, you awake?' Tyrell whispered.

'Yeah.'

'I can't sleep.'

'Nor me. I'm listening for that lorry.'

'Same here.'

The morning was so calm and beautiful it made the horror of the previous night seem like a bad dream. But I ached all over, my bruises were real enough.

The field in front of us sloped down to a line of trees bordering a small river. Beyond was a track leading to some buildings on the edge of a wood. We made towards the dwellings, crossed the river by a footbridge, and ascended a path. As we neared the wood, I saw it was bristling with tanks. Men in white pleated skirts surrounded us. I wanted to comment on their funny outfits but I kept quiet because they all had guns – pointing at us.

We'd stumbled into Greece. Our captors were disarmed by our pleasure at learning this. An English-speaking officer arrived and told us that we'd walked through a minefield. We were lucky to be alive.

Doubly lucky.

10 Trial

THE TRIAL OF THE JULIE mob finally got under way in January 1978, some ten months after the bust. The fifteen of us made an initial appearance in Bristol Crown Court to be charged and enter pleas. Scenes around the courtroom depicted the tobacco and slave trades on which the city's wealth had been based. We were to be tried amid scenes celebrating the traffic in an addictive drug and in human beings.

In addition to various individual charges, we were all charged with 'Conspiracy to contravene the Misuse of Drugs Act'. All but two of us pleaded guilty. Our lawyers said we'd been charged with conspiracy rather than substantive offences because, with laxer rules of evidence, the Crown would be sure to get a guilty verdict.

Against legal advice, some of us had decided that, rather than make the ritual expressions of remorse in our pleas of mitigation, we would take the opportunity of explaining what we thought about the drug that had brought us to court. My counsel explained my viewpoint well. He and lawyers acting for other defendants also referred to the report on LSD made by Dr Martin Micheson, consultant in charge of the Drug Dependency Clinic at University College Hospital in London.

In summary, Dr Micheson's report said that the vast majority of casualties from illegal drugs were caused by opiates, barbiturates and amphetamines. Fifteen years' clinical experience had shown him that LSD was not addictive and caused little or no physical injury. Despite its widespread availability, psychological reactions to it were uncommon.

The judge's view was that such submissions were irrelevant. LSD was an illegal class A drug and the defendants would be dealt with accordingly.

On the way back to the nick, Andy got into conversation with one of the screws.

'The thing is,' I heard him saying, 'who would you trust more, an experienced senior doctor who specialises in drug problems or a newspaper editor in need of a sensational story? Don't believe all the scare stories you read. Look, we distributed millions of tabs, millions. If this stuff is so dangerous, why aren't the hospital wards full of acid zombies – they're not, you know. Listen to what the doctor said – LSD is not addictive and psychological reactions to it are uncommon.'

'But not unknown.'

'That's true.' I leant forward and joined the conversation. 'LSD is a very strong drug and can be terrifying. The thing is, for practically everyone, those moments over the abyss pass quickly. I've no doubt there are some whose mental state means they shouldn't trip, but the same is true of drink. Most people handle it without too many problems, but alcohol ruins the life of quite a few people and of their families. Yet the distillers aren't in the dock. I've bumped into a number of drink derelicts in my time, I bet we all have, but I haven't actually met anyone whose life has been ruined by acid, or even anyone who was really harmed by acid. I'm not saying they don't exist, but they're not common.'

'What if I told you I know an acid casualty?'

'Well, first I'd want to know if he was genuine – because I know someone who claimed to have been spiked with acid as a get-out-of-jail card, and someone else who used it as an excuse for disability benefit. Do you know an acid space-case, then?'

'No, I was just wondering.'

We rose early on the raw morning of 8 March and began the familiar performance of getting out of the prison. This time we had to clear our cells completely. We were going for sentencing and would be returning, as convicts, to a different wing.

Laden with gear, we clattered down the iron stairs and waited for a screw to count us and unlock the door. The whole prison was caught up in our drama. This was the biggest trial anyone could remember and a lot of bird was about to be dished out.

A fistful of screws were waiting for us in reception, noisily arguing among themselves. They'd made a book on us and were running a sweepstake, one pound a go, to guess the total number of years the fifteen of us would receive. We were greeted with shouts and jeers and raucous invitations to join in and have a bet. Ignoring them, we changed out of our prison uniform and into our own clothes. Taffy, the mad Welsh screw, told me he'd put us down for four hundred – an average of over twenty-five years each.

'I wouldn't weigh you off, I'd hang the lot of you,' snarled another. 'Save the expense of keeping scum like you locked up.'

Most of the screws were in jovial mood. In prospect was a day away from the nick. They were to be present at the climax of a famous trial, something to talk about for years to come. Banging gloved hands together, stamping booted feet, joking and laughing, they were making a lot of noise.

We were silent. We'd been talking about this for almost a year. Now there was nothing left to say. I was aching for it to be over. Not a prison day had passed without my thinking of the moment that was only a few hours away. I was particularly sensitive to the coarse laughter and low humour of the screws, and to the way they endlessly jangled their keys, chains and handcuffs.

I tried to blank out their discordant racket and concentrate on getting straight in my head the opposing meanings of consecutive and concurrent. I'd heard those words so many times that I could no longer separate them. Pleading guilty to two major counts – conspiracy and possession with intent to supply – my prison term would be doubled or halved, depending on whether my sentences were concurrent or consecutive. I faced anything between six and twenty years. Shaking my head, I found something else to worry about: the cache in Ampthill Woods.

Richard's acid was gone; but Henry and Brian still had a million microdots. What effect would this have on our sentences? Should they have handed their stash in? Would that have made a difference? Would the acid still work in so many years time? I really didn't know. It's a prisoner's lot to be ignorant of the answers to the questions running round his brain.

'Cuff 'em up!' the principal officer yelled.

Our coach went on a mad dash through the city, surrounded by the wailing sirens and flashing lights of a large escort of police cars with a swarm of motorcycle outriders. Armed marksmen were posted on rooftops around the court. Overkill, or what?

A double file of policemen split the waiting crowd. We were bundled into the court between them. Friends called out encouragement; flashbulbs flared. Inside, we were hustled down to the dungeons and locked up, three to a cell.

Underground, I felt claustrophobic. I forced myself to breathe deeply so I could overcome the almost overwhelming urge to hammer on the door and scream, 'Let me out! LET ME OUT!'

Russ was called for a final talk with his solicitor. Plastic food arrived on plastic plates and was left untouched. My turn for a quick word with my brief. There was nothing more to say, except 'good luck' and 'thanks for all your help'. Back to the cell.

I prayed the judge had had a good night's sleep and a satisfactory bowel movement this morning. What if he'd been kept awake by sciatica or proof of his wife's infidelity? Maybe he'd decided to find out for himself what this LSD was all about and taken a trip last night… Some hope.

We waited. After a year in prison we were used to waiting. I wondered whether I'd get a chance to see Mary.

Tony Bradshaw, my solicitor's clerk, had assured me he'd fix it up if it were at all possible. When you're caught up in momentous events, unable to influence their outcome, the mind tends to focus on little details, things that are within your small range.

'I wonder if we'll get a chance to talk to Jan and Mary.' Russ echoed my line of thinking.

'Hope so,' I replied.

We were on speaking terms again. It wasn't as though the statement he'd made implicating me had had any real bearing on my situation. And he'd been under terrible pressure, desperate to keep his newly pregnant wife out of the firing line. You can't hold a grudge forever. I can't anyway. I'd be useless in a vendetta.

Suddenly there was a great racket of booted feet on the stairs. Three names were called. A clamour of screws opened cell doors and slammed them shut. The first trio went up.

'Good luck!' My cry was echoed from the other cells.

'Shut up! Shut up!' the turnkeys screamed.

We waited in silence, listening for any whisper or echo that would give us a clue as to what was going on above. Noise flooded in as the court door opened and was cut off as it slammed shut. A voice bellowed, 'Thirteen years! The bastards!' That was Henry.

Then it was our turn. At the top of the stairs I emerged in the centre of a large, bright room. Momentarily dazzled, I looked for Mary among the sea of faces in the public gallery. Someone waved. It was Jan, signalling to Russ. I was pushed to my seat, facing the bench.

The judge came in. Everybody stood. He sat. We all followed suit. The courtroom filled with coughs and scrapings. In an electric moment my eyes met the judge's. I wondered if he had to suppress a smile each time he entered a court and everybody rose for him. Maybe not. He looked severe, as though he'd never smiled in his life.

Slack-legged, wobbly, I hauled myself to my feet when my name was called. I couldn't properly take in what the judge was saying, something about 'previous good character' and 'serious crimes'. I was waiting for the consecutive/concurrent. At the end he said, 'I sentence you to eight years' imprisonment for conspiracy to contravene the Misuse of Drugs Act; to eight years' imprisonment for possession of LSD with intent to supply, and to one month's imprisonment for possession of cannabis. Sentences to run concurrently.'

Concurrently. My heart hiccupped. Wasn't that the bad one? No, it wasn't! It meant eight, not sixteen years.

'Thank you,' I said.

Only eight years… The relief passed in an instant. Eight years imprisonment! How could I survive that?

On my way down, I stopped and looked at the spectators. Now I could see every face in the crowd. There was Mary, next to Martin. They smiled and waved encouragement. In a state of shock, I waved back.

11 Prison blues

AFTER SENTENCING, we were bussed back to the nick. Our clothes were put into deep storage and we were issued with blue jeans and jacket: prison blues. We were now convicts, subject to the full rigours of the penal regime. Daily visits with food and wine became a thing of the past, convicts were entitled to one twenty-minute visit per month.

While waiting for allocation to long-term prisons, we were kept in the main section of Horfield, A wing. It looked and smelled like a larger version of the Gormenghastly remand wing, but it had much more movement and life. With some four hundred prisoners, there were rush hours at meals and at the start and end of work periods. You had an hour of association after tea, when it was your landing's turn. There are few choices in a prisoner's life, but here was one; you had the option of staying in your cell or hanging out with the other guys on the ground floor until evening bang-up. You could watch the big TV up at one end of the dining area or do as I did and sit at tables and talk or play chess, cards or table tennis.

During the year on remand, we'd festered in our cells. As convicted men, we had to work. The first job for everyone in Bristol nick was sewing mailbags. With big, blunt needles we had to do ten stitches to the inch. The seams were measured by a screw with a yard rule, to ensure that the regulations were met. All day long we convicts, a hundred strong, sat on rows of benches, talking, heads bent over our sewing like old ladies.

Loudspeakers continually blared out pop music from a radio station. It was our bad luck to be in the mailbag shop while the charts were dominated by one of the direst recordings ever made. To the slow beat of Wings, the monotonous dirge 'Mull of Kintyre' was piped through the shop several times a day, week after week, month after bloody month.

You had to complete the mailbag quota in order to earn the maximum wage of seventy-six pence a week. Not able to sew fast enough, I did a deal with the Number One, the con in charge of the workshop. In return for five roll-ups a week, he loaned me enough bags to get me on to top pay.

Cons weren't allowed money in Horfield. Wages were credited to your shop account. Mine were sufficient to buy a stamp and half an ounce of Old Holborn. To acquire other things, like toothpaste, meant cutting down on tobacco or not writing home.

The noisiest times in A wing were at meals. Screws controlled the ebb and flow of the cons with screamed instructions. Prisoners were called down from their metal landings in groups to line up and get their meal on a tray. While they were clattering upwards, more hungry men would be rattling down. Breakfast, or just before, was the time to make an application to the governor or report sick. I joined the queue outside the screws' office and shuffled forward as the line shrank in front of me. Then it was my turn.

'I want to see the governor,' I said.

'Why?' asked the SO, the senior officer.

'About the food.'

'Is it a complaint?'

'Yes.'

The screw standing right behind me rumbled, 'You're wasting your time… and ours.' He leaned out the door and yelled 'Next.'

'No, I haven't finished. I'm entitled to see the governor.'

'Well, it won't do you any good,' the SO said. 'Let me give you a word of advice, Fielding. You'll only be stirring up trouble for yourself. You're going to be inside for a long time and it's not a good idea to start off on the wrong foot.'

'Even so, I'd like to see the governor.'

After breakfast, instead of going to the workshop, I waited with the other cons who'd been stubborn or foolish enough to insist on their rights.

'Fielding, FO1465!' the screw barked, when I was standing in front of the governor.

'Yes, Fielding…?' The governor's enquiring silence invited me to speak.

'I have a complaint about the vegetarian diet,' I said.

'So I've been told,' he replied, wearily. 'I've got the diet sheet here,' he added, giving me a glimpse of the file he was holding. 'Fielding, you must understand that the men's nutritional requirements have been carefully worked out. Government regulations ensure that the diet is adequate.'

He read me the menu for the previous day. 'It sounds pretty good, I must say,' he commented. 'I wouldn't mind it myself.'

'It does sound good,' I agreed. 'And if that was what I'd been given, I wouldn't be standing here. But the potato-cheese cake you mentioned had no cheese in it. Lunch was potato cake with potato and cabbage. Governor, I have a health-food shop – food is my business. I do know what I'm talking about. The vegetarian diet is deficient in protein, vitamins, minerals and fibre.'

'I'll look into it,' he said.

As all the cons knew, the kitchen crew commandeered the best of everything – tea, milk, cheese, eggs and meat. Most of them had the look of pink porkers being fattened for slaughter. Apart from gorging on the supplies, they flogged them off. You could buy tea and milk off some of the kitchen crew, but it sticks in the throat to pay for stuff that should already be yours. The lazy bastards were also throwing away hundredweights of vegetables, dumping them straight into the bins rather than going to the trouble of washing and preparing them. I didn't tell the governor that. He should have known already.

He did look into my complaint. For a few days the food improved dramatically, but it soon deteriorated again.

The lack of fibre in the diet made me constipated. Soon I was suffering from piles. I reported sick, though the hospital was a place to avoid. My request for bran was treated with suspicion, as is any petition by a prisoner; all the staff know that convicts are devious as well as deviant. Even so, what trouble can you cause with bran? I was given a pillbox of it to sprinkle on my porridge at breakfast. The next day I stood in the applications queue outside the screws' office and went on doctor's report, and the next day and the next and every day until the doctor got sick of seeing me. He gave me a big bag of bran and told me to stay away until it was finished.

What a relief – and not only for my bowels. Each day I'd had to nerve myself to face the increasingly irritated comments of the screws. I knew I was starting to get a reputation among the uniforms as a smart-arse trouble-maker. If I'd continued going on doctor's report every day, sooner or later I would have found myself separated from the rest of the sick parade, locked in a room with some angry screws. The hospital was where many of the nick's beatings took place. You could die in prison and people did, some of them young and healthy. Jailors and jailed both knew that no screw had ever been convicted of the murder of a con.

Your choice, as a prisoner, is to do your bird as a man or as a worm. Neither way is easy, each brings its own problems. Let yourself be pushed around by the screws and you're given a hard time by the other cons. If you don't want your fellow inmates to make your life unbearable, you have to stand up to them as well as to your jailors – but it can be a fatal mistake to infuriate the screws. Convicts must tread a fine line. Survival is the name of the game.

At least I didn't have too many problems from my fellow cons. Being part of a large group meant no one could intimi-date us. But nobody wanted to. We were highly regarded for the notoriety of our crime, for the money it had generated and the amount of bird we'd pulled – a hundred and twenty years between the fifteen of us. We had status.

Andy walked around with me on exercise a lot while we waited to be allocated. He knew we were unlikely to be sent to the same nick and he wanted to hear what had happened after I left Turkey. I could have told him in half an hour, but I let the story run on over a few days. You learn to spin things out in the nick, to extract the maximum nutrition from a very thin diet.

The day after our arrival in Greece, the girls and I got a lift in a lorry and bowled along in the sunshine, bound for Thessalonika. After an hour we saw the sea. From then on the blue waters of the Aegean twinkled invitingly on our left. It got hotter in the cab as the sun rose in the sky. When the driver suggested a swim, we readily agreed.

Wearing cut-off jeans and t-shirts, the girls raced into the water and dived in. Tyrell stood up and dragged the hair out of her eyes with her fingers. Her T-shirt was wet and translucent. The dark circles of her nipples were magnets to male eyes.

The lorry driver splashed up to me in a state of happy excitement. 'Is that one yours?' he mimed. 'I'll have the other.'

'No,' I said, but he wasn't listening. Aflame at the thought of hippy girls of easy virtue, he lunged at Tyrell. While he was off-balance, I pushed him over. He came to the surface choking. The lorry driver was a big man, a big, angry, spluttering man. For a moment, as he roared, I thought he was going to beat me up, but he just got out of the water, dried himself with controlled fury, dressed, strode off to his truck and drove away. A couple of hundred yards up the road he stopped and threw the girls' rucksacks into the ditch.

A group of Dutch heads in a VW camper van took us to Mount Olympus. We were ravenous when we got a ride in the back of a tomato truck and gorged on a loaf of bread, a gift from the driver, and his giant misshapen tomatoes, the best food we'd ever eaten.

In Athens, Tyrell's bank transfer hadn't come through. I sold blood to a clinic and made enough money to pay for our room and feed us for a few days. We explored the old quarter, the Pláka, and hung out at the Acropolis, watching the sun sparkle on the waves and gazing at the city where western civilisation had been born.

I sat on stones where Plato and Aristotle may easily have rested. Thinking of their physicality made me see the philosophers not as subjects of study but as real people, grappling with the dilemmas of life. With a reeling shift of perspective, I realised how radically my existence had changed since I'd been a university student. For the past two years I'd been swept along on a rip tide, surfing into the future with scarcely a look back and hardly a coherent thought in my head. Deliberately. Out of my shifting kaleidoscope of hallucinated thoughts had come a few very definite ideas about how to live.

In Tuscany I'd learnt a lot from John Amati about ecology, the scientific study of the interactions between life forms which make our earth the place it is. My acid vision, that we are all one, appeared to be supported by science, at the ecological level at least. All life on this planet is one.

Once we realise that, we'll be more inclined to nurture our environment and less likely to damage it.

I'd dropped out because I didn't want to be part of the consumer society that's vandalising the world. I was sure that wasn't the way to go. For the last two years, I'd been running on inspiration, not logic, doing things on the spur of the moment, if they felt right, trying to give my intuition precedence over my intellect, attempting not to dwell on the past or ponder the future but to be right in the moment. This approach had given me some incredible times, but of late it had brought me close to disaster, more than once. I wondered if I was really on the right track.

Then I realised, with a laugh, that so much self-analysis made me guilty of the very kind of thinking I abhorred. Had I absorbed all this cogitation through my arse, sitting on sun-warmed stones soaked with the ideas of men like Socrates and Aristotle? Perhaps it was simply a sign that the analytical side of me was coming awake again. I really had no idea. And I didn't even want to think about it.

When Tyrell's money arrived, we hitched down through the Gulf of Corinth to Patras and took the night ferry to Italy. The boat sailed past Cephalonia and Ithaca. We saw twinkling strings of lights and heard laughing and singing coming from the bars on Corfu. Across the narrow strait was Albania, unlit, forbidding, almost close enough to touch.

In southern Italy, having to discourage another ardent lorry driver, I vowed never to travel with two girls again. Near Naples an orange VW camper stopped and hooted. It was the Dutch guys we'd met in Greece. We piled in and travelled a thousand miles with them to Amsterdam. At the

Paradiso Club I bought a gram of hash and rolled up our first joint since the nightmare in Turkey.

'Holland is a civilised country.' I choked, took another deep toke on the spliff and passed it on. 'Weird, isn't it, we can openly score and smoke here… and yet in Turkey, where they must have been getting stoned for thousands of years, a bit of blow can get you locked up for ever.'

Amsterdam was a cool place, but I didn't want to be there. I was homesick. Longing to get across the North Sea, I started to draw on the pavements. I was doing well, nearly had enough money for the crossing, when my shoulder-bag was stolen. Now I was down to the clothes I was wearing and a few sticks of chalk.

The police recovered my discarded bag and passport. The money was gone, of course. Though England was tantalisingly close, just across the water, it felt like I would be stuck in Holland forever. Though I persevered with the chalks and was making a little cash each day, I had to keep eating and I never had quite enough money for the ferry. Finally the girls took pity on me and made up the difference for a ticket to Harwich.

The port wasn't far from Woodbridge, my old school. I thought to take advantage of the Queen's tradition of always offering a meal and a bed to returning old boys. The new housemaster, my former maths teacher, made an exception in my case. He took one look at me and told me to clear off.

'And don't come back,' he added as I retreated down the drive. 'We don't want your sort here. You're the worst kind of example to the boys.'

There was just one person I really wanted to see in the school, my old English teacher. He'd been the only master who had the gift of inspiring his students. Desmond Proctor-Robinson, P-R, loved his subject and communicated his enthusiasm. As I walked over to Marryott, where he was housemaster, I could see him clearly in my mind's eye – small head, prominent Adam's apple, slicked-back hair and beady eyes behind pebble glasses. I wondered if he would remember me – so much had happened in the three years since I'd left. A little apprehensively, I banged the knocker to his study.

'Fielding – good heavens! How delightful. Come in. What brings you to my door?'

He poured a couple of sherries while I told him about my reception at Queen's.

'No wonder they turned you away,' he said, handing me a drink and raising his glass. 'Cheers. I'm pleased to see you, Nigel, but not enamoured of your appearance. Take a look at yourself – the mirror's over there. What on earth do you think you look like?'

In P-R's full-length mirror I saw myself for the first time in weeks or maybe months. I could have been an Albanian mountain brigand – wild-eyed, tangle-haired and burnt a deep brown. My jeans were a mass of colourful patches, my T-shirt a red rag under my shaggy Afghan coat. I thought I looked great.

'You're one of those hippies now, aren't you? Is it fun?'

'Amazing.' I nearly added 'sir' but managed not to.

'What's it all about then?' His eyes gleamed. P-R could be withering when he chose, but he seemed genuinely interested. What could I say? 'Try some LSD and you'll see.' I could take insane risks in Turkey, but I wasn't brave enough to speak that directly to P-R, so I said nothing and just smiled.

'How old are you now, Fielding?'

'Coming up to twenty-one.'

'You're twenty! Lucky lad. Make the most of it, it won't last.'

12 Freaks

DURING THE WEEKS in A wing, while we waited
to be allocated to other prisons, Brian and I hung out a lot
together. Neither of us were well, we were both suffering
from sinusitis and post-trial trauma, but we had some epic
battles over the table-tennis net and we got each other
laughing when we sat at table to play cards. Wrapped up
in the triumph of trumping an ace or slamming back the
ping-pong ball, Brian sometimes looked like the sparky
young daredevil he'd been when I'd first met him, eight
years before. Then he was suddenly gone, whisked away
to one of the high security prisons. That night I lay in bed,
remembering my friend, wondering if I'd ever see him
again and thinking about how he had come to be such an
important figure in my life.

When I got back to Reading, in the late summer of '69,
it looked like the psychedelic revolution had happened in
my absence. It was an extraordinary transformation. There

were freaks everywhere. They swarmed all over the university and all around the town.

'What's more,' my old buddy Jack told me, 'it's much the same in every city in the country. The spore is on the wind, man. So many people are dropping out that straight society will soon lack the manpower it needs to keep going.'

The Electric Eel and Paula put me up at first. I knew I couldn't stay – they had a tiny baby – so I put the word about that I was looking for a pad. Brian asked me if I'd like to take the spare room in 30 Upper Redlands Road, the student house where he lived.

Most of the rooms in Upper Reds had had a psychedelic treatment. I daubed my new home with jungle foliage, painted little scenes in the raindrops at the end of the fronds and moved in as soon as the paint dried.

Jack lent me the money to buy half a pound of Pakistani hash. I sold it in quarter and half-ounces and made enough to pay him back and score another quarter pound. Upper Reds was just across the way from Whiteknights Park, the university campus; we had a constant stream of students who came to smoke or score from the three of us who were dealing dope from the house.

Chip was another Brummie like Brian, a friendly, shambling freak with a brilliant mind under a thatch of black hair. Pals of his were bringing back vanloads of good hash from Asia. I could get Afghani or good Paki black from them any time. With very little effort I made enough to pay the rent, buy food and stay warm and high through the winter.

Brian came home late one night and burst into my pad, a huge grin lighting up his face. He grabbed the nearest joint, took a long toke and held his breath while he looked around the room. The cold night air had come in with him. It stirred the six of us out of the stoned fug into which we'd gradually sunk through the evening. He knew he had all our attention when he casually said, 'So, who fancies a trip?'

Reading had been without acid for months. I hadn't had any for over a year.

'Me,' I said, and so did everyone else.

Each of us swallowed one of the yellow capsules that Brian handed round. Finally he popped one in his own mouth.

We were all wide awake now, waiting for the trip to start. Chip made tea. Someone else rolled a joint. When I could feel the first definite tingles, I put the Incredible String Band on the turntable.

I met a man whose name was Time,
And he said 'I must be going.'
But just how long ago that was,
I have no way of knowing...

The laughter must have died down a century ago. I'd been afloat on a sea of patterned thought. Back in my body, I realised I'd grown too big for the house and lumbered to my feet.

'Too much. I'm going out.'

We all bounced down the stairs like marbles and ran into the night. Dawn, naked and beautiful, stole up on me while I was sitting on the megalithic stones in the wilderness beyond Whiteknights Lake. I'd been wondering about the bloody passage of human history and thinking about the spaces between the stars and the idea of light. 'Man, this is strong acid!' I said to myself, for about the twentieth time. A fox silently trotted across the clearing in front of the stones and melted into the blackberry bushes. The undergrowth was throbbing, growing to the beat of life.

The arena of sound swelled as the light strengthened. Rustlings, chirrings, barking, engines – fresh elements kept being added to the orchestra of the morning. I listened, entranced, until it suddenly occurred to me that I was cold and my stomach was a gurgling void. Time to go home for breakfast.

The kitchen was a mess. It was always a tip, I was just seeing it with freshly washed eyes. The walls were covered in scribbled jokes, inspirations and messages. Every horizontal surface was piled with crusted pots, stained mugs and mouldy plates. How could we live like this? I put on the kettle and backed out of the room.

Out of this world, men in suits walked on the moon. Out of our heads, we careered around the inner universe, to a soundtrack of Pink Floyd, Hendrix, the Stones, Love, Spirit, Jefferson Airplane, Country Joe and the Fish... We took a lot of acid that winter; Brian seemed to have any amount of it. He laid fifty trips on me just before he moved up to London.

'Pay me when you've sold them,' he said. 'Then, if you want, you can have some more.'

Viking John, the best-looking student on campus, was now sleeping on a mattress on the floor of my room. He'd brought his record collection with him.

'What about some Rachmaninov?' he suggested while I

was flipping through my thin stack of albums, wondering what to put on next.

'I'm not big on classical music,' I replied and went on looking.

'No, I think you'll like this, his second piano concerto.' He took the album out of its sleeve and passed it to me. 'This guy's a real freak.'

I put the record on the turntable, lit the joint of Afghani I'd just rolled and sat back. John was right, Rachmaninov was out of his skull. The music was passionate, almost demented in its intensity. With eyes closed, I felt I was in a coach, rocking through the snowy Russian landscape, wrapped in some vast Slavic tragedy. A few days later John said, 'I think I'll try you out on some Yeats. You know his stuff?'

'No, can't say I do.'

'OK. Listen to this. This is William Butler Yeats himself, reading a short and beautiful poem.'

Through the hissing and crackling of the old recording, a tinny but strong voice declaimed:

I will arise and go now, and go to Innisfree,
And a small cabin build there, of clay and wattles
    made;
Nine bean rows will I have there, a hive for the
    honey-bee
And live alone in the bee-loud glade.

And I shall have some peace there, for peace comes
    dropping slow
Dropping from the veils of the morning to where
    the cricket sings;

> *There midnight's all aglimmer and noon a purple*
> *glow*
> *And evening full of the linnet's wings.*
>
> *I will arise and go now, for always night and day*
> *I hear lake water lapping with low sounds by the*
> *shore;*
> *While I stand on the roadway, or on the pavements*
> *grey,*
> *I hear it in the deep heart's core.*

'Wow!' I said. 'Amazing. Let's hear that again.'

'You think that's good,' John chuckled, 'wait 'til I play you some of my T. S. Eliot recordings.'

Viking John taught me that there was great music and poetry outside rock 'n' roll. As well as Rachmaninov, he turned me on to Beethoven and Tchaikovsky and tried, but failed, to do the same with Mahler.

From lunchtime onwards, a succession of freaks would arrive to score, smoke, converse and listen to the sounds. Most evenings there'd be between six and a dozen of us sitting around the clearing in the jungle that was my room. Long stoned silences interspersed with laughter and animated talk.

We felt we were reinventing the way life was lived. Our counterculture was a kind of anti-establishment rainbow coalition. The red end of the spectrum was personified by Trudge, a dour northerner, wrapped in hard-left dogma and a trench coat. On the ultra violet wing were freaks like myself and Rob downstairs, who floated on the breeze and considered any kind of organisation an incipient tyranny.

The more politically oriented elements of the counterculture were getting angry at police harassment and becoming increasingly militant. Trudge and the heavyweights who thought like him began to mutter darkly about revolution. We lightweights argued against descending to the establishment's level of physical violence. The whole point of our rebellion was that we were different from them. We just had to keep going with what we were doing. More people were with us every day. Those old dinosaurs would be extinct before long.

Through the long winter nights we smoked and tripped and talked. I went on a lot about travelling, praising the simple virtues of life on the road and regaling my friends with stories of my adventures. I talked myself into itchy feet. When May came around and the weather got warm, I packed my bag. I was off to Cornwall, where I aimed to find work in a pottery. Rob slung his guitar over his shoulder, he was coming too.

Gangling Rob was an ace guitarist, he played most of the time he was awake. Music filled his life and his life was full of music. He had straw for hair, pebble glasses, a goofy grin and a cartoon way of throwing back his head when he laughed, which he did a lot. Rob was another refugee from a military family. Maybe this was why we had a similar sense of humour. We were laughing non-stop as we walked down to the Basingstoke Road and stuck up our thumbs, headed for Land's End.

The trip took several days. Our wild hair and multicoloured clothes put a lot of people off. It didn't matter because we were in no hurry and the weather was perfect. We came to West Penwith, the very tip of Cornwall, in the company of a couple of London freaks. They insisted that we meet the friends they'd come down to visit, saying Billy would be a great contact for us to have. Our knock went unanswered. The cottage door was ajar. The Londoners looked at each other, shrugged and went in. We followed. The curtains were drawn against the beautiful day. In the gloom it took a moment to discern the figures slumped on the two sofas.

The man stirred, muttering darkly. We clearly weren't welcome. I was all set to leave, but the others had already accepted the offer of a cup of tea from Nora, the lady of the house. Our host brightened after eating some of the pills that our travelling companions gave him. He introduced himself as Billy Bolitho and apologised for his indisposition. Billy turned positively sunny once he'd smoked some of the dynamite grass I had with me.

Rob and I spent our first few nights in Penzance, sleeping on the beach. We had to shelter under the railway arches when the weather changed and sheets of rain swept in from the Atlantic. Billy offered us the use of the top floor of the three-storey house in Penzance that he and Nora were about to move into. He'd taken to us because of our military backgrounds.

'Being in the army,' he told us, 'was the best part of my life.'

I went round the potteries, looking for a start, and got taken on as an apprentice at Leaper's in Newlyn. The money was a joke, six quid a week, but I thought it was worth it because I'd be learning all about the potter's craft. Wrong.

The boss only wanted me to fill slip moulds for the long dishes he made for the tourist trade. I turned out dozens every day; each one sold for the same amount as my week's wages. I kept going because the others in the pottery – the boss's wife, the young potter and the genuine apprentice – were very friendly and helpful. They taught me and let me practise on the wheel whenever the boss was out delivering his tat to gift shops.

At first Rob couldn't earn anything with his guitar. The tourist season hadn't started, so busking was a waste of time. He got a few spots to play in bars, but only for free cider or beer. Not having to pay rent, we could just about survive on the money I made in the pottery. We mostly lived off burnt pasties, which we could get from the bakers for next to nothing, and small mackerel, bought for pennies off the fishing boats. Frying the fish filled the top of Billy's house with an oily harbour smell.

Billy Bolitho was unlike any adult I'd ever known. Since first turning on I'd had little or nothing to do with the older generation. They lived in another world altogether. None of them were my friends until I met Billy.

He was tall and strongly built, his jaw jutted like a landing craft. A tuft of greying blond hair sat on top of a rectangular face. Billy's pale blue eyes perched above a slightly crazed smile. The smile disappeared on his days on desolation row.

Billy had been in school through the Second World War. It had lasted just long enough for him to take part in its dying moments. As the Allies advanced across France, he'd hurtled around on his motorbike, shuttling dispatches between headquarters and the advancing front. If he ever overshot the target, his sergeant told him, he'd be riding straight into the Nazi lines. Dispatch riders were given benzedrine to help them keep awake for their job. Billy had been a speed freak ever since.

He'd been getting a scrip from the doctor for twenty-five years. Over time, as his tolerance grew, the prescription was increased. When we met it was for forty-nine black bombers a week. One bomber was enough to keep me jabbering non-stop for about twenty hours, but Billy required at least eight bombers a day. This meant one or two days a week without speed. Very bad days. To get through the wasteland he needed to score some other amphetamines, take lots of barbiturates or anything that could soothe his screaming nerve ends.

Billy was a rogue scion of the first family of West Penwith. His uncle was Lieutenant-governor of Cornwall. The Bolithos owned land, ships, mines and a bank. They were enormously wealthy. At thirty, Billy had come into an inheritance of two million pounds. In three years of partying, gambling and clubbing in London, he and his small army of hangers-on had got through the lot. Rather than let him liquidate any more of the Bolitho's assets, his family had put him on an allowance of two hundred pounds a month. In 1970 that was a lot of money, far more than most people would earn. Billy usually spent his allowance straight away, then lived on credit for the rest of the month. He was a Bolitho; his credit was good.

At the beginning of June, I saw how he went about getting through his money. He drew out his allowance in cash, paid off his long-overdue milk bill and bought a crate of cream. In the late morning we walked down Market Jew Street. Billy stopped to settle his accounts with a succession of tradesmen. In the window of an antique shop, he saw a painting of his grandfather riding to hounds and acquired it for fifty quid. On the way home, we called in to the pub. They must have known he was coming for the place was full. Billy bought a round for everyone and presented the painting to the landlord, who hung it on the wall to the cheers and toasts of all the freeloaders. By lunchtime, Billy had done his entire allowance. He and Nora had twenty-four pints of cream to last them a month.

Although an out-and-out druggie, Billy didn't like hippies at all. Thinking of him as a rich old mark, the Penzance dealers routinely overcharged him.

'You don't need to pay those kind of prices,' I told him. 'I don't know about speed, but in Reading you can get good dope at ten or twelve quid an ounce and ace acid's a pound a trip.'

'Maybe you could get me some,' he announced, in his booming aristocratic voice. 'I like a good trip. There's nothing quite like it.'

I hitched up to London and got Brian to lay fifty hits on me. Billy wanted them all. In spite of being warned these sunshine capsules were powerful – two hundred and fifty micrograms – and that one was plenty for a strong trip, Billy swallowed twenty with a glass of milk. An hour or so later, he stripped off all his clothes and took a mop and a bucket of hot water up to the third floor. Singing Gilbert and Sullivan at the top of his voice, he spent the day cleaning the entire house. The following morning he fog horned, 'One of my best trips ever. Marvellous.'

The police paid us a visit not long after that.

'I'm sorry to bother you, Mr Bolitho, sir,' the sergeant

said, twisting his cap in his hand, 'but we've had reports that drugs are being used on the premises.'

'Stuff and nonsense!' Billy snorted. 'Do you think I'd allow that kind of behaviour? Anyway, I'm glad to see you, Sergeant. I'd value your opinion on a... let's say a private matter. We'll go to my study. Nora, please give the men a cup of tea in the kitchen.'

After the constables had trooped off in Nora's wake, Billy waved the sergeant into his study. He leant back out of the door and hissed to me, 'Clean up.'

Billy Bolitho. What a case! Part of him was still zooming around the war on his motorbike, goggles covering his benzedrine eyes, leather despatch satchel slung over his shoulder.

One night, Rob came back from a gig with a young girl in tow, a buxom seventeen-year-old country girl from Devon who'd run away from home to join the hippies. Stacia moved into Rob's heap of bedding on the floor. I moved my heap into another room, then I took a break from the lovers and hitched back to Upper Reds to see my pals.

Reading was buzzing in anticipation of the upcoming Isle of Wight Festival. Chip and another friend, Scooter, were going along to sell the five thousand caps of acid that Brian had laid on them. I decided to go too, along with half a million others. Just about the first person I saw at the festival was Stacia. She was up on stage with Hawkwind, down to her panties and dancing.

Chip had dropped out of his science course at Reading.

Looking like one of the Furry Freak Brothers with his mane of tangled black hair and scimitar nose, he set up shop in the middle of the vast crowd in front of the big stage. There, under a huge banner, which read ACID in letters three feet high, Chip, Scooter and I watched Hendrix stumble through his last big gig. Finally the great man pulled himself together and made us sit up and listen, playing with the awesome power that had electrified a generation.

In three days, Chip knocked out nearly four thousand of Brian's trips at a pound a time. He was immediately rich. We'd all made some money from the festival. I used mine to go halves on a pound of Red Lebanese with Duncan, a soft-spoken Suffolk dropout with a mass of brown curls. We went up to Scotland and sold it around the fringes of the Edinburgh Festival.

News that Hendrix was dead took the spring out of our step and made what we ate seem tasteless.

Summer came to an end. Rob went to Wales, but I returned to Cornwall. For a fiver a week, I got a winter let on the only cottage on the ancient power centre of Trencrom, a megalithic hill fort between Penzance and Ives. The views from the top of the hill were spectacular. To the north, St Ives bay swept up to Godreavy Lighthouse; to the south, St Michael's Mount was Trencrom's twin in the water.

My friend Jackie Van Gelder owned the Black Cat pottery near the seafront in Penzance. She agreed to let me use her premises at night. Here I made chillums, the conical hash pipes much used in Asia. At first I used subtle wood-ash and sea salt glazes, then discovered an aventurine flux that made colours flow into each other. Painting the flux on the overlaps of bright glazes produced a swirling psychedelic effect.

The chillums took up little space in Jackie's kiln. Twice a week, when she was doing a firing, she'd fit in some of my pieces. Beautiful and functional, my psychedelic chillums sold well in Granny Takes a Trip and the other headshops in London. I'd take fifty or sixty at a time. With the money I made I usually bought a little hash and picked up fifty or a hundred trips from Brian.

Viking John turned up one day at Trencrom with a big suitcase and half a pound of fine Jamaican weed. For weeks we did little but get high, go for long walks and stagger home with all the wood we could carry. When Atlantic gales windblasted the house we played Rachmaninov at full volume and burned the poetry of Yeats and Eliot into our brains.

Chip and a whole bunch of friends from Reading came for Christmas. We partied for three days before they all piled into their cars and drove off, with waves and shouts and cheery cheerios. Viking John went with them. The party had reminded him how much he missed the social life in town.

I missed it too when the January storms battered Trencrom. With no one else to talk to, I started having long conversations with the two cats I'd inherited. I was doing a lot of acid up on top of Trencrom, travelling backwards in time, peeling away the layers which separated me from my neolithic forebears who'd crouched on these same rocks four thousand years earlier.

West Penwith, where England sticks its toe into the Atlantic, is a magnet for all shades of mystics. The lean and haunted Marko was a follower of the cabbala. Marko, with his flowing hair and long cloak, pinned by a Celtic brooch, fixed me with his missionary-grey eyes, leant on his curiously carved staff and whispered, 'Your skin, like velvet, has a nap. It is possible, literally, to rub a person up the wrong way…'

He did. I suspected there was less to Marko than met the eye. In West Penwith there was a stiff competition to be weirdo of the week. I ran into astrologers, cultists, magicians, numerologists, occultists, psychics, seers, Tarot readers, UFOlogists, wizards, witches and zealots. Picking up the vibe, I studied ley lines, spaced out on Carlos Casteneda and tried to read the signs in the wood and the wind to descry my future.

I consulted the *I Ching*, the Book of Changes, an ancient, extraordinary work, central to Confucian and Taoist philosophy. I threw the coins and looked up the resulting hexagram: Lü / The Wanderer. The judgement read, 'Success through smallness. Perseverance brings good fortune to the wanderer.'

I've only ever consulted this book ten or a dozen times in my life and on each occasion it has astounded me – not by answering the question I thought I was asking, but by showing me what was really in my mind, below the surface noise. I'd been worrying about where I was going to live after I had to give up the cottage in the spring and I was fretting about my love life, or lack of it. At first the hexagram appeared to have nothing to do with my central concerns. Only on reflection did I see that my way forward was indeed through exploration, not material security or physical attachment. Once again, the *I Ching* had opened up the wrappings of my life and shown me my heart.

The judgement added, 'Perseverance brings good fortune to the wanderer.' It looked very promising. I read on. 'A wanderer has no fixed abode; his home is the road. Therefore he must take care to remain upright and steadfast, so that he sojourns only in the proper places, associating only with good people. Then he has good fortune and can go his way unmolested.'

All this resonated with me, especially the phrase 'his home is the road'. Right, I'd return to being a wanderer. I was ready for a change.

In the frozen rut of January, I'd been having fantasies about going to Indochina, tracking down the source of buddha grass, the strongest marijuana in the world, and sending it back to Britain to blow my friends' minds. It didn't matter that I'd never been to Asia. I could suss things out from Singapore. It would be an excellent way of re-establishing contact with my family, whom I hadn't seen for over two years. Some months before, my Dad had been posted to Singapore, charged with the job of closing down the British military presence on the island.

Indochina! From my early schooldays, that word had had such a ring for me. It still did. Now all I had to do was to get together enough money to make the journey possible. On my next trip up to London, I talked to Brian about my plan and the obstacle in its path.

'So, how much do you need?' he asked, frowning as he always did when talking about dosh.

'Er… Hold on, I've got to work it out.' I thought about it hurriedly. Two fifty should do it: half for the plane tickets and half for the rest. 'Well, I'm about a hundred quid short.'

'I'll lend you the money. Tell you what, I'll give you

a hundred and fifty. It's never a bad idea to have a bit in reserve.' He rummaged around in a drawer and came up with a sheaf of tenners. 'Here you go.'

I knew Brian had been doing well for some while and I knew what a generous man he was, but the matter-of-factness with which he made my dream possible took my breath away.

'Wow, Brian. Too much! Thank you. Listen, I'll pay you back, of course. And, if all goes well, you'll get a weight or two of the strongest grass in the world.'

I wound up my affairs in Cornwall and returned to Reading to prepare for my imminent departure to Southeast Asia.

13 Indochina

AFTER SEVERAL WEEKS in the mailbag shop, the Julie mob began to be transferred to different prisons. Brian was already gone. One by one, I said goodbye to Henry, Richard, Eric and Andy. Finally, I received my allocation. Along with Russ and Dave Solomon, I was to stay in Horfield, moving to the long-termers' wing.

B Wing, a modern four-storey building, was reserved for people serving over four years. The ground floor comprised the screws' office, the bathroom, dining hall and a television room. The top three floors each contained an ablution block and thirty-three single cells. Over a quarter of the cons were lifers, there was a sprinkling of druggies, some mouldering old fellers and a lot of violent young men. Every prisoner had his own tiny cell, measuring six foot six by seven foot six.

My mate Smiles, another of the Julie mob, had been moved over to B Wing a couple of weeks before. He paid the wing Number One to get me the peter next to his, on the short spur on the top landing, a corridor of just nine cells. Having a reliable friend alongside was a huge bonus. We knew we could rely on each other, come what may. It made all the difference.

I'd met Smiles a couple of times before the bust, but we hardly knew each other until we were locked up. Even then it was a while before we became friends. He was a Mancunian, a bearded, tattooed ex-squaddie. On remand I'd known him as the loud-mouthed extrovert at the other end of the landing and it was a few months before we strolled round the exercise yard together. Then I discovered we had a very similar stance on life… and beneath Smiles's brash exterior was hidden an extraordinary mind.

'Some of us are looking for the divine spark within,' he said to me, during one of our first conversations, fixing me with his piercing blue eyes. 'The others are rummaging around in the bins.'

If you're lucky, you might meet one or two totally exceptional people in your life. Giants walk among us, disguised as men and women. Smiles towered over guys twice his size. Fearless and opinionated, he strolled through the snake pit of prison, saying whatever he thought to anyone.

Just before bang-up on the first night after my move to B Wing, we were all standing at the doors of our cells. Sandy Brown, large professional breaker of limbs and the hard man of the wing, called out, 'Who said Fielding was having George's old peter?'

In the silence, Smiles walked the length of the spur, rolling his shoulders in an absurd exaggeration of a Hollywood tough guy.

'Oy did,' he said in a travesty of a Scouse accent. 'Wanna fight then?'

He made the idea sound so absurd that Sandy laughed

and clapped my mate on the shoulder, saying, 'No, Smiles. Why would I want to fight with you.'

Cell 3-1, a rough seven-foot cube, was my home for over three years, my retreat. The brick walls were covered with dirty yellow gloss. Right at the beginning I made a vow never to count the number of bricks and I never did, in eleven hundred nights. My bed was on the right as I went in. Next to it was a small bedside table. Above the table a two-foot-square barred window faced the door. A work surface ran the length of the other wall, with a shelf above and a chair, two cupboards and a pisspot below.

From the window I looked out over the rooftops and chimneys of Bristol to a grassy knoll on the horizon. On its crest was a small stand of trees. The arrangement was so perfect it could have been Japanese. I spent hours and hours looking at that little patch of heaven, imagining myself sitting propped up against one of the trees and looking out over the countryside. That copse on the knoll was a permanent reassurance that there really was a world beyond the prison walls, a reminder that I'd be out there one day.

'I'll sit in your shade when I'm free.' I beamed my thought to the trees.

I didn't take long to settle into the routines of the long-termers' wing. Evelyn Waugh was right when he wrote, 'Anyone who has been to an English public school will always feel comparatively at home in prison.' Ten years at boarding school had been good preparation for a stretch in a penal institution. I knew what it was to sleep in an unhappy bed, a world away from home. From an early age I'd got used to putting up with unpleasant company in disagreeable surroundings and had learnt to function outwardly at a superficial level while my real life went on inside my head.

I spent hours and hours in my cell calculating and recalculating figures. I'd got an eight, which meant that – with remission – I'd be released after five years, four months. But I'd be eligible for parole after a third of my sentence: two years, eight months. As I'd already served a year, I could be out in twenty months. But I'd been granted leave to appeal against the length of my sentence, so if I got it down to a six, with first parole, I could be home in a year...

We were all obsessed with time. Smiles had the same sentence as me. He made up a chart with fifteen-hundred little squares on it. Each square represented a day. Along the top, in tiny writing, was the date. The space below was divided into four smaller squares, each containing a number. The top left gave the days remaining until his release date, top right was the number of days until first parole, bottom right to second parole, bottom left to third. Each night, before going to bed, he'd colour in another day. On alternate days he used a red or green felt-tip. The chart contained a message, conveyed in black. Gradually – but with excruciating slowness – the chequered part of the board grew, the occasional black square appeared and the numbers in the squares diminished.

After bang-up, I often listened to the radio. One programme I always caught was *From Our Own Correspondent*. Annoyed with myself for missing the opening one week, I snapped the radio on to hear the correspondent saying '—and all at once the whole clearing was full of the smell of durian.'

It was the smell that did it. I closed my eyes and I was back on my first trip to the tropics.

As soon as the rickety train pulled into the station and air stopped moving over me, sweat broke out all over my body. Moisture began pooling in my creases and folds. I wiped my brow with a handkerchief and fanned my face and neck with my notebook.

'And see those trees over there?' My neighbour leaned past me, brushing me with his arm and pointing down the line. 'They're rambutan, and the big tree behind them is a durian.'

My new friend was small, dark and had disconcerting red lips. His smell was a blend of coconut, spices and something I couldn't identify. He was a teacher on his way to see his sick mother in Malacca. On the journey from Kuala Lumpur he'd been telling me about Malaysia and naming the plants we were passing: coconut, bananas, papaya, jackfruit, rice, pineapples, mangoes and mangosteens.

'Anyway,' he continued, 'I change here and we must say goodbye. Enjoy your visit to my country. I wish you the best of luck.'

'You too,' I replied. 'And I hope your mother gets better soon.'

We shook hands. He stepped down from the train, put his suitcase on the ground and raised his arm in salute as we pulled out of the station. I waved back. The passing air felt wonderful on my sweat-filmed body. 'You're on the other side of the world,' I reminded myself. 'In the tropics, on the other side of the world!'

~~~~~

It had begun when I moved out of the cottage on Trencrom. I'd packed my rucksack – leaving the rest of my stuff with my landlady – said goodbye to my friends and hitched up to Reading. The next day I walked around town, visiting, picking up the threads of old acquaintance.

Ursula was a former girlfriend. We'd had a short scene together in the days before I took off for Turkey and had remained pals. I called by her flat in Hamilton Road, sailed in and was promptly shipwrecked. There was a mermaid curled up in a chair, a slender girl with long wavy black hair and a look that melted my soul. The smile she gave me transfigured her sad pre-Raphaelite face. When she laughed the room was full of light. I was helplessly in love with her from our first moment of meeting.

Thelma was a seventeen-year-old schoolgirl. When she had to go, I took her home. We caught the bus to Burghfield and walked up the road towards her house. She stopped me at the corner of the street.

'This is as far as you go. We'll say goodbye here. I'll catch hell if my parents see you.'

'I'll behave. I'll be really nice to them.'

'It wouldn't do any good. You don't know my father. One look at your hair and your Afghan coat and he'd be frothing at the mouth. No, I'm going to keep you out of my parents' sight.'

We kissed goodbye at the laurel hedge.

'When will I see you again?' I asked.

'Tomorrow. After school.'

The next day I was waiting for her at the gates. From that moment on we spent every instant we could together.

It was never enough. The few hours that we managed to have to ourselves always left me thirsting for more.

I'd never been so wildly happy, but there were a couple of things bothering me as time slipped away. My trip to Indochina, for one. I should have left England weeks ago, but I dallied, leaking money, incapable of ripping myself away from my love, but knowing that I'd have to go through with my plan. I no longer had the money to pay Brian back and my credibility was at stake: I'd boasted to all my friends about my intentions in Asia.

My other problem was sex. How do you make love to a mermaid? I'd fucked a few girls before, but my feeling for Thelma was of a completely different order. This was love, it wasn't just getting laid. Of course I wanted to, but my mind wouldn't let my body go. Too screwed up to screw, I was limp-dicked, unable to connect. She insisted it didn't matter at all. We loved each other, that was what counted. The physical side would come together in its own time.

I wasn't so sure. I didn't understand and was miserable. I was worried because I couldn't get it up and I couldn't get it up because I was worried. It did matter. It mattered a lot.

The issue still wasn't resolved when she stood waving goodbye on the platform of Reading station, getting smaller and smaller until she was gone. What was I doing? How could I leave her, just like that? How could I do anything else? The train bore me off, distraught and elated, into my latest adventure.

I landed in Kuala Lumpur in the middle of the night on 21 April 1971 and knew, with the first lungful of earthy jungle air, that I was a world away from home. Everything looked strange and different. Everything. I hadn't thought that the chickens, ducks and pigs would be orientals too. All at once I was lumpishly aware of being an ignorant westerner who knew virtually nothing about his surroundings. With just forty quid in my pocket, I needed to learn fast.

Through fear of losing face and looking an idiot, I'd managed to propel myself to the other side of the planet without enough money to buy a ticket home. My plan had to work or I was stuffed.

Although I'd had my shoulder-length hair chopped off for the trip and was acutely conscious of my bare and sweating neck, Singapore's immigration officers called me a hippy. Apparently the only acceptable hairstyle in the island state was a crew-cut. They weren't going to let me in until I explained that I was going to visit my father, a senior British Army officer. They rang him to make sure I wasn't lying.

The last time I'd seen Dad and Katie had been on an Easter visit to Larkhill. We'd exchanged angry words at one in the morning on Easter Sunday and I'd stormed out into the night. After walking ten miles to Salisbury, I swore I'd never speak to Dad and Katie again, but I had. They'd invited me to stay when I wrote and told them I was going to tour Indochina.

I got the rickshaw driver to drop me at the entrance to Alexandra Park and walked into the exclusive estate where my family lived. I was perspiring freely. How was the meeting going to go? At least I'd see my sisters, even if the atmosphere meant I couldn't stay long.

The girls ran out to meet me. Susi wouldn't let go until

Katie said, 'Come on, Susi. We all want to say hello to Nigel, you know.'

'Good to see you, boy.' My dad's grip was firm, his eyes warm. 'You look in good shape.'

'Hello Nigel,' Katie said with a bright smile. 'Welcome.'

We touched cheeks. I said, 'You're all looking well. The tropics must suit you.'

Dad and Katie were happy to keep the peace and so was I. We avoided politics, lifestyles and other contentious areas, and talked sport, travel and the natural world. Truce.

The atmosphere at home was much improved. Judy was on the point of going off to work in Indonesia. My sister had grown into a beautiful young woman. No longer subject to Katie's capricious tyranny, she was spreading her wings, about to fly off to Jakarta. Seven-year-old Susi was a lively kid and great fun. We sometimes painted together in the hot, sticky afternoons. I read Rupert Bear bedtime stories to her in the warm evenings when the whole garden was suffused with the heady scent of frangipani.

We were sitting on rattan chairs on the verandah of Raffles Hotel, watching a cricket match on the maidan. Mild applause acknowledged a crisp drive through the covers. I was doing nothing but sitting, yet I was pouring with sweat.

'Is this the hot season, Dad?' I asked.

'No. It's like this all year round,' he said. Calling over a waiter, he ordered another stengah for himself, a gin and tonic for Katie and lime sodas for my sisters and me.

I'd wandered into another world altogether. We all live in our own worlds. My dad's consisted of uniforms, parades, inspections and jeep rides to endless meetings with government officials. Katie's life revolved around keeping her three servants busy, planning dinner parties, going to the Tanglin Club, scheming against other officers' wives and having appointments with hairdressers or fittings with seamstresses for the cream shantung silk skirts and blouses she'd taken to wearing.

At the end of one of her soirées, after the ladies had moved to the living room and the servants had cleared the dishes, I found myself holding a brandy balloon at a table with half a dozen half-cut army officers. As conversation at our end languished, we became aware of the talk of the group around my father. The officer on my left snorted, blew out an impressive stream of cigar smoke, leaned forward and threw his words down on the table.

'If you ask me, those chaps who were ready to move against Wilson spoke a lot of sense. That man is utter poison. I can tell you that if he ever gets elected again—'

'And I can tell you, Major,' my father was on his feet, suddenly perfectly sober and speaking with a crisp authority I'd never heard before, 'it is my firm opinion that the army officer's sworn duty to serve his country means that he will not, MUST not, meddle in politics.' In his normal voice, he added, 'Anyway, we were speaking about Tub Wilson, not Harold.'

Most days my dad went off early to work and I escaped from Katie's household to spend time exploring the low-life areas around Bugis Street and the waterfront. I was trying to find out where to score, but I was wasting my time. Singapore was very heavy on drugs and druggies. I couldn't even find any grass to smoke, let alone get any information on where to find kilos.

Giving up on the Chinese, I wandered around the Malay kampongs in the interior of the island, hoping to catch that unmistakeable marijuana smell. Another blank. Eventually I met a couple of furtive young dopers and learnt from them that there was plenty of good cheap grass in Sumatra and Thailand, but none in Singapore.

When I was alone I thought about Thelma, wondering where she was going, what she was thinking. I'd agreed to spend three weeks with the family but halfway through my stay I was itching to be on the move, to get my business done and get back to my love. I wrote her a letter and bought silks, silver and a sandalwood box to take her on my return. The presents seemed absurdly cheap. I still had over thirty quid when I finally set off for Thailand.

My first stop was on the island of Penang, in the north of Malaya. There was no problem getting stoned in the capital, Georgetown. You could score fingers of good grass from the rickshaw drivers for pennies. But I needed to buy in bulk if I was to do anything significant with my shrinking stash of money.

I fell in with a bunch of freaks and went to stay in the shack they rented in the jungle in the south of the island. I was the only Englishman in a mix of Europeans, Antipodeans and Americans. One of the Yanks, a morose deserter called Jake, had been hiding out for years, moving around Southeast Asia. The rest of us were all here for the same reason – to send marijuana back home. I spent days helping Aussie Hugh clean the seeds from several kilos of Sumatran weed, bound for Sydney. For my work I was given half a pound of grass. I sealed it in a bag, wrapped it up in a sarong and sent it to the first address on my list. My partner at the English end was Chip's friend Scooter, a likeable ex-public schoolboy who was determined to live down his posh past by being out of his brains all the time. I signalled him with a postcard. It was a start, if only a small one.

'You can't score weight round here. What you need to do,' said American Pete, handing me a stick of buddha grass, 'is come with me to northeast Thailand. I know the farmer who grew this. It's five times as strong as the Sumatran, has no seeds and only costs ten dollars a kilo. I'm on my way up there if you want to come...'

I rolled a joint of his grass and lit up. Good taste. I felt myself start to go spinning upwards and suddenly it was like the start of a trip. I clung on, then I was astride it and even enjoying the ride. Wow! I'd never smoked anything like this before and it cost less than four quid a kilo. I still had enough money to get quite a lot of dynamite dope.

Pete was a short, scrawny Californian with bad teeth and a good mind. He wore a dozen little bells in his long, matted hair and jingled when he shook his head. We boarded the ferry to the mainland, caught the train to Bangkok and took a bus northeast to Khorat, a sprawling town next to a vast American airbase. Pete knew a couple of airmen there, Brady and Tim. We stayed with them, at their bungalow on the edge of town.

Enormously wealthy by Thai standards, the thousands of US servicemen had completely distorted the local economy. Many of them didn't live on the base but rented houses in Khorat. Most had *teeruks*, darlings, temporary girlfriends paid to cook and clean and fuck. At the peak of their numbers, there were over half a million US troops in Southeast Asia. Most of them went to Thailand for 'rest and recreation'. Servicing American servicemen was the start of the international Thai sex industry.

We were staying on an American street of smart new wooden bungalows. As well as their official inhabitants, they also housed quite a few deserters from Vietnam. Everyone was stoned out of their minds on Buddha grass or heroin. Smack was readily available on the street. At five dollars a matchboxful, even a private could afford to be a junkie, at least until his tour ended. A lot of guys were smoking smack, believing you didn't get addicted unless you injected. Santana's *Abraxas*, the music of the moment, blasted out of powerful stereo systems. Harley Davidsons cruised up and down the road. There was American ice cream in the fridge. Everything was so cool, but teetering on the edge of an explosion.

We spent one afternoon drinking green tea and getting stoned with a black sergeant, a friend of Brady's. He pulled out a half of whisky, took a slug and offered me the bottle.

'Hey, man, have a drink with me.'

'No thanks, man.' I'd never drunk whisky in my life, having associated its smell with the aftermath of my mother's death.

The sergeant's expression changed abruptly. He put down the bottle, whipped out a revolver and levelled it at me.

'Think you're too good to drink with me, you limey asshole!'

Slow to react, I looked down the barrel of the gun, then into the mad eyes of the stranger who seemed angry enough to kill me.

'No, man. Hey, we're getting stoned together aren't we? Are you going to smoke the rest of that joint?'

'Sorry.' He passed me the roach and put down the gun. 'Sorry about that. You couldn't begin to understand all the shit I've had thrown at me.'

'It's cool,' I said, thinking it was anything but. He was so wired he might have shot me on the spot. My life could have ended there and then, another minor incident on the fringes of one of America's military interventions.

The next day Pete and I got up early and took a series of buses to Udon, close to the border with Laos, and then took a taxi ride into the country. The village headman was delighted to see Pete again and insisted we took refreshment together. We sat down in the shade and drank green tea. I looked around. Thousands of drying grass plants hung on strings in open-sided thatched huts. The scent of marijuana flowers permeated the humid air.

When etiquette permitted, we broached the reason for our visit.

'No problem,' the headman laughed, sweeping his arm across the vista of hanging plants. The whole village was involved in the grass business. Talking pidgin and using fingers, we negotiated with the men while mothers and children sat in groups in the dirt, making up Buddha sticks. A stick held a dozen or more heads of grass, bound with fine hempen fibre around an eight-inch sliver of bamboo. Each stick weighed around four grams. Twenty of them made a brick. The bricks were being put together by the old people.

A brick cost seventy-five US cents each. Choosing the

plumpest, I picked out sixty. Pete did the same. With a sackful each, we got the taxi to take us on the back roads to avoid the police roadblocks between Udon and Khorat.

I had close to five kilos of grass, but not much money to spend on hiding it. In a grocer's shop in town I found gift packs of green tea. There were two big tins in each pack. By breaking up the sticks and compressing the grass, I was able to get ten ounces in each tin and leave enough space for a top inch of tea.

I sent a postcard to Scooter and posted off six packs, using all my pre-arranged addresses. The postage all but cleaned me out, leaving me with just two dollars. My situation wasn't yet desperate; I could eat for a few cents at the side of the road, but I was glad of a free meal when Brady offered to smuggle me on to the base for lunch. White-skinned and short-haired, I easily passed for an American serviceman in the far-out East. I lined up with my pal in the chow queue and made a pig of myself with hamburger and chips.

That evening I started to get stomach cramps. I sweated, puked and crapped so much and so badly I thought my life was dribbling away between my legs. I was ill for days. Lying on my pallet, with lots of time to think, I remembered that as a child I'd disliked most forms of meat, but had to finish everything on my plate. After leaving home, I'd been able to eat what I wanted and had mostly stopped eating flesh, but hadn't gone the whole hog. My miserable week galvanised me, brought me face to face with the old saw: you are what you eat.

I didn't want to be dead meat, so I stopped eating it.

~~~~~

Pete went north to Chiang Mai. I set off south for Penang, where Scooter was due to send my money. Without the five dollars for the train fare, I had no choice but to hitch eight hundred miles down the Isthmus of Kra. In Bangkok, I met Steve, a laconic American freak with dirty blond curls.

'I need to get out of town, man,' he drawled. 'Too easy to get smack here. I'll hitch down with you. Be a good chance to get clean.'

We covered a lot of ground on the first day, travelling down the east coast. A local bus, brightly painted and crammed with people, kids, fruit, chickens and piglets, stopped for us.

'*Bo baht*,' I said. No money.

After lots of chatter and laughter, we were invited on board and taken to the end of their route for nothing. The same thing happened four times in succession.

By the second day we were in the hills, on the edge of bandit territory. Here, communist insurgents ruled the night. There was a six o'clock curfew; no traffic moved after dark. Stuck in a little village, we slept on rickety benches in the tiny tea shop of an old widow. Thank you, Mama. Thank you for the warmth you showed to two young men you must have known you'd never see again.

As in my penniless wanderings round Europe, I was shown kindness by people who had little to give, but willingly shared what they had. All my life, all over the world, I've found people are mostly kind and generous, except when they've got wealth to protect.

On our third day, the mountains of Burma marched on our right. Towards sunset, we arrived at a village on the west coast. Steve hadn't been talking much, but his withdrawals didn't appear to be too severe – he was doing OK.

He went to buy fish from a boatman while I got fruit in the village. We walked to the end of the bay and he made a fire on the beach to grill the fish.

Coconut palms hung out over the sea. Little waves lapped the shore. The sky flared with sudden colour. A motorbike, roaring out from the houses, killed the magic of the scene. The bike stopped on the beach in front of us. In the fading light we faced a young Thai Elvis.

'You fellas betta come with me,' he Americanised.

'Why?' I asked.

'Don' be wise guys. Come on.'

'Fuck off,' Steve said. 'We're fine here.'

The bravado leaked out of the boy. He asked, then pleaded with us.

'My dad kill me, you don't come,' he said. 'They make dinner for you. Long-nose foreigners never stay in our village.'

The Kingdom of Thailand was the only country of Southeast Asia not colonised by Europeans. In the south of the country we were the first whites many people had ever seen. A score of skylarking children were clustered around a large house on stilts, waiting for the long-noses to arrive. They grew silent at our approach. As we followed Elvis up the bamboo stairs an excited chatter broke out from below. Inside, eleven men sat cross-legged on the floor, in a partial circle. The twelfth man was standing.

'This is my dad, headman and chief of police,' Elvis said.

We shook hands and bowed our heads. Dad spoke a couple of sentences.

'It is an honour to welcome you to our village,' Elvis translated.

'It's an honour for us to meet such hospitable people.' I nodded to Elvis, wondering what reception a couple of ragged Thais would receive if they turned up at dusk in a Cornish village. Elvis translated. We all smiled and put our hands together, bowed and sat down to complete the circle.

Women placed large bowls of rice and dozens of small dishes of vegetables and fish in the centre of our circle. The food was fiery and delicious; we ate long and well. Through Elvis, I answered the questions of my dining neighbours about my family, my travels and my country.

After the plates had been cleared away, Elvis's dad called a woman forward. She brought a chopping board, a big knife, a bag and a bong, a Thai water-pipe. Taking a handful of grass from the bag, she chopped it finely and put a pinch in the small bamboo bowl. Steve got his load down in one manly lungful, as protocol demanded. When it was my turn I blew it, literally, coughing and spluttering until my eyes streamed. The rough local weed was nothing like the fine Buddha grass I'd grown used to smoking. I produced my stash bag and put it on the tray. It did the round and suddenly everyone was really smashed and laughing and having a great time.

After a word with his dad, Elvis translated, 'This is very good grass. Got any more?'

'No, that's all,' I lied, suddenly paranoid at this question from the chief of police. I had close to a kilo in my rucksack.

In the morning the chief of police took me to his garden, uprooted one of his dope plants and gave it to me with a few words.

'A poor present for a man who shares his last smoke with new friends,' Elvis explained.

~~~~~

A doctor and a nurse picked us up in their jeep. 'Just down the road,' the doctor said, 'I'll be turning off to do vaccinations in a village on the east coast. My nurse is giving instructions on postnatal hygiene.'

'They're having a festival,' she explained. 'All the people in the area will be there.'

Sliding along a mud track, a wet red ribbon through a quivering jungle, we drove to a village festival. While the doctor and nurse got down to work, Steve and I took a stroll. We slid on to a bench at the back of a crowd to watch a classical dancer performing on stage. The sinuous way she moved her neck, arms and fingers was extraordinary, absorbing. A man in the row in front turned his head, caught sight of us, goggled and nudged his neighbour. Awareness of our presence spread quickly through the audience. In ones and twos and whole groups, the villagers stood, turned and sat down facing us. We'd become the star turn of the fair. Most of the eyes weren't on me – darkened by the sun and wearing only a sarong, I didn't look so different from the villagers – they were on my blond companion.

'Hey, it's hot,' Steve said to me. 'What about getting a pineapple or something?'

Discomfited, we got up and went off to look for fruit. The whole audience followed. Soon a couple of hundred people were staring in fascination at us as we sat at the base of a coconut tree, eating huge slices of watermelon and spitting out the pips.

Criss-crossing the isthmus of Kra, we saw the sun rise out

of the South China Sea and set into the Indian Ocean. The next night we were given a lift by a lorry-load of tin miners and stayed at their mine in the jungle. They started up the machinery for us so we could see how it worked. In Hat Yai, I spent the last of my money on a train ticket to Alor Star, in Malaya. It was stupid to carry my grass across the border, but I got away with it.

High on the relief of fear released, I found myself saying to Steve, 'Fancy taking a taxi to Butterworth?'

'What are you talking about? You don't have any money and nor do I – not for a fifty-mile taxi ride.'

'Just a sec.'

I went over to the cab that had sparked the conversation and asked the fare to Butterworth. It was a few dollars.

'OK, I'll see you back here in half an hour, with the cab fare,' I said.

He looked at me disbelievingly.

I was thinking of the Electric Eel as I approached the most prosperous looking businessman on the street and told him I was flat broke. He gave me some money. I moved on to my next patron. Alor Star probably hadn't had too many white panhandlers. In a few minutes I had the taxi fare.

Back in Penang, I returned to the hut in the jungle. Pete's girl-friend Cheryl was there, but he was still up in the far north of Thailand. All of us, bar Jake, were in the same situation: we'd sent grass home and were waiting for money. At our lowest ebb, we were down to thirty dollars between eight of us. I had grass, but no cash at all until I managed to flog a bag of weed to a passing flock of Kiwis. Our food reserves in the hut consisted of a sack of peanuts and a small sack of coffee beans. We wouldn't starve because the garden had a good stand of banana trees as well as pineapples, mangosteen, rambutan and the highly prized durian.

Rain poured down from dark clouds and the frogs began croaking for joy. When the sun came out the ground steamed and I set off to climb Penang Mountain with Aussie Hugh. Most of the time we could see little but the foliage around us. The jungle appeared empty but buzzed continually and echoed with screeches, cries and thumps. Not far from the peak we got stoned by a troupe of monkeys and retreated in disarray. Snakes on the path, giant lizards in the trees, leeches in the streams and now stone-throwing monkeys... Penang wasn't Berkshire, it had teeth.

The next day I went to the north coast with its beautiful string of beaches. The ones near Georgetown were crowded, so I hitched west. Seeing a picture-book cove, with a small island in the bay, I got my ride to drop me. The beach was deserted but for a couple of Chinese girls. I said hi as I was passing. In perfect English, they invited me to join them. Attractive, educated – those girls were a pleasure to talk to.

'So, how did you get here?' I asked.

'We have a car,' the more talkative one said. 'We saw that van drop you. If you need a lift back to Georgetown before dark, we can give you one.'

'Brilliant. Either of you fancy a dip?

They both declined, saying they'd swum enough.

'Well, I guess I'll visit the island,' I said. I put my passport and shirt into my shoulder bag, asked them to look after my things and strode into the warm water.

Although not a strong swimmer, I was sure I could reach

the island. I did, although it was a good bit further than I'd thought. What hadn't occurred to me was that the place would be knee-deep in pitta-bread-sized crabs, continually climbing over each other. I swam wearily around the island, looking for a place to land. The whole place was crawling. Not finding anywhere to go ashore, I put my feet down in the shallows, but when I touched bottom, it moved. In panic, I jerked my feet away and started to swim for the shore, anything to put distance between myself and bloody Crab Island.

Tired from the outset, I was making slow progress with my sidestroke when I swam into a cold current. The first twinges were a warning signal, then my toes cramped up. Automatically, I reached for my left foot to stretch my screaming muscles and went under, swallowing a great mouthful of water. Bending my leg had spread the seizure to my calf. Thrashing for the surface, I gulped some air, but swallowed some water too. I felt the warning signals in my other leg and thought I was a goner, but just at that moment I came back into a warm current and the cramp eased. Even so, I barely made it to the shore. Totally exhausted, unable to move an inch further, I lay gasping at the water's edge, a do-it-yourself castaway.

The girls, sunning their backs, hadn't noticed a thing.

After a week, I hitched into Georgetown with my chunky pal, Aussie Hugh, and went to the bank. There wasn't anything from Scooter.

'Never mind,' Hugh said. 'I expect it'll be here tomorrow. Come and share a gram of O with me at Eddie's.'

'Sorry?'

'Eddie's opium den. It's just round the corner. Haven't you been? It's a traveller's hangout. Amazing place. Come and have a look.'

After three pipes of opium, my growing fear that I was stranded on the far side of the world receded and I drifted into great cathedrals of dreams. Later I had tea, looked at Eddie's fantastic collection of Marvel comics and talked to some of the other travellers in the den.

I returned to the bank the next day and the next. It wasn't long before the clerks got to know me. As I went in, the guy on the foreign exchange would call out, 'Sorry, Mr Fielding. Nothing for you.'

After each unsuccessful visit to the bank, the over-whelming temptation was to go round the corner to Eddie's where my worries would recede into insignificance and the day would go by with my head resting on a ceramic pillow of curious softness. Soon the days were melting into each other.

To start with, Eddie prepared my pipes. Before long, I was doing my own, opening the cellophane packet and pulling off a glob of the sticky black paste with a steel spike. I heated and turned the opium on the side of the spike, using the solid glass top of the lamp to work it, until I had a ball with a thin crust. Spiking the ball, I'd ram it into the small hole of the opium pipe, twist the spike and pull it away, leaving a mini doughnut of O ringing the pipe's mouth. Salivating by this stage, I'd turn the pipe upside down so the doughnut was directly above the thin hole in the glass-topped lamp. When the drug began to bubble, I emptied my lungs and slowly inhaled.

I paid on the first couple of visits, after that I was smoking on credit. I began on half a gram a day, three pipes. A month later I was having twelve, then fifteen pipes a day. Although the opium was cheap, only three pence a pipe, my bill mounted steadily.

Every now and then, when I read over what I'm writing, I think, who is this fucking idiot? It's me. Of all the many dumb things I've done in my life, this has to be one of the craziest... God knows what would have happened to me had I been unable to pay. I can hardly believe how consistently, stupidly reckless I was in my youth. And yet, at the time, I always felt I knew what I was doing...

Six weeks after I returned to Penang, American Pete reappeared. He was expecting a consignment of acid, so he hitched in to Georgetown with me to check his mail. I went along to put off the seemingly inevitable moment of disappointment in the bank. I looked to see if there was anything for me. Still no letter from Thelma, but I had a parcel. It was a book. Inside the hollowed-out hardback was a plastic bag containing five hundred blue microdots of LSD and a note from Brian. Pete's parcel had arrived too. He had three hundred hits of Californian acid on blotting paper.

After trying out our trips to make sure they were OK, I sold a few tabs to a group of American travellers and made enough to square my opium debts and pay the fare to Thailand. Pete and I both had hundreds of trips to move and we knew somewhere that was in sore need of some good LSD: Khorat.

We took the twenty-four-hour train ride back to Bangkok.

En route I began noticing the lack of opium in my system but there was nothing I could do about it so I put up with it. I hadn't got so deeply into the drug that its absence was a torment. I was more or less over it by the time we arrived in Khorat. Our acid went in a couple of days, hoovered up among the thousands of US servicemen. I don't know what I expected but no peace movement broke out among the ground crews; the planes still took off from the base daily, going to bomb Cambodia.

I had the best part of a thousand dollars and I couldn't wait to get away. I was desperate to be home. There'd been times when I'd wondered if I'd ever see Britain again. I'd told Thelma I'd be a few weeks, but four months had slipped away. I'd been gone for so long, it might as well be forever. Would she still be waiting for me? I bought myself a ticket to Heathrow and swallowed my last acid tab just before the flight. I'd never tripped in the air before. I took off before the plane did.

Staring over the wing at the blue sky, I dreamed of a wonderful homecoming and nightmared every manner of problem. Why no word from Thelma or Scooter? At least I'd be home in a few hours and then I'd know the score. The focus of my eyes shifted to the wing. Wasn't that a crack running up it? But I was tripping, or had been. How much time had passed? Was I sufficiently straight to talk to the stewardess? Thinking I was, I rang for her.

'Look,' I said, pointing to the wing. 'That looks awfully like a crack to me.'

'Oh, that's just a mark in the paint. Nothing to worry about, sir,' she reassured me.

I watched her as she went up to the front of the plane and disappeared into the cockpit. One of the flight crew came to have a look. Moments later the loudspeaker crackled and a tinny voice said, 'Ladies and gentlemen, this is the captain speaking. We are about to start our descent to Karachi Airport. Although this is an unscheduled stop, there is no cause for alarm. Please return to your seats and remain there.'

In a few minutes we were on the ground. After a couple of hours there was an announcement that we would have to stay overnight. We were to make our way to the entrance where coaches would take us to a hotel. I wondered how long we'd be stuck in Karachi. I'd go mad if I didn't get back to Britain soon.

14 Bird

WITH MY MOVE to the long-term wing came a change of work. I was sent to the sewing machine shop. Suddenly I was rich – getting twice what I'd been paid for sewing mailbags. My job was to put the front pockets into jeans. Once I'd mastered the treadle, I could do my daily quota in two hours. I spent most of the rest of the day hidden behind a pile of boxes at the back of the storeroom, gambling.

I'd made my living at university at three-card brag. Now I was gambling again, this time at backgammon. We played behind a great stack of baskets at the back of the shop. Ronnie, my principal opponent, was a black New Yorker doing six years for failing to smuggle cocaine into the country. Ronnie was a straightforward man, impossible to dislike. His long pianist's fingers moved the counters with assurance, but he played with an ill-judged mix of excessive caution and headlong risk.

'Man. You are SO lucky!' he would scream in disbelief after yet another defeat – stretching the SO and spitting out the lucky like it was a bad taste in his mouth.

'It's not luck, Ronnie.'

'Aw! Don't shit me, man. Don't give me none of that bullshit!'

'It's not luck. Watch the way I play.'

'You jive muthafucker. You'd talk your own children into slavery. You are one lucky sonofabitch.'

Each week we'd have to stop playing once Ronnie had lost three-quarters of an ounce, as much as he could afford. It usually took two or three days. Now I was able to smoke the Old Holborn I won off Ronnie and use my wages to order food from the prison shop. I needed to supplement the poor vegetarian diet. Money wasn't allowed in Horfield; wages were credited to your account in the prison shop, which was open once a week. We queued up to buy the basics they carried – tobacco, papers and matches, biscuits, sweets, stamps, toothpaste – or we ordered other foods, provided we had the credit to cover them. I spent my wages on oranges, peanut butter and wheatgerm.

For a while I watched the poker school that met in the corner of the dining room during evening association. As gambling was forbidden in prison, the bad lads at the poker table were apparently only playing a friendly game for wooden chips. The snout changed hands in the cells.

I watched until I knew what was going on. Then I watched some more. When a chair fell vacant, I sat down to play. From the first hand I felt myself running on gamblers' adrenalin, working out odds, assessing opponents, weighing up the right moment to steal a hand, deciding whether to call, raise or fold.

But this wasn't the brag I knew. I was a newcomer at poker and, like most beginners, I was tempted to stay in too long, hoping my rubbish would improve on the draw. Then the betting would get serious and I'd be frightened off. Playing this way, your pile of chips tends to shrink. The boost from the odd win doesn't make up for the small losses of all those hands you chased. After clinging on for several evenings, I lost my stake and had to vacate my seat.

I continued to watch the school. This time I didn't focus on the cards so much as on the players. Only two of them were difficult to read, the others gave a lot away. The most interesting guy at the table was Chris Davies. A small, precise man with a large head, he piled his chips into neat stacks and only took a quick peek at his cards before leaving them on the table. Mostly he was cheerful, occasionally he looked worried, sometimes he appeared to be trying to hide his confidence. None of it meant anything, necessarily. Chris was a wizard of deceit. His master stroke – it worked time and time again – was to take a worried look at his cards, as if he wasn't quite certain what he'd got. Chris was too good for the others and was a winner most evenings. His weakness was that he didn't like to be chased off a good pot. Some macho reflex would prompt him to call more often than he should. From time to time he took a real pasting.

I waited until I'd built up a decent-sized stake. When a guy called Singh dropped out, I claimed his chair. The school ran on for week after week with nothing dramatic happening. Sometimes I was up a bit, sometimes I was down. Generally I held my own and I felt I was getting better. The game was good fun, helping to grease the passage of the hours.

~~~~~

During the long evenings in my cell I listened to the radio, read, drew, painted or thought about my weekly letter to Mary. A considerable amount of time went into planning the four-page letter. I often did several rough drafts before I wrote out a fair copy on the prison letter form. I couldn't help but be aware of the censor looking over my shoulder. Convicts weren't allowed to describe the prison, its geography, routines or staff. You couldn't complain about the nick either, so the contents of your correspondence had to come mainly from your imagination or memory. After the miserable time on bail, I wasn't optimistic about my relationship with Mary surviving, but I put everything I could into those letters to amuse and entertain. I recalled good times we'd had together in Greece, Spain, Kashmir and Peru. All the while I was trying to strengthen the bonds that linked us.

Always trying to find something new, I spent several evenings making an elaborate interwoven Celtic design around the border of one letter form. Once I took off on the description of a gaggle of hot air balloons that floated free over the nick, another time I regaled her with the conversation I'd had with a wasp I'd befriended…

After reading an extraordinary book called *From Death Camp to Existentialism*, I experienced a fundamental shift in my whole stance on life. Viktor Frankl, the author, had survived Auschwitz. That put me and my predicament in perspective straight away. From the horrific crucible of an extermination camp, Frankl had distilled pure gold:

'Everything can be taken from a man but one thing: the last of the human freedoms – to choose one's attitude to any given set of circumstances.'

I was freed by the truth of it. I couldn't change what was happening to me, but I was at liberty to choose my attitude to it. Knowing this added another dimension to my existence.

Living in your head allows for endless opportunities for distraction and for countless forms of depression. When the direness of my situation crowded in on me and I felt in danger of being swamped, I drew strength from the wisdom of Victor Frankl and from the mantra that Smiles had given me: this too will pass.

Christmas came around again, my second season of good will inside. Last year on remand had been a very different affair. Then, thanks to my visitors, I'd had many festive trimmings: wine, walnuts and dates, tangerines and chocolate, cake and mince pies.

The kitchen had been keeping us on short rations all month, saying they were holding back food so we could have a real holiday blow-out. There was turkey but, for the vegetarians, the Christmas treats were an orange and an ice cream, the only ones of the year. A couple of prison visitors, looking frozen with embarrassment, called by the dining room to wish us the merry business.

Several competitions were organised to occupy us during the holidays. Smiles and I got to the semis in the cribbage doubles, but it was at table tennis that I did best. In the final I met the reigning champion. Matty was one of four lifers on our spur, a freckled man with a slow smile and a cold heart.

'I've worked out how to play you,' he sneered, trying to psyche me out before our match. 'You only got this far because you're left-handed. And you had the easy half of the draw. I've already beaten all the best players. I'll wipe the floor with you.'

I kept the ball away from his lethal forehand. Even so, the first game was a close run contest that Matty very nearly took. In the second, he fell behind, railed at my 'negative tactics' and threw the last few points away in a rage.

I won the match and a prize of a pound, but I'd made an enemy.

The poker school resumed after the wing competitions were over. It was the close of the year and there was a recklessness in the air which was reflected in the play. Smiles got on the wrong end of a big hand and had to quit his chair. By recklessly calling me, Chris Davies dropped a packet. He upped the stakes in an attempt to claw his way back.

Soon after, a hand was dealt where everyone seemed to have good cards. Despite the raises and back raises, four players stayed in. A big pot. With one more card still to come, I had a pair of queens showing and another in the hole. I'd been playing passively, letting others make the running. The dealer flicked out the final cards. Mine was the fourth queen. Knowing I had the top hand, I checked. Chris had two pairs showing, aces and tens. He raised, as I was sure he would. I came back at him with another raise. Seeing he'd been suckered, he folded. The other players thought I was bluffing. Both called. There were over thirty ounces of tobacco in that pot. The poker school was broken. I'd won all the snout.

Because cons weren't allowed to be in possession of more than two ounces, I had to lay my excess off around various non-smokers in the wing.

One of the school, a lifer called Nick, got himself put on Rule 43, claiming that his life was in danger. A day or two later he was shipped out to another prison and so avoided paying the half pound of snout he owed me.

Rule 43 is a special regime where a prisoner is kept away from the other convicts. Solitary confinement. You can be placed there by the governor, if he considers you a danger to other prisoners, if you've been caught trying to escape or have been recaptured after escaping. Alternatively, you can elect to go on Rule 43B, if you feel threatened by your fellow cons. Rule 43 men take their exercise separately and work in their cells. Most of the people who choose Rule 43B are nonces – sex offenders.

The prison grapevine functions very efficiently. Nonces have no chance at all of keeping the nature of their offence a secret. The screws will pass on the word about them if, for some reason, the local cons don't already know.

When a nonce arrives in the nick, he can expect a working over from the vigilantes in the prison population. It usually happens in the first few days. Some people take their punishment, insisting, 'it wasn't rape, she called foul after the event'. If they're believed, they may be accepted into the cons' society and allowed to get on with their bird. But those who have been caught interfering with children can expect no mercy. Their miserable lives really are in danger on the landings, in the workshops and shower blocks. Going on Rule 43 doesn't entirely ensure their safety. Screws are no fonder of paedophiles than cons. Sooner or later, when a nonce is slopping out or taking a shower, he'll find himself unguarded, no screws round, surrounded by a gang of cons.

Physical violence is part of prison life. It simmers below the surface, then suddenly erupts.

The cells seethe with thousands of currents. For your own safety you need to be aware of them, to be constantly assessing events and the effect they have on the state of mind of the often treacherous and unpredictable men around you. Most days are outwardly quiet, but any moment can bring danger or disaster. Every day there are fresh alliances and betrayals. Shifting sands. Today's friend may be tomorrow's enemy, he may inform on you or even try to kill you.

After a glorious spell of spring weather had made the wing hot and stuffy, I spoke to the principal officer and got the heating turned off. The next night we were all hanging out at the doors of our cells, chatting as we usually did. Ears are fine-tuned in prison; the background sound of bootsteps and jingling chains told us the lock-up screw had finished the second spur and was headed our way.

Ping-pong Matty, the lifer, had the cell across the aisle from me. As the screw approached our spur, he stepped over, punched me twice in the face and ran into his peter, just as the screw came round the corner and locked him in. Taken completely by surprise, I turned to look for my glasses which had gone flying. The door slammed shut behind me. My specs were all right. I wasn't. What if he'd had a knife? I could be bleeding to death right now. The blows, two lightning light punches, hadn't hurt. I could hardly feel them. The impact was inside my head. He could've killed me before I'd even responded to the threat.

I started shaking uncontrollably, a delayed reaction to the blows. Matty had caught me totally off guard. It had never happened before. Most people need to work themselves up into fight mode. I'd always known when the talking was about to explode into punches by the humming in the air around my head and the rancid taste in my mouth. This time violence had erupted out of nowhere.

I tried breathing deeply to get the shakes under control. It was dawning on me that this could be a major turning point in my bird. Matty had hit me in front of seven witnesses. I couldn't ignore the incident and hope that it would go away. To do nothing would be to announce that anyone could hit me with impunity.

What could I do? I needed to think this through. If I mishandled the situation I was in big trouble. Word of this would be all over the wing within moments of slop-out in the morning. Turning the other cheek may be a noble action, but in prison it's a sign of weakness. If I did nothing, then my standing in the wing would plummet and I'd have to face challenges from all the cons who enjoyed pushing weaklings around. On the other hand, a violent confrontation with Matty could be lethal. He was a deranged man who boasted about killing his wife for her presumed infidelity. No, I didn't want to fight Matty.

I hate violence. I don't think I ever picked a fight in my life, although I'd been involved in a few. Even when you don't like scrapping, there are times when there's no choice. But this wasn't a schoolyard scuffle with no more serious consequences than a nosebleed and some bruises, this could cost me my life.

I spent a restless, worried night trying to find a satisfactory way of resolving the situation.

'What the fuck was that about?' I confronted Matty head on in the ablution block, as soon as we were unlocked in the morning.

Everyone on our spur had crowded into the bogs to see what was going to happen.

'You think you run the fucking wing. Who do you think you are?' Matty hissed.

'What are you talking about?' I was genuinely confused.

'Why should the heating go off just because you say so?'

'Fuck's sake, Matty,' I said. 'What's the matter with you? Do that to a grass and they'll never let you out. Jesus, man, get a grip. Listen, if you've got something on your mind, talk about it first. Don't ever try anything like that again! Lucky you didn't smash my glasses.'

'All right! What's going on here? Break it up,' a screw bellowed from the door.

'Some of us live in this place,' Matty spat at me as a score of cons squeezed out of the doorway. 'You lot waltz in, you haven't been here five minutes and you think the place belongs to you.'

It may not have seemed long to Matty, who had done eleven years of a life sentence, but I was already into my third year inside.

As it turned out, I'd made enough noise, done enough snarling, to show I was no pushover. I didn't have any more problems with Matty, who was happy to make his peace with me. He knew his momentary loss of control could have put his release date back by years or even blown his chances of parole for good. For my part, I was relieved to have come out of a potentially disastrous situation with a whole skin and my credibility more or less intact.

Night after night, I doodled and drew in my cell while I thought about Mary. I would read and re-read her most recent letters, examine the echoes of her last visit and swing between a faint optimism and utter despondency.

Our appeals were finally coming up. A lot of thin hopes were invested in this, our only chance to get our sentences reduced. I didn't expect a result, but I couldn't help dwelling on it longingly, doing the arithmetic, dreaming… 'If I get my sentence knocked down to six, then I'll be immediately eligible for parole. I could be out in a couple of months.'

My visions of early release were blown to tatters when all the sentences of the Julie mob were upheld. The restitution appeal, by those of us who'd had money seized, was passed up to the highest court in the land, the House of Lords.

By the summer of 1979, I'd become one of the older faces in a constantly changing prison population and was able to get myself a better job. I was invited to join the ten-strong company of carpenters in the woodshop. Under the guidance of one of the older hands, I learned how to make furniture – half-size kitchen units, Welsh dressers, chests of drawers – for the kids' ward of the local hospital. The woodshop was a great place to be. It smelt nice, I liked the work and I was with a congenial bunch of guys. The days flew by, though the nights still took forever.

One afternoon, I was called from my workbench for my monthly visit. Mary's long blonde hair had become a chestnut perm. She was wearing a different perfume. These changes could only mean bad news. I was almost speechless through the twenty minutes, waiting for the blow to fall. At the end of the visit, she said, 'Sorry, Leaf. I'm going to get a divorce. I'll wait until after your parole result, but I'm letting you know now.'

'Time's up, Fielding.' A screw was at our table.

Sand-bagged, I stumbled back to my cell.

Smiles was a beacon. A few months before, I'd helped him through the break-up of his marriage. Now it was my turn. He guided me through the succeeding weeks, buoying me up when I threatened to sink, defusing my sudden rages, steering me away from dashing myself against the rocks of authority.

'Anger is the easiest answer to despair,' he said, 'but it doesn't change the situation and afterwards you're worse off than before. Bear it. This too will pass.'

Smiles looked straight at you with his bright blue eyes and spoke his mind, whoever you were. As he demanded the highest levels of integrity in his dealings with everyone, his bluntness didn't make him popular. Nobody stood openly against Smiles, but there was a note in the box about him every few days.

The many snitches in the prison usually grassed people up under cover of posting a letter in the mailbox. Once you'd been the subject of a note in the box the burglars would appear. These security screws would search you and your workstation. Then they'd take you to your cell. After scrutinising an article of your property, they'd throw it into the corridor. By the time they'd finished, your cell would be empty. You'd been burgled.

The days grew shorter. The heating came on in the wing. First parole was approaching for Smiles and I. We were both doing eight. We couldn't help hoping though we knew our chances were minimal.

Another Christmas. I retained my table tennis title. With the new year came news of the knockback. Parole refused. Mary began divorce proceedings.

Though I tried to draw inspiration from the magnificent words of Victor Frankl, I found I just couldn't coolly choose my attitude to losing my wife. Internally, I was on the floor. I might have looked the same – I hope I did, in prison it's not good to look vulnerable – but I was as demoralised as an earthquake survivor.

Smiles knew exactly what was going on in my head. We could read each other pretty well after being next-door neighbours for eighteen months and he knew exactly how to reach me. 'The paddle for shit creek is small and made of wax,' he said one evening. We were sitting in his peter in the time between supper and bang-up.

I couldn't help a little smile.

'It has to be used carefully to steer from the war of shit to the shore of wit. Come on, fuck 'em all, let's have a game of Scrabble.'

When we'd put a few words on the board he scratched his beard and said, 'I'm sure I've got a seven-letter word here, but it might take a bit of finding.'

I put together a matchbox pipe and loaded it with a piece of hash the size of a grain of rice – a lungful. Lighting it, I inhaled the smoke and held my breath for as long as I could before leaning out of the window and breathing out. By the time Smiles had done the same I was flying. His question took me off balance.

'Do you remember your first love?'

'What?' I said, as I thought of my mermaid. 'Of course. Everyone does, don't they?'

'Do you remember how fucked up you were after you split up?'

Now I knew what he was up to, trying to help me get some perspective on my situation. Smiles had had a knockback too, his hopes had been smashed like mine, but he wasn't wrapped up in self-pity, he was helping out a mate. I appreciated it.

And his plan worked. After bang-up, alone again in my cell with the image of Thelma in my mind, my thoughts returned to the autumn of '71, when I flew home from Thailand.

15 Tabbing

I BREEZED THROUGH customs at Heathrow barefoot and grinning. I'd made it! So had my packages. Whole swathes of Reading were immobilised by the dynamite grass I'd sent. Scooter was among the casualties. Too spaced out to leave his flat, he hadn't got round to selling much. Word got out, of course, about the immense dope he was holding and people had beaten a path to his door to get hold of some.

'Most of it had gone and I still hadn't got round to dealing with the bank,' Scooter said apologetically, 'when Brian called by to see what was happening. He said he'd send you some acid, so I reckoned you'd be okay. I'm sorry, man. I should have transferred some money to you straight off.'

'Yeah, well, I made it back, didn't I?'

I ought to have known that Scooter would be decommissioned by the arrival of the strongest grass in the world. Everywhere I'd been, I'd left a trail of bewildered people, clutching to the railings on hotel balconies, sitting dazed at the side of the road where they'd been hitching, staring into the sky, or at their fingernails. I was like that when I'd first tried American Pete's Buddha stick in the Penang jungle. Scooter was the same. He should have had an 'Out of Order' sign on his forehead.

'I've got the money, Leaf. It's all here.' He opened a drawer and thrust a bundle of notes at me. 'Everyone says it's the best dope they've ever smoked. And it is!'

It should have been a triumphant return but the vibe was all wrong. Nobody at Upper Reds could quite look me in the eye, none of them seemed to know where Thelma was. Beginning to get very bad feelings, I went to see my old girlfriend Ursula. She was out but her feller, Lance, was there.

'Leaf. My God. Come on in,' he said. 'I'm just making a pot of tea. Look, it's fallen to me to give you the news. I'll get the tea first. Make a joint, help yourself – it's your Buddha weed. Amazing stuff, man. I've never smoked anything like it. Urs and I made a little one-skinner, had a couple of tokes and then it was four hours later and I still had this half-smoked spliff between my fingers... OK, tea. I'll be right back.' He fled into the back of the flat.

I felt strangely calm. Lance had told me without telling me. I followed him into the kitchen. He was pouring the tea.

'What happened?' I asked.

'It was Rob.' He put down the pot and turned to look squarely at me. 'I'm sorry, man. I'm really sorry. Rob turned up a few weeks after you left. It was obvious to everyone that he and Thelma were attracted to each other, but she was your girl and nothing happened. And time went by and there was no word from you—'

'But I sent her letters here. Didn't you get them?'

'Only one from Singapore, soon after you left.'

'But – no, never mind. You were saying...'

'Yeah. Well, Thelma said to tell you that she still loves you – but she also loves Rob. She can't help it. Maybe that's not how it should be, but that's how it is. That's basically it, Leaf. I think I got it straight. Oh yeah. They're in Norwich. She should be back in a few days. She'll talk to you if you want.'

'I don't know. Anyway, thanks for putting me in the picture.'

In a daze I left Reading, travelling down to Cornwall with Scooter, to see if we could find our final package, which had gone astray.

Half the freaks in Penzance were out of their brains on the amazing grass that Mick was selling. We paid the light-fingered opportunist a visit and recovered the second tin. He'd already sold almost all the first one.

Sitting on the beach in Mount's Bay, climbing Trencrom Hill, walking the ley lines... Whatever I did, wherever I went, I couldn't get Thelma out of my mind: I heard her bubbling laugh, knew the exact angle she held her hand when she was making a point, the little hop she made when excited...

I kept wondering whether she'd have waited for me if we'd made love. What made everything worse was that she'd gone off with one of my best mates. The bastard.

Rob was a lovely guy. Magic poured from his guitar, his music was a magnet that drew people from afar. I understood why the ladies loved him. And I could see how any guy would fall for Thelma. I could see all that, but it didn't help at all. How could they do this to me?

Betrayed by my cosmic companions, I was marooned on the asteroid of myself, in the deep wastes of space, thousands of light years from anywhere.

I kept on the move through the autumn of '71, changing the scenery, flitting restlessly around. Visiting Reading, I heard Brian had been asking for me. I went up to London to see him.

He was chewing as he opened the door. His face lit up in a big smile.

'Hey, Leaf! Come in, come in. Cup of tea? Kettle's just boiled. I'm having a bacon sarnie. Want one?'

'No thanks, Bri. I'm a vegetarian now.'

'What! You're kidding.'

'No. I got sick on a burger in Thailand and decided to stop eating meat.'

'Leaf, you can't live on vegetables. You'll get ill.'

'It's not just veg, Bri. I eat everything except dead animals. I haven't eaten any meat for three months and I feel great.'

'Man, it's just a fad. One day you'll be gagging for a nice steak, you'll crack and that'll be the end of it. Here, have a bite of this.'

He held the sandwich under my nose.

'Fuck off!' I pushed his arm away.

'So what do you want, then, a cheese sandwich – is cheese OK?'

'Cheese is fine. But eat your sarnie first. I'll roll up.'

He finished his food, smacked his lips in exaggerated enjoyment and said, 'Man, you're crazy to give up meat. Anyway, never mind about that. Listen, I've got a proposition for you. But not a word to a soul... whether you accept or not. OK?'

'Sure, Brian.' Somehow I knew what he was going to say.

I looked at him, grinning away at me. As ever, I had to grin back. Brian had been something of an oddity in Upper Reds, a house of spaced-out ragamuffins. He was the only one who wore sharp clothes, the only one with a car and, other than Viking John, the only one with a steady girl-friend. We mocked him for being too hung up on money; he scoffed at us for being impractical idiots. We'd been good friends for over two years, yet in some ways we could hardly have been further apart. One trip I'd watched Rob laughing as he skipped his last coins across the surface of Whiteknights Lake. Brian would never have done that. As an impecunious fresher, he once jumped fully clothed into the lake for a ten-bob bet. He did it on the spot and collected immediately.

'If you could see what you look like,' Brian chuckled.

'What are you laughing at?'

'Just an old memory. Go on, you have a proposition.'

'Yes. I'm serious about not saying a word. This is just between you and me. OK?'

'Sure, Brian. I heard you the first time. Not a word.'

'Well, you know the acid I've been getting?'

'Sure,' I said. 'Excellent acid.' I passed him the joint.

'The best. The very best. My partner and I were dealing directly with the people who produce it. Now we've gone into business with them. They're so disorganised it's a wonder they're still functioning. Anyway, that's another story. We've come to an agreement about re-jigging the whole set-up. We're going to move it away from Cambridge, where all sorts of people know what's going on, and start up again, only this time as a discreet, efficient operation.'

'Sounds good.'

'We're putting together a small group to run things and we need a couple more people. I thought of you. Stop me now, if you're not interested.'

'No. Go on.' This sounded right up my street, I needed something to keep me busy.

'Actually, finding the right person isn't easy. There aren't too many reliable acid heads around... more or less by definition.'

'Brian, I wouldn't claim to be Captain Consistent myself.'

'I know that. But you always paid for the acid I laid on you... and you pulled off your Thai run. That was really something. Your Buddha grass...' he let the sentence trail away. 'One thing though, if you do come in with us, you mustn't do any other dealing at all. That's a condition. You'd make enough money so that you wouldn't need to do anything else. So, how does it sound? Interested?'

'In principle, yes. But where would I fit in?'

'We need someone to help with the tabletting. It's a two-man operation. If you want, give me a hand with the next batch. We'll pay you fifty quid for it. After that, if everyone's happy, you'll be in. As co-tabletter, you'll get a halfpenny a tab – that's two hundred quid for a few hours' work.'

'How often do you do the tabbing?'

'Depends. As often as necessary. At the moment it's every five or six weeks.'

'So, where do we do it?'

'I'll show you the place later. I'll introduce you to my partner too. The three of us will go through all the details together. There's quite a bit to learn.'

'Sure. Listen, it sounds great. I'm your man.'

The money was good, but that wasn't why I was going to do it. This was my chance to help turn the world on. I was going to change the course of history.

I knew that by joining Brian's group I'd become part of an outlaw band. But I'd been living outside the law for some time now – my whole lifestyle was illegal. It didn't bother me. The police might have lots of leads into the underworld, but they had no handle on us acid revolutionaries. We were off their radar.

'Remember the original sunshine capsules?' Brian asked.

'You bet. That was powerful acid,' I replied. We were in heavy traffic, somewhere south of Hammersmith Bridge, on our way to the tabbing house.

'Some of it. But it hadn't been mixed properly. A lot of that sunshine was as weak as piss. I got a duff batch and took it back to Cambridge. They didn't have any more caps so they gave me some crystal. Then I had the same problem as them. How do you divide one gram into four thousand equal parts? Know how I solved the problem? Know what I did?' He looked at me, grinning like a jackpot winner.

'Lights have changed, Brian. What did you do?'

He rammed the car into gear and roared off. 'I challenged Chip to find a solution. He said he'd think about it. Within a week he'd invented the microdot. Can you believe it? Then, just for fun, he built a machine to make micro-cubes. That's Chip for you. We're making cubes today.' He swung into the driveway of a semi and scrunched to a halt on the gravel. 'Here we are.'

~ ~ ~ ~ ~

'You've got to get this absolutely right, Leaf,' Brian warned me. We were in a big tiled bathroom. 'Be thorough and methodical. Think about every single move you make. One slip and you'll be so out of your brains that you'll be a danger to yourself and the whole operation. You with me?'

'Sure.' All the moisture had suddenly disappeared from my mouth.

'We're going to do a dry run first, without any acid. This is the equipment.' He pointed at the array on the wall unit in front of the mirror. 'Mixing bowl and glass rod, plastic sheet for covering the bowl, powdered calcium lactate – that makes the bulk of the pill – red and blue dye, gum, gloves, masks. Over there is Chip's machine for making the cubes. I'll show you that later. The acid can stay in my bag for the moment and we won't use the masks until we do it for real.'

We did a practice run. Brian wasn't totally happy, so we did another.

'OK, it looks like you've got the hang of it. Let's get to it.'

He took a phial from his bag. He held the tube up to the light and turned it on end. The silvery crystals threw rainbow sparkles as they flowed. It was the first time I'd seen crystal acid.

'Beautiful, eh? The magic ingredient,' Brian murmured dreamily. Then, in his normal voice, he continued, 'Gotta be careful with this stuff. It's about as light as air. There's ten grams in this phial, enough to make forty thousand trips. Ready to do it?'

I nodded.

We kitted up. When I put on my face mask, my ears were suddenly full of the snuffling sound of my breathing. Only then did it really come home to me what I was embarking on. I'd stepped up a league. All my illegal activities to date had been playing about, thumbing my nose at authority. It was serious now, not a game any more. Thoughtfully, I pulled on a pair of rubber gloves.

Brian poured a measured amount of water into the glass bowl. He opened the phial of acid very carefully. Under cover of the clear plastic sheet, he gently poured the LSD crystals into the bowl; they dissolved instantly. There didn't appear to be any sediment. He added a few drops of red and blue dye, a little gum and stirred the solution with the glass rod. Continuing to stir, he sifted in two measured cupfuls of the excipient, powdered calcium lactate. Then it was my turn.

I set to work, kneading the ingredients into a stiff paste. My glasses were steamed up and my fingers aching by the time Brian was satisfied the acid was evenly distributed throughout the paste. We had a cricket ball of purple dough, the consistency of short-crust pastry mix.

Brian took a generous pinch, put it into a mould and pressed down with a metal stamp. After trimming, he was left with a tile of the paste, four centimetres square and two millimetres thick.

While I made the next tile, Brian put the first on the base plate of Chip's machine. It looked like nothing so much as a big Meccano frog. He pulled down the lever that suggested the head. Nineteen parallel razor blades in the frog's stomach sliced into the tile of acid, all but cutting it into twenty equal strips. He raised the lever and rotated the base plate through ninety degrees. Lowering and raising the blades again left the tile almost diced, ready to split into four hundred micro-cubes. He lifted out the base plate, set the tile aside to dry and put in the next one.

We worked on in silence. After a while, we changed over, continuing steadily until we had made and processed all the paste – one hundred squares, forty thousand hits of purple-haze. By then I was a little tripped out, hyper-aware of sound and light.

We began the lengthy business of clearing up, washing everything over and over again. By the time we'd finished, the tiles were dry. We bagged them up in thousands and concealed the results of our work inside a box of breakfast cereal.

I went round to Brian's flat to meet his partner. It turned out I knew him already. Henry was a big and bearded Scot, a rugby-playing mountaineer who dressed like a country squire in tweeds and brogues. His soft, educated voice sat oddly with his forceful personality.

'What do you think about acid?' he asked me straight out.

'Mmm, difficult,' I said. 'Acid isn't susceptible to easy analysis. Let's see… LSD is probably the best hope the human race has got of coming to grips with its problems.'

'Fair enough,' he said. His face cracked a smile. 'I think pretty much the same myself.' He grew stern again. 'Now, one of the areas I deal with is security. You should be aware that this is a very serious, high-stakes game we're playing. Think you're up to it?' He stared at me searchingly.

'I reckon so,' I replied.

'Well, you're doing all right so far.'

'I told you he was OK,' Brian said. 'Let's get on to the codes.'

'Meetings first. Now, Leaf, we're going to talk about hiding places, precautionary procedures, handovers, fall-back arrangements, emergency signals and so on. We'll start with meetings. We won't see much of each other, but we'll need to rendezvous occasionally and the last thing we want is to have to organise that on the phone. So we have a meeting place and a fall-back. We always have a fall-back position. Our meeting place is the Maids of Honour teashop near the entrance to Kew Gardens. Know it?'

I shook my head.

'They have the most amazing cakes and scones. When we arrange a meet – and we'll be talking about telephone codes next – that's where we'll go. If one of us doesn't make the meet, we default to the fall-back option four hours later. Do you have a good meeting place for our fall-back?'

'Er, I'll have a think about it.'

'OK. Now if I say I'll see you at the pub, the match or wherever, at five on Saturday, it means we'll meet at the Maids of Honour on Friday at three. One day and two hours before the stated time. Got it?'

'Sure, a day and two hours.'

'Now, if you ever have to mention the organisation on the phone, we're Intertrans – short for Internal Transport. Another thing, we've all got to look respectable. We don't want to draw any heat by looking like freaks.'

I agreed that it was common sense to keep a low profile. I'd discard my hippy gear for conventional clothes and wear my hair short – disguise myself as a straight. Though the schoolboy within me was excited by this undercover

Le Carré stuff, I didn't really like it. I would have preferred to be me.

Chip was the other Intertrans recruit. He and I became the tabletting team. He'd been working with Brian and Henry on a freelance basis, but had agreed to get fully involved when they asked him.

'I was unable to resist their call for help,' Chip confessed. 'Brian said I was the obvious person, as I was already in the know.' Copying Brian's voice, he brummed 'We're already using your equipment, Chip, for Christ's sake!'

Shorn of his mane of hair, his beard and moustache, Chip was transformed. Dressed in conventional clothes, he looked like office fodder, neat and boring. So did I. At first we couldn't stop laughing at our appearance. In our disguises, we rented a bedsit in Fulham to live in and another in Oxford Street for our work.

A week later I met Brian in the Maids of Honour tearooms and came away with a phial of crystal. In the tiny bathroom of our Oxford Street bedsit, Chip and I converted the ten grams of crystal acid into forty thousand micro-cubes, each containing two hundred and fifty micrograms of LSD. Chip sealed the trips inside a packet of cereal. I took it off to the teashop where, over tea and cakes with Henry, I switched my carrier bag of shopping for an identical one of his which held the next ten grams of crystal.

We were in business.

After processing several more batches in Oxford Street, we moved the tabbing operation, then moved it again to a bedsit in Richmond. We also shifted our living quarters, changing our room in Hurlingham Gardens for a basement flat in Twickenham. A dark and damp place, it did have a saving grace, the proximity of the river. I could wander along the towpath or just sit on a bench and watch the water flow.

It was a lazy life – we only spent one day a month tabbing. The rest of the time was our own. We'd get stoned and listen to music, take long towpath walks, go to the cinema or visit friends. Occasionally we'd take the train to Reading to get high with our old buddies. Every few weeks I'd meet up with Brian or Henry and we'd exchange crystal for tabs. While we sipped tea and buttered scones, we'd keep each other up-to-date on our news. Things were going well. In six months we'd doubled our sales and halved the price of acid. On the street, a trip once again cost £1, as it had in '67. Anyone who felt like it should be able to afford to take a trip.

Micro-cubes were the unique fingerprint of Intertrans. At the beginning of '73, Henry and Brian decided it was time to change back to microdots and reduce the strength of the trips to two hundred mikes.

'The chemist reckons we should stay at two-fifty,' Brian whispered over lunch in the cafeteria that had become our new meeting place, 'but two hundred's plenty for a full trip.' At normal volume he said, 'I don't know how you can live on that mush. Don't you feel weak? Don't you sometimes feel like getting your teeth into a real steak?'

The equipment for microdots was very simple: a plastic spatula, a tray and fifty identical plastic boards, all drilled with one thousand and eight 2mm holes. To make the tiny pills, we put a board on the tray, buttered it with acid-paste until all the holes were filled and scraped off any excess. When the microdots dried they shrank slightly. With another board, made to the same template but with spikes instead of holes, it was easy to push the trips out of the board and straight into a plastic bag.

The day after our first microdot session, I was up and making breakfast when Chip wandered into the kitchen in his underpants. He looked a mess.

'Oh man,' he moaned. 'I'm out of my brains. What's happening?'

'Sit down,' I said. 'Take it easy. What's going on?'

As he stared at me, the confusion in his eyes turned to fear.

'You're all distorted,' he whimpered, 'it's like I'm tripping. Oh fuck. Is this a flashback? What's going on? Help me, man.'

'You'll be fine, Chip,' I replied, trying to sound confident and reassuring. 'Maybe you picked up some acid dust on your clothes or something. Listen, everything's fine. You don't have to do anything. Just relax, take it easy. Tell you what, have a shower. I'll wash your clothes.' I laundered mine too.

By the afternoon he was calmer and in the evening he was almost back to his usual cheerful self. But the next day he woke to hallucinations again. And the next. Chip was looking haunted. After a week he'd had enough, he quit Intertrans and left town.

The next day I woke on a bobbing raft that had been my bed. The outer edges of my vision were rippling upwards, paisley patterns multiplying like amoeba. I was adrift on

the sea of my life. It would have been terrifying had I not
realised I was tripping. And I'd found the source of Chip's
problem, for I'd added his pillow to my bedding. He must
have brought some crystal into the flat on his hair. I rang
him to explain.

'It doesn't make any difference,' he said. 'I can't take any
more. I'm finished with Intertrans. In fact I'm steering clear
of all drugs from now on.'

I did the next batch on my own. I'd finished the mixing and
had filled quite a few boards when I realised I was going
up fast. The symptoms were unmistakeable. I was about
to start tripping and, judging by the speed of my ascent, I
would soon be rocketed through the portal to acidland.

What could have happened? My gloves looked all
right – no they weren't! There was a tear in one of them.
My left hand was cut and bleeding. How long ago had
that happened? As I rose to my feet a school of thoughts
swam into my mind. Losing the radar that made them turn
together, a thousand notions collided. With a brain full of
expiring ideas, I tried to focus on the job in hand, the mob
inland, the goblin band... it was no good. Fuck, this was
going to be a strong trip.

'Come on. Concentrate!' I scolded myself. I sat down
and started to fill the next board. It was taking forever. We
are raindrops, falling through the air of life into the ocean
of being. Should I bandage my cut? What if the street was
full of police? I'd better check the window.

There was just enough sense left in me to know that if I
quit my workstation, I'd never get back. 'Forget all the other
stuff, you idiot,' I reminded myself. You're just tripping. Get

on and fill the board.' I did it. It was an absolute triumph
of will.

Turning to put the board with the others, I knocked the
drying rack with my elbow. It crashed to the floor. Acid
went everywhere. Thousands of little pink pills spilled on
to the pink and green speckled floor. I went down on my
hands and knees to pick them up. The floor was a mass of
writhing tendrils. I sank down into them, unable to move
for over four million years.

Generations grew up, grew old, died and were reborn on
the little rock spinning around a fire in space. Through the
confetti of millennia I grew tired of the interminable human
story, but it rolled inexorably on and on, cruelty upon
kindness upon cruelty until, mercifully, at the smoking end
of time, Lord Shiva danced the world out of existence.

Sweet nothing.

Then he danced it back into being and started the whole
process all over again. Life reared up in ever more complicated forms, struggling towards consciousness. Distant
reptilian ancestors, one after another, all facing the same
sudden decision, fight or flee, all making correct choices for
long enough to breed. All of them, biting, running, ducking
and hiding, all my gran^{n}parents on the long mutation march
into humanity. Men again, discovering fire, roaming the
earth with dogs, planting seeds, founding cities, inventing
planes.

On cue, a plane roared overhead. As the drone of its
engine receded, another rose to take its place. I sat up. I
was back in Richmond, in the bedsit under the Heathrow
flight path. I looked at the mess around me…

Four million, three hundred and twenty thousand years
old, I was in no condition to clear up. I staggered off to get

help from Brian. Everyone seemed to be staring at me as I shambled down the road.

'Christ! What's the matter?' Brian, standing sleepily in the doorway in his dressing gown, was suddenly awake. 'Come in. Come in. Are you OK? What happened?'

After clearing up, Brian took me home and told me to rest up for a while. A week or so later, he turned up with Henry.

'Bad news. We have a problem with the chemist,' Henry said bluntly. 'He thinks we've been ripping him off. He won't work with us any more. There's no more crystal. It's all over.'

I nodded. I'd fucked up and was being given the boot. Security considerations made Henry say that Intertrans was being wound up. I understood. For form's sake I pretended to believe him.

Young and resilient, I quickly recovered from that massive acid overdose. I think. But if I had lost it, would I be able to tell? What is reality?

16   Mary and cream

A LOT OF THINGS changed in the wake of my four-million-year trip. Somehow I wasn't so fucked up about losing Thelma. Time was putting a scab on my wound, now it only bothered me if I picked at it. Booted out of Intertrans, I no longer had to play straight, I could grow my hair again and wear whatever I felt like. I was desperate to get out of London and feel there were fields around me.

In the spring of '73, aged twenty-four, I took a ten-week let on an Elizabethan mansion in the Chilterns with my old mate, Viking John. There were seven or eight guests' bedrooms, a great dining hall for feasting, a croquet lawn for afternoon games and, beyond the garden, beech woods full of bluebells. Christmas Common was a wonderful setting for the long party I planned.

I knew I wouldn't have to worry about money for a while; I had three thousand quid – enough to live in style for a year. We moved into our rented mansion and invited our friends over. At the weekends there were usually around twenty people, fewer during the week, but the party never entirely stopped. I was enjoying it, but Viking John was having a rough time.

John and his girlfriend, Mary – both tall, blond and beautiful – had been the golden couple on campus. But things had been going badly for them of late. They'd been making each other miserable for months, but seemed unable to make up or bring their relationship to an end. The definitive split-up occurred in the final week of our let. John went storming off to town, leaving me to clean up the party mess and get the house in shape to hand over to the owners.

Mary stayed to help me clear up. The break-up had left her in a sorry state. She was one of my favourite people and it pained me to see her so listless and tearful. I was doing what I could to cheer her up, trying out the terrible puns and corny jokes I sometimes came up with.

'Did you know I've got warts? I didn't like them at first, but they grew on me.'

'Oh God. That's awful.'

'Don't you think people who sunbathe are beyond the pale?'

'Stop it!'

But I wouldn't and succeeded in getting her laughing. We started to have a really good time together. In three days of hard work, we cleaned the house from top to bottom.

I'd arranged to stay with Duncan and Debbie, old friends from university days, in the little cottage they were renting in Dorset, deep in Thomas Hardy country. Their basic rural life suited me fine. I felt jaded after too much party fare and was ready to get back to simple living.

Mary, having failed her exams at Reading, was now at uni in Southampton. On my way to Dorset, I dropped her off at her flat and accepted the offer of a cup of tea. I hung around a while, not wanting to say goodbye. 'Well, I'd better be going.' I said eventually. 'Come down and see me.'

'I'd like that very much,' she replied.

It sounded as though she really meant it. Was there an invitation in her eyes or was it just my wishful thinking? I fancied her like mad, but I found it difficult to believe that someone as beautiful as Mary would be interested in a round-shouldered, bespectacled skinny-ribs like me.

Our goodbye kiss turned into a long hug, but I pulled away before it went any further. I argued with myself about that on the drive down to Dorset.

'You did the right thing,' the virtuous part of my mind insisted. 'It would have been stupid to go too far too soon. You might have lost a good friend.'

'Idiot,' the opportunist in another area of my brain sneered. 'You've just blown your best chance. Turn around now and go back.'

I even slowed the car down, but I didn't stop. I worried about what to do all day and the next until a phone call put me out of my misery.

'It's for you,' Duncan said, handing me the phone. 'Mary,' he mouthed.

'Hi,' I said brightly, my heart bouncing like a kangaroo on speed.

'Leaf, hi. I was wondering, were you serious about that invitation?'

'Absolutely.'

'Well, if it's convenient, how about this weekend?'

'Wow! Yes. That'd be fantastic!'

~ ~ ~ ~ ~

I stood on the platform at Yeovil station for a quarter of an hour, rehearsing what to say, getting more nervous with every passing minute. When she stepped down from the train, she flew into my arms and I hugged her as if my life depended on it.

'I didn't realise until you left me in Southampton how much I was enjoying being with you,' she whispered in my ear.

'I wanted to stay,' I whispered back, 'I don't know why I didn't.'

We had such a good time that she came back the following weekend and the next. She didn't return to uni after that third weekend together.

It wasn't long before we found a furnished cottage to rent, outside Nethercompton on the Dorset–Somerset border. It was perfect. Rock Cottage had been an isolation ward in the nineteenth century; it was half a mile from the nearest dwelling. Day or night, we could turn up the music and no one would complain, we could take our clothes off and nobody would see. Summer scudded by in a warm glow. We did yoga, we walked, gardened, gathered, made our own bread, yogurt, wines, jams and chutneys, ate the vegetables we'd planted after moving in... Life with Mary was smooth, creamy and lovely.

What's in a name? There is something in mine. I'm a Fielding, happiest outdoors, under open skies. Through the autumn, we picked blackberries, scrumped apples and gathered hazelnuts. We rose early to search the fields for mushrooms, filled our pockets with gleaming chestnuts and stockpiled wood for the coming cold weather. That was our only nagging worry; we had no income and winter, bloody winter, was on its way back.

Though we lived frugally through the cold months, the little dosh I had left from Intertrans dwindled away. If only I hadn't spent so lavishly at Christmas Common...

In the spring, I got a phone call from Russ, a dealer friend from London who I used to score hash from in the late sixties. He'd evidently done well for himself, as he now lived in a flash house in Oxfordshire.

'How are things?' he asked.

'Fact is, I'm a bit low. Mary's on holiday with her family. I wasn't invited. How are you?'

'Oh, man! Phoebe's left me. I'm going nuts all alone in the house. Listen, I need a change of scenery. Fancy shooting off for a few days?'

'I'm pretty broke, Russ, I can't afford to go anywhere.'

'Well, don't worry about that. It's my treat. You up for it?'

'Yeah. Sounds good.'

'Pack your bag. I'll be down in a couple of hours.'

I don't know why, but I'd assumed we'd be going to Cornwall. Russ had Morocco in mind. I grabbed my gear and my passport, jumped into his battered Land Rover and directed him towards the Channel.

We broke down in France, somewhere south of Tours. The day's enforced rest, while we waited for the vital part to be replaced, gave us a chance to relax and take in our new surroundings. The fields were full of flowers, little puffy clouds drifted in a blue sky. At lunch our waitress flirted with us shamelessly. Russ lost his preoccupied frown and showed signs of regaining his habitual chirpy demeanour.

Russ's narrow face was dominated by a great big Roman nose. Hunched over the wheel, as we negotiated the Somport Pass through the Pyrenees, he was all bones and angles and expensive hip clothes. In Zaragoza he bought speed from the chemist so he could keep going. We didn't stop to sleep until Jaén. By late morning on the following day, we were in Algeciras and boarded a ferry to Africa. A Swedish couple on the boat were looking for a lift to the Rif Mountains.

'We'll take you,' Russ said.

As we pulled away from the Moroccan customs sheds, we were boarded by a young street hustler. He was gabbling as he tumbled into the open-backed vehicle.

'Number one quality. Best price. You want hash? Kif? What you want?'

'Nothing. Get down!'

'No,' he yelled. 'You need me.'

For miles we resisted his attempts to sell us hash, carpets, girls, boys, leather goods, metalware, jewellery... Finally, as we neared Tetouan, I cracked and said I wanted to score a few smokes. We stopped in town and sat outside a bar, sipping mint tea. In no time he'd got us a ten-gram deal. Omar was an engaging kid, maybe fourteen years old, it was hard to tell. I liked his spirit and his persistence. I talked with the others before saying to the kid we were interested in half a kilo, but only if it were a better quality.

'We go Ketama,' he said. 'My uncle is farmer. One ton, no problem. Two ton.'

'No, half a kilo.'

'Sure, sure,' he said. 'First you don' want, then OK a little, then more. I know what you want.' He refused to accept that we really only wanted half a kilo.

Beyond Chefchaouen we began climbing the skirts of the Rif Mountains. The landscape grew wilder, stonier. Ragged, barefoot kids kept running out of isolated huts, waving great slabs of hash and shouting at us. Omar volleyed them with abuse.

'Fuck off! They're my foreigners,' I expect he was saying.

After hours of hairpin bends, we left the road and headed down a dirt track. The light was failing when we arrived at a huddle of buildings clustered around a dusty courtyard. The farmer and his three grown sons welcomed us and took us into a large room furnished with carpets, cushions and low tables. We sat down and took tea and cakes while they plied us with their hash.

Laughing dope. Soon we were all out of it, giggling helplessly. The world is a hilarious place if you don't know any better. Dish after dish of food began to arrive. We talked in poor French about our families and our journeys. After the meal, between puffs on the hubble-bubble pipe, we got down to business.

'It's great dope, but at the moment we only want a sample,' I said. 'If things go well, we'll be back for substantial amounts.'

'How much of a sample?' the eldest son asked.

'Half a kilo.'

'Are you serious?' He rounded on our guide and berated him. Omar argued back until one of the other sons grabbed him and threw him out into the night. The boy started scrabbling at the door, whining that he ought to get paid for his work. I gave him a little money, poor kid. Night had fallen and it was over a hundred miles through the mountains back to where he'd begun the day.

'You could have got half a kilo in Tangier or Tetouan,' the eldest son said. 'Why come all the way up here?'

I told him I was thinking about doing a big run. I was, after a fashion. Sooner or later I'd meet someone with a boat or a smuggling route. One day it would be useful to know a farmer.

In the morning, our host took me round his spread.

'Look,' he said, opening the door to a long shed and waving me inside.

The smell hit me straight away. The length of a cricket pitch, the shed had a narrow aisle down the centre. Both sides were piled high with hundreds of sacks of kif, weighed down by dozens of sacks of pollen. There were several tons of dope in that shed – just breathing the charged air left me feeling quite woozy.

Leaving the Swedes at the farm, we headed northeast to the coast. Russ wasn't well. Every few miles he kept having to stop and dash into the bushes to squirt out a bit more of the chicken he'd eaten the night before. Around a corner we ran into a police road block. A machine gun was trained on us.

'Oh fuck.' I cursed the pathetic inadequacy of the hiding place I'd casually chosen for the dope we'd bought – the bottom of my rolled-up sleeping bag. We were motioned out of the vehicle by the men in silvered sunglasses. They got in to search. I waited helplessly for the moment of discovery.

Somehow they missed the pollen. Chastened, we drove away and on to Al Hoceima. We smoked ourselves stupid by the seaside for a couple of days and left the rest of the dope in a culvert.

At Southampton, customs kept us for hours while they

gave the Land Rover a complete going over. We were clean. Eventually they had to let us leave.

In the wake of the Moroccan trip I was flat broke. Mary and I got a bit of rent from Duncan, who came to live with us after splitting up with Debbie, but things were very tight until Duncan and I found a summer job as tent erectors, setting up marquees for weddings, fêtes and flower shows. Each morning we'd get up at seven and drive to Martock on Duncan's motorbike. There we'd meet up with the rest of our gang and head off to our latest assignment, anywhere between Cornwall and Hampshire.

Once on site we'd work flat out until we'd all but completed the job. For lunch we retired to the nearest cider house where the gang would eat their pies and drink scrumpy for two hours. Dunc and I would have our sandwiches and slip away to smoke a joint or two.

After a somnolent afternoon, Eddie the ganger would plan our route home. He knew all the cider houses in the West Country and would go miles out of his way to visit a particularly favoured one. There we'd spend two or three hours drinking, clocking up overtime, before returning to Martock to sign off for the day. We'd ride home on the back roads in the dusk on a bike with no lights.

When summer came to an end, the tent erecting job folded. There was nothing else to be had in the way of employment in rural Dorset. As I wouldn't sign on – I was a drop-out and wanted nothing from the state – I had to move where the work was.

In the autumn of '74, Mary and I returned to Reading and
rented a room in the house of a couple of friends, Paul and
Sonia Newson. I got a job as a painter and decorator with a
team of builders run by an old university mate.

We struggled that winter. I didn't earn much and half
the money I made seemed to go on the upkeep of the car
I needed in order to be able to work. Broken down again,
in the freezing rain, in a January morning rush-hour on the
London Road, I remembered that one of the reasons I'd
dropped out in the first place was to avoid becoming a wage
slave. I slammed down the bonnet of my tired old Mini. I'd
have to find a way out of the dead end I'd driven into.

'I could work,' Mary offered. 'My old friend Jane's a
stewardess with BOAC. She loves it. Apparently she more
or less lives on her expenses and saves her salary.'

'But you'd be away half the time.'

'We've got to do something. Anyway, I wouldn't be doing
it for ever, just long enough for us to get our heads above
water... that's if I can get them to take me on.'

She was beautiful, intelligent and well-spoken; I knew
they'd take her on. They did, in first class. But after training,
she started doing long-haul flights all over the world that
took her away for up to ten days at a time. When she was
home, she was jet-lagged and exhausted. In the spring we
moved out of town to Farley Hill, where we rented a flat in
a converted stately home. Mary's flying schedule improved
when she was put on the regular polar route from Heathrow
to LA. Things were looking up again.

Martin Wise was a driver for the Newson brothers, delivering their imported Indian and Moroccan clothes to

shops all over the country. We'd met at Paul's house, hit it off immediately and started hanging out together at the weekends. One day I was moaning to him about the exorbitant prices in the only health-food shop in Reading.

'I just found a fantastic wholefood shop in Manchester,' Martin said. 'On the Eighth Day. It's really cheap. Give me a list of what you want and I'll get it for you next time I'm there.'

'Ask them how they went about starting up,' I said.

They were very helpful. Martin returned, all fired up with enthusiasm. We could do that, we thought, and went up to Community Foods, a health-food wholesaler in London, to find out their range of foods and their prices. We did the same with flour mills, honey suppliers, bottlers of fruit juice, herbalists... then sat down to do our calculations. We didn't have the money to rent or lease a shop in Reading, at least to start with, but we reckoned we'd be able to run a delivery service, offering a good range of wholefoods at very reasonable prices.

The light shining in Martin's eyes reflected the gleam in my own. For the first time in my life I'd found something that was both worthwhile and legal. What a great thing to do!

'We'll have to carry on with our day jobs for a while,' I said. We only had seven hundred quid with which to get the business up and running.

Martin wrote out our first price list in his beautiful copperplate hand. We distributed photocopies and went shopping for our supplies. Our first order was from my sister Judy who, having rounded up all her colleagues at school, sent in a massive shopping list. Soon other orders started to come in.

Reading Wholefoods' business wasn't complicated. We bought the food in bulk, directly from producers or importers, packaged it in our Farley Hill flat and delivered it in the old Transit van we'd acquired. We didn't use any plastic packaging at all and recycled everything possible. Our customers were asked to return our egg boxes, the paper bags we used for packaging our grains, flakes and flours, the cellophane bags that held pulses, nuts, dried fruit, herbs and spices, and the glass jars we filled with honey, nut butters, tahini and soya sauce.

The price list was all the advertising we ever used. Knowledge of our service spread organically, from friends to an ever-widening circle. Our trade grew steadily. At first we didn't take any wages, but used our profits to build up the stock.

In the spring of 1975 I got a phone call from Brian. He said he was on his way over – wanted to have a talk. I instantly knew what he was going to say – it was something in his voice, or maybe all that acid had made me telepathic in certain areas.

Mary was away in LA when I answered the doorbell. Brian was wearing his big conspiratorial grin. It was as if no time had passed at all. Muffled against the cold, we went for a walk down to the river. The high banks of the lane were full of primroses, tiny reflections of the pale March sun.

Brian smiled at me, shrugged his shoulders and plunged straight in.

'Guess what? We're back in action – just getting going again.'

'So you managed to sort out the problem with Richard. I got the impression that was terminal...'

'Oh, Leaf. I knew you didn't believe us when we said it was all over. It was true, man. God knows where Richard is now. We did stop. Then after a while we thought, you know, we've got everything else, all we need is another chemist. Well, it took some time...' Brian flashed his famous grin, 'but we found one.'

I had to smile back at him.

'Yeah, we're up and running. Listen, we want you to come back... but not as tabletter,' he added hurriedly. 'Henry and I will do that from now on. We'll swap jobs. You can run the distribution network. How about it?'

I took one of the tabs he gave me while I thought about it. The trip confirmed what I'd already decided in my heart. I'd do it. I was nervous about stepping outside the law again, sure, but we all have fears. You can let them form the boundaries inside which you cower, or you can confront them, push them back, give yourself space to grow. I squared my mental shoulders and rang Brian.

'I'm in,' I said.

There was another reason for my decision. Money. A couple of months before, I'd had to stop working as a painter after being overcome by fumes while painting Arborfield Army camp. Reading Wholefoods wasn't yet at a stage where we could draw a salary, so I wasn't earning anything. I couldn't live off Mary's wages forever.

I reminded myself that I still believed in what I was doing. True, I no longer thought, as I once had, that acid was going to usher in a golden era of tolerance and understanding.

But I still considered LSD a valuable tool in helping people look inwards and understand themselves as well as look outwards and really see the transcendental beauty of our home.

Trippers wouldn't trash the planet.

17 High inside

IN THE MONTHS following the parole knockback I came to see that my relationship with Mary had effectively ended with the bust, three years before. I couldn't blame her for wanting to bring to a formal end a marriage that had been smashed long ago. I might be inside for another three years. We'd be strangers to each other by then.

Accepting my fate, I looked around me and realised I'd do better to spend less time thinking about the inaccessible world outside and focus more on my immediate environment. The opportunities that prison presents are limited, but they exist and I'd done enough porridge to know how to take advantage of them.

After a year working with saws and chisels, I accepted the invitation to take what was widely regarded as the top position in the nick: gym orderly.

I landed the job because, after a lot of practise, I'd become the best badminton player in the prison. Both the gym screws were badminton fanatics and I was the only one who could give them a decent game. In a short while

I could match them. The senior officer refused to play me again after I finally beat him. The other screw was a decent human being and carried on giving me a game, even when he could scarcely win a point. I did a little weight training, played five-a-side football and had a dozen games of badminton a day: I've never been so fit in my life. It was a pleasant way to pass the time, better than a con could have any right to expect. Everyone was astounded when I quit.

I left because I'd finally got the post on which I'd set my heart from the very beginning of my sentence. After more than three years inside, I became one of the garden red-bands.

All prisoners in Horfield, when not in their cells, were under the direct supervision of a screw. All except red-bands. My movements were still restricted, but I was able to wander outdoors on my own, wherever there were plants. God, it was wonderful to be outside. I dawdled in flowerbeds, inhaling the heady scent of roses, wallflowers and sweet-williams. I trimmed the verges of lawns, dead-headed, dug, raked, planted, weeded and wheeled my barrow around...

We three gardeners raised hundreds of thousands of seedlings and cuttings in a vast heated greenhouse. They were sent off to brighten prisons throughout the south of England. I sought and obtained permission from the PO, the principal officer, to give one pot plant to any long-termer who wanted one. Most of them did. For my cell, I chose a climber to soften the hard outlines of the barred window, ipomoea, commonly called morning glory.

Three of the Julie mob had appealed against the seizure of

their money at the time of their arrest. The decision had been passed up to the Law Lords. The appeal was finally heard in the summer of 1980. Their Lordships ruled that the hundred thousand pounds in question should not have been taken. They didn't rule that it should be returned, only that it was not correct for the police to have taken it. A conspiracy is an agreement between people, something abstract. Goods and money have nothing to do with it.

This was a kick in the balls for the Home Office. Whoever had come up with the clever idea of conspiracy charges must have been quaking in their brogues; the Lords' ruling left the way open for a successful appeal to have the money returned. Could the government stand idly by while convicted drug manufacturers had the proceeds of their crime returned to them? They could not.

The Home Office is not without resources. They changed the law to avoid being embarrassed by this issue in the future. For us they needed another expedient. Soon after the Lords' decision, I received an income tax assessment on my earnings as a drug salesman. The prison grapevine quickly confirmed that the central conspirators, scattered around the country, had all received assessments. Henry's was for one million, six hundred thousand pounds.

Unless you lodge an appeal within a month, a tax assessment is legally binding. I appealed. A tax official came to see me. At first he blandly insisted that this was a regular tax assessment.

'In that case,' I said, 'I'm entitled to deduct business expenses: entertainment allowance, travel costs, use of home as an office, phone calls…'

I offered to substantiate the last by calling as evidence the police phone-taps on my home. By now the taxman was laughing. He admitted that there was a deal in the offing, but only if everyone agreed.

Everyone did. We each signed a document agreeing that all monies seized by the police at the time of our arrest would be accepted as full settlement for outstanding tax on drug profits for the period of our offences. I didn't get a copy of that document, but I kept my tax assessment – showing that the government wanted their cut from our drug deals. In my book, that makes them accessories after the fact.

I wonder what happened to that hundred grand in cash.

The formerly immutable prison system was changing under my feet. Lights out was shifted from ten to eleven, then abolished altogether. We were given the awesome responsibility of deciding when to switch the light out. I used to say the authorities didn't have a chink in their prejudices, but my faith in their malevolence was shaken when long-termers were given permission to have battery-operated record players.

We were only allowed six records. Unlike the guests on the radio show, we were going to have to live with our choice. We were real castaways.

Top of my list was Dylan's *Blonde on Blonde*, the best record ever made, I believed. That it was a double album, enabled me to sneak in an extra disc. Joni Mitchell, Steely Dan, Bruce Springsteen, Joan Armatrading and Love completed my selection. The book I chose to have with me in my cell was my trusty atlas. With it, I vicariously roamed the world. When this was all over, Smiles and I agreed, we would travel.

~~~~~

Of all the naturally occurring psychedelics, morning glory seeds are chemically the closest to LSD. In the autumn, I harvested the seeds from my window plant and ate them. They definitely did something, though there weren't enough for a proper trip. My appetite for psychedelics whetted, I got Scooter to bring me some acid. I took it an hour before bang-up and was just starting to fly when we were locked in.

For a time I hung out at the window, joking with Smiles in the next-door cell.

'Sure I've got a bee in my bonnet. It's a buzz!'

When talking became too complicated, I lay down on the bed and allowed the world to pour into me. I laughed and cried and let my mind hang out to be aired. The small cube filled with a tornado of thoughts.

'I'm in here for acid, but I'm on acid in here. Hold on. Can that be right?' I'd confused myself. Better go through it again. 'I'm doing acid in here and I'm in here for doing acid. Wait a minute. I'm doing acid. OK. Yes, this acid is OK, pretty good in fact. But I'm in here for doing the acid I'm doing in here.' Round and round, faster and faster. I needed some fresh air, but I couldn't go for a walk. Well, if you can't go for a walk when you want to, then it's hardly worth tripping.

'OK, you've tried it,' I said, pretending to be cross with myself, 'but that's enough. No more acid in prison.'

The spyhole flicked open. A screw was creeping round the corridors in slippers, hoping to catch someone jerking off, smoking dope or digging a tunnel. He couldn't see I was tripping. I smiled at him. You can imprison the body but you can't lock up the head. Our attitude is our own to choose.

Most evenings I made myself a little pipe out of a scrap of silver paper and a matchbox and smoked a couple of rice-grain sized crumbs of dope. I usually had a bit of dope around. I had plenty of time to think of ways of smuggling hash into the nick and concealing it once I'd got it in.

Russ had a neat trick which worked perfectly for over a year. From his position as the library red-band he'd noticed a blind spot in the prison security system:

All the mail for the nick was taken by the library screw from the gatehouse to his office. There he looked at every item and sorted it, wing by wing. He then took the mail to the censors, who opened and checked everything. Finally the post was handed out to the cons. Foolproof.

Not quite.

The library screw would pick a bundle from the sack, look at the top letter and call out: 'Fielding. 1465.'

'B Wing,' Russ would reply, consulting the movements board.

The warder would toss the item into the B Wing trolley and read out the next name and number. Occasionally Russ would say: 'Transferred to the Scrubs,' or 'Sent to the Moor.'

Men are constantly being shipped from jail to jail. Their mail lags behind them. Such letters and packages would be thrown on to a heap in the corner, for eventual forwarding to the appropriate nick. The heap was only sorted when it grew large, every two or three weeks. It wasn't urgent, it was only mail for cons.

Russ would get a message to his confederate outside,

with the name and number of a freshly transferred nonce. A few days later a rolled-up Sunday paper would arrive for the man who had just left.

'Gone to Strangeways,' Russ might say, and the newspaper would get tossed on to the forwarding pile.

The library screw, formerly a mechanic, used to spend a couple of hours each afternoon in the prison car park, earning a bit extra by working on the motors of the staff. While he was away, Russ would take out the thin sheets of hash hidden inside the newspaper.

This was only one of several routes by which dope was coming into B Wing. There was no shortage for those who liked a smoke. I'm sure the wing principal officer knew there was plenty of blow around and tolerated it as long as it stayed discreet. The screws preferred the cons to be stoned. It made for a quiet, contemplative wing and it made their life a lot easier. When someone brewed up a load of hooch, there were drunken brawls and blades could be dug out of their hiding places, but when a couple of ounces of hash arrived, the hard cases and tough nuts mellowed out and got laidback.

From one of my visitors, I learnt that Henry and Brian had agreed to hand over their remaining acid, a million trips, in order to improve our parole prospects. But so much time had gone by that they were unable to find the cache. Trees had grown, undergrowth had changed... they just couldn't mark the spot. Of course the police were suspicious, but were persuaded it was a genuine attempt to clear the slate.

They agreed to take Brian and Henry out to Ampthill Woods to have another go. This time they found the stash.

Second parole was approaching for Smiles and me and all the acid was accounted for. Under such circumstances, it was difficult not to be at least a little hopeful.

You have to apply for parole and state why you should be granted it. I agonised over my application. I was sure I could improve my prospects of freedom if I could only find the right words.

Reports are made out for the parole board by a number of people in the prison system. The psychologist's report was considered particularly important for two categories of prisoner: murderers and druggies. I was called for an interview with the shrink, a long-haired young man in his mid-twenties.

He had the most enormous facial tic I've ever seen. At intervals, one side of his face would be convulsed by a major spasm. This was the guy who was going to make a report on my mental state. I didn't know where to look. Whatever I did would be wrong. I kept my eyes down while we limped through his assessment of my psychological profile. After that interview, there was nothing to do but work on the wording of my application. I spoke about it to Dave Solomon, the other member of the Julie mob in B Wing. Later I tried to get it down on paper:

I asked the advice of my sad old friend,
as we stood in the governor's queue.
'What can I say for my second parole?'
'Silence!' screamed the screw.

After a sleepless night in the cell,

Awake in a swarming bed,
I stood by Dave in the breakfast line
and, whispering, I said

'What is time? What is justice?
And what is the speed of life?
How many wrongs make a right?
And who ran off with my wife?

And when will I get the freedom
to travel to Reading or Rome?
How many years must this go on?
When can I go home?

Dave said:

'To get away from the locks and chains
and doors that are made of steel,
you'd have to pretend, right to the end,
a remorse you just don't feel.'

Of course I made my submission.
What – pass up a chance to go free?
I carefully wrote my petition,
hoping I'd found the key –
the words to open up my cell,
and give me the freedom I lack…
Then down I fell, into hell,
when the bastards knocked me back.

Following this second knockback, I wrote to the Home
Secretary:

15/3/81
Sir,
Ref. Parole decision R1/RLP/M1946, I am petitioning
you for an immediate parole review.
Your Government White Paper of June 1980 said
'No one should remain in prison longer than necessary.'
Is it so absolutely necessary that I remain in prison?
I have spent nearly four years inside now, eaten over
four thousand prison meals, on this my first offence.
I can see no possible benefit accruing to anybody
from my continued imprisonment. I am ready and
eager to take my place in society. The next year or more,
if spent inside, must surely result in a physical and
mental deterioration that can only reduce my chances of
leading a worthwhile life.
Sir, the decision is yours.

After so long inside, I no longer expected any favours from
the authorities. Even so, I felt I had to try. What could I
say? As I wasn't prepared to grovel or lie, I didn't have a
lot of options. I was right not to be optimistic. After being
'fully and sympathetically considered', my petition was
rejected. With this knockback came a small sweetener –
I'd be transferred to Leyhill open prison for the final part
of my sentence.

Before my move, things went radically wrong in B Wing.
Roberto, the only Italian in the wing, was a young well-
connected mafioso. He'd been caught moving smack
through England. He had a servant, a junkie called Billy,

who cleaned his shoes, brought him tea and generally did his boss's bidding. Roberto usually paid the kid with tobacco. One night he gave him a bit of dynamite dope.

Hashish is an amplifier, a heightener of sense and mood. It can make you feel great… or very frightened. Billy had a smoke in his cell after bang-up and got the horrors. He leant on his emergency bell and begged the screws who answered it to take him to the hospital as he was dying.

The duty warders that night were the burglars, the security screws, responsible for preventing the prisoners from acquiring anything they weren't supposed to have – weapons, booze, drugs… Realising Billy was smashed, they got heavy with the panic-stricken kid and made him tell them where he'd got the hash and all he knew about the dope scene in the wing.

Roberto and Russ were bundled off to the block: the punishment cells. The burglars came in with sniffer dogs and searched the wing from top to bottom. The screws leaned on Russ to make him say how the hash had been coming in. He told them, then he was gone. Suddenly Smiles disappeared into the block. I took my wheelbarrow round there to try to talk to him. A screw caught me before we'd exchanged more than a few words. Next thing he was shipped out to Dartmoor. A few days later I got a message from him.

'I'm OK. See you on the out when all this is over.'

I'd managed to avoid the fall-out from Billy's collapse. My transfer to Leyhill was still on. I was due a change of scene after more than four years in Horfield Prison.

I hung out with Dave on those last few evenings in Bristol. On the last night he said, 'You know, I never understood why you rejoined Henry's gang. You'd left, you were in the clear, living with a wonderful woman... Why did you go back in?'

'I'm not sure,' I replied. 'I needed the money, I guess. Know what? It seemed like a good idea at the time.'

Dave had dug up the subject I'd managed to bury after several months of agonising about it on remand. What an idiot I'd been to return to Intertrans.

18   *Distributor head*

RUNNING THE DISTRIBUTION network seemed a pretty straightforward proposition. I only had to supply one person, the top dealer, and he was my old friend Russ. Effectively, I was the cut-out between the producers and the dealing network.

The first thing I had to do was find a good hiding place for the two hundred thousand trips that Brian was going to lay on me. It wasn't easy. Southern England is a crowded place. My cache had to be well away from any towns or villages, I needed to be able to park discreetly nearby, approach under cover and have an observation point which gave me a good view of the area. For the stash itself I was looking for well-drained soil and foliage dense enough to enable me to remain unseen while I did the business. I spent weeks poring over Ordnance Survey maps in my flat in Farley Hill, driving to promising locations, nosing around and going home disappointed.

Finally, I found everything I was looking for at Caesar's Camp, a sizeable wood by Nine Mile Ride, near Bracknell.

After Mary had flown off to LA again, I returned to Caesar's Camp with the necessary implements and went to ground in the wood on a rise overlooking a great tangle of rhododendrons. After fifteen minutes, sitting with my back against a tree, listening to nothing but birdsong, I wriggled into the heart of the dense undergrowth, chose my spot and cut out a turf of earth, some fifteen inches square and three inches thick. Carefully setting the turf aside, I started to dig, putting the spoil into a bin liner. After the first few inches the going became much more difficult. The ground was full of roots and stones. It's impossible to dig silently in stony soil; anyone in the vicinity would hear me. I kept stopping to listen – the only sound was the harsh rasp of my breath.

'Gotta cut down on the smoking,' I gasped.

I waited until my panting had slowed sufficiently for me to hear properly, then had a good rest before beginning the next stint. After several more turns, each a bit shorter than the previous one, I finally got down to Henry's recommended depth of three feet. I was knackered and covered in a film of sweat and soil.

Into my burrow went a bin liner containing two large airtight plastic cylinders. At present they were empty. I filled the hole with earth, tamped it down, replaced the turf and tidied up. A sprinkling of leaves concealed the edges of the hiding place and made it blend in with the surroundings. I carefully took my bearings, marked the nearest tree with a notch above head height, gathered up my things and left.

After the next heavy rains, I went back to check the stash. If it was waterlogged, I'd have to start all over again. It was dry. I phoned Brian.

'Hiya. How are things?' I asked.

'Great. How are you?'

'Good. Listen, what about getting together for a game of Go?'

'Sounds good. When are you free?'

'How's Saturday?

'Fine.'

'I'll try and get up for one o'clock.'

Our agreed code hadn't changed, so Brian and I made our rendezvous at eleven on Friday morning. We had shifted our location though and met up at a greasy café in Notting Hill. We had an egg sarnie and a cup of tea and picked up each other's Sainsbury's carrier bags as we left.

All was quiet as I arrived at Caesar's Camp. I walked to the knoll and waited a while. Slipping into the mass of rhododendrons I looked for my marker tree but just couldn't find it. I searched and searched, horribly aware that it wasn't clever to be blundering around in the woods with two carrier bags containing enough LSD to send the entire population of Reading into orbit.

I was cursing the whole business of having stashes. It was a hell of a performance finding a good site and burying then unearthing the trips, but we'd agreed at the beginning of our association that none of us would ever keep any acid in our homes. That way there was no danger of a simple dope bust causing Intertrans to unravel.

I went back to the hillock and started again. It didn't help. I just couldn't find the fucking mark. All the trees looked the same. I'd have to go against Henry's rule and return home with the microdots – I daren't wander around forever. On the point of giving up, I spotted my notched tree, found the stash and buried the acid.

~~~~~

A few days before the first handover, I met up with Russ. Over dinner, at a restaurant in Oxford, we reminisced about Morocco then talked through the details of the deal. Russ was on good form, looking sharper than ever and producing a constant stream of jokes and quips.

On the day, wanting to have plenty of time in hand, I got up very early and drove to Caesar's Camp. I found my marker tree immediately, leant against it and waited until I was sure there wasn't anyone else in the wood. I pulled on a pair of rubber gloves, dug up the acid and counted out forty packets of a thousand tabs. The trips went into a plastic bag. I set it aside and reburied the container. My heart was thudding. Until two minutes ago I'd been clean: now I was holding enough gear to get me locked up for years. I paused and listened to the reassuring silence.

'Right,' I whispered. 'To work. Better get this stuff out of sight.' Like many people who've lived on their own, I had the habit of talking to myself. With a knife, I teased apart the flaps on the top of a box of dog biscuits. After pouring most of the contents into a carrier bag, I put the acid in the box, topped it up with biscuits and glued it shut. I turned the box upside-down and rested it on the hardback book I'd brought.

Doing deep breathing exercises to calm myself, I waited until the glue was dry. Cleaning up and scattering fallen leaves around the stash obliterated any traces of my visit. En route to the car, I chucked the surplus dog biscuits into a ditch. After a long, slow breakfast in a roadside café by Wallingford, where I read the *Guardian* from cover to cover, I took a very circuitous route to the meet, constantly checking my mirror and stopping at every lay-by to make sure I wasn't being followed.

I arrived in Wantage half an hour early, parked in a side street and walked towards the town square, newspaper clutched in my clammy hand. Anything could happen next. My antennae turned this way and that, straining to pick up any false notes, any indication that I might be walking into a trap. Crossing the square, I went into a teashop, ordered a coffee and cake and sat down at a window table with a view of the pub where we were to meet. I pretended to look at the crossword, while keeping an eye open for any unusual activity. The whole town seemed fast asleep. I randomly filled in one of the answers and had a bite of cake. I tried to swallow but my throat didn't seem to be working properly and my mouth was full of dry crumbs. I gulped some coffee to get rid of the cake, but only scalded myself. My choking fit drew the attention of the waitress and the old ladies taking tea. They'd remember me if anyone asked.

Russ appeared, dead on time. He parked outside the pub and went in. No one seemed the remotest bit interested in his arrival. I waited another five minutes. Nothing happened.

The town still looked quiet as I walked back to my car. I drove into the square, parked and went into the pub. Russ was on his own, sitting at a table. At his feet was a Sainsbury's carrier bag, just like mine. There wouldn't be any money stashed in his bag; this first batch was being laid on him. He'd pay me for them when I handed over the next consignment. The trips cost him sixteen pence each. My cut was a penny a tab. I stood to make four hundred quid for my morning's work. That was about three month's wages for an agricultural labourer.

'I was just starting to wonder where you'd got to,' Russ said as I joined him with my shandy and my shopping. 'Everything OK?'

'Sure. You?'

'Yeah, fine.' In spite of his words, Russ was full of little nervous movements. He was as keyed up as me, poised for instant flight. Adrenalin pumped through our systems. After some strained small talk we knocked back our drinks and went our separate ways. He had my shopping bag. I had his. No one grabbed us on the way out.

I didn't start shaking until I was clear of the town. The process of doing a handover, I now understood, was much more nerve-wracking than making tabs.

At our second handover, Russ's bag included a packet of Alpen, filled with tenners. I put the money in a sandwich box and buried it in the wood near my home in Farley Hill, ready to hand over to Brian the next time I saw him.

Reading Wholefoods was expanding steadily. Once Martin and I were confident that there was a sustained interest in our food, we looked for some cheap premises. For eight quid a week, we rented a space in The Emporium, an indoor market off Friar Street.

We fitted out our stall with shelves and hung up the beautiful Reading Wholefoods sign Martin had painted. Early on a spring morning of 1975, we brought in our stock, stacked the shelves and waited for our first customer.

We didn't do a lot on our opening day. The takings were £4.50. The following day they doubled and our turnover continued to grow and grow. After three months we annexed the adjoining stall, to have enough room for our expanding stock. By this time we were selling tons of our two top lines, wholemeal flour and our own muesli mix.

Though there was a growing interest in health foods and vegetarian diets, few people knew much about preparing meals that were both nutritious and tasty. Aiming to change that, we produced a 'Recipe of the day', which Martin chalked up on a blackboard in his copperplate script. It was an effective sales aid. We always sold plenty of the recipe ingredients.

No longer a dropout, I was working long hours at an honest trade. Martin and I had become the acceptable face of the alternative society in Reading.

Most weeks I'd spend one day picking up supplies. The rest of the time I was either in our storeroom, mixing muesli, packaging and weighing, or I was at The Emporium, selling and talking to our customers.

Our stall became a meeting place where people lingered and exchanged ideas and information. We started out as a marginal outfit but when doctors began recommending high-fibre diets we were instantly fashionable. It was becoming cool to be aware of your diet, eat natural food and recycle everything you could.

Wearing my shopkeeper's hat, I was a useful member of society who spent the working week providing a valuable service to the community. It was an excellent cover for my secret life. Every few weeks I flitted out to Caesar's Camp, dug up another forty thousand hits and handed them over to Russ.

In the autumn, Brian called me for a café meeting. Moments after my arrival, Henry bustled in, brisk and businesslike.

'Hi, Leaf. How are you doing?' He looked me straight in the eye while we shook hands. Then he got right down to it, in his bull-at-a-gate manner. 'We want to set up another supply line, one that goes straight to the continent.'

'What? You want me to go to Europe?'

'Hold on, hold on,' Brian held his hand up. 'Let's keep our voices down here. No, we don't want you to leave the country, just to do another handover, same as you do for Russ. You know the guy too. It's Eric.'

'You'll make twice as much money,' Henry added.

'And double the risk,' I replied. 'How cool is Eric these days?'

'He's fine, man,' Brian said. 'Come on, think we'd do business with him if he wasn't?'

'OK. Point taken.'

'And,' Brian continued, 'you won't have to handle any money. That goes by a different channel. What else? Oh, yes. Eric's acid comes in a new form – volcanoes. You'll like them.'

Eric and I had got on well from the days in the early seventies when I'd scored off him in London. Eric was a social animal and had always been good fun to spend time with. But now we didn't hang out together on our meets – a drink, a brief chat and then he was itching to get away, to hide what I'd given him.

All my life I've been fairly good at ignoring problems I don't want to think about. Usually they go away, but sometimes they loom over you and their shadow grows. In early 1976, my old friend Ursula was arrested with a thousand tabs of our acid. She'd scored them from someone way down the distribution chain, so I wasn't directly connected, but it felt very close to home. Ursula's bust, conviction and imprisonment shook me more than I wanted to admit.

Soon afterwards, I awoke in the middle of the night, standing on our bed, trembling, slick with sweat, sick with fear.

'What's the matter?' Mary asked sleepily.

'Nothing. Just a bad dream. Go to sleep.' I went to the kitchen and shakily made myself a cup of tea. The details of the nightmare were absolutely clear in my mind: I was sitting in an armchair in a prison television room, when the door burst open and the lights came on. I looked around to see what had caused the disturbance. In the doorway were three figures – a giant, flanked by two scrawny henchmen. The muscle-man in the centre wore a coalman's sleeveless leather jerkin, he had curly black hair and a thick black beard. I stared at him in sick fascination. Radiating evil, he looked around the room and his eyes met mine. He smiled, licked his lips and pointed straight at me. 'You,' he growled. 'I'll have you!'

Petrified, I escaped into wakefulness.

'It was only a dream,' I told myself, shivering as I sipped my tea. 'Everything's fine.' It wasn't. I didn't want to go back to sleep in case the appallingly vivid nightmare continued. Was this a premonition – a foretaste of what was in store for me? For days I couldn't get the nightmare out of my mind.

'What do you expect?' I kept telling myself, 'Ursula's bust made you worried. Your anxiety surfaced in sleep – that's normal enough. It was just a bad dream.'

I was talking to myself a lot these days. There wasn't anyone else I could confide in. My double life halved my integrity – and integrity's nothing if not whole. All this concealment was grinding me down.

Mary flew off across the pole again. I slunk back to my secret life and did what I could to make myself feel safer. To minimise my risks, I took seven hundred thousand trips from Brian and Henry – I wouldn't need to pick up from them for some time – and gave Russ and Eric fifty thousand a go – that reduced my handovers; I was only in danger of being caught tab-handed for a few hours a month. But business was growing and the interval between deliveries kept shrinking.

I figured it was time to change the location of my stash. Sooner or later I was bound to be clocked by an inquisitive local. Even the best caches have to be abandoned eventually; with use a hiding place develops a worn appearance, obvious to any curious person. I went searching again and found an excellent spot near Fleet, close to the M3.

Only four people knew what I was doing. I was sure of the caution and discretion of Henry, Brian and Russ. Eric the showman was another matter. I arrived at the pub for one handover to see a small crowd gathered around a vintage chocolate and cream Bentley in the car park.

Eric had a drink waiting for me at his table. I sat opposite him.

'Seen my new motor?' he purred.

'That's your Bentley?' I hissed. 'You must be fucking mad! Everyone here is going to remember your car. Some of them could probably describe the driver.'

'Hey, relax man.' Eric laughed at my twitchiness. 'I'm the owner of a fashionable cocktail bar, remember. I'm supposed to be a flamboyant, high-profile publicity-seeker.

The surest way for me to draw the wrong attention is to look furtive.'

I pushed the bag across to him with my feet, got up and left.

'Eric thinks it's cool to be uncool,' I told Brian at our next meet. I was shaking with the anger that sneaks in on the heels of fear. 'Listen, Brian. I'm only going to see him one more time. I'll show him my new pick-up point in the woods. Then he can drive down the motorway, stop at the Fleet services, take his dog for a walk and collect the acid. I'll be watching from cover to make sure everything goes OK.'

'Sounds like a good idea,' Brian said soothingly.

I made a collection point for Eric, in the same wood as my cache. Now I wouldn't have to transport the acid by car and run the risk of being involved in a traffic accident or being stopped by the police. And I'd only be in possession of the tabs for a few minutes – as long as it took me to dig them up, put them in the dog biscuit packet and transfer them to the large plastic sandwich box in his cache.

The ever-increasing demands of the health-food business meant I didn't have much time to brood on my fears. We'd just been given the opportunity of taking over a shop lease for nothing. We grabbed it and worked all hours to transfer our operation to 7, London Road and convert the premises to our requirements. With the shop came an office, a large storeroom and a flat.

After the move, Reading Wholefoods became even more of a social centre. The business blossomed. Along with our dried goods we started making and selling sesame snaps, flapjacks and slices of carrot cake. Soon we couldn't cope with the demand and were delighted when one of our customers offered to take over the home baking. Hilary's delicious bread, quiches, cakes and biscuits brought more and more people to the shop. Then she began to do sandwiches and veggieburgers. Her produce went so well we started thinking about opening Reading's first vegetarian restaurant with Hilary as chef. Martin and I agreed to look further into it when I got back from my honeymoon.

Mary and I had been talking about getting married for some time. The sun shone on our wedding in the early summer of 1976, one of the great days of my life. Normally I'm a joker, dressed in motley, but that day I got into a suit, a green suit with a snappy broad-brimmed hat. Mary looked wonderful in white. Martin was my best man.

My dad and Katie were there, as were my brother and my sisters. Mary's family came in force and lots of our friends too. I was having such a good time I didn't want to leave the reception, but we were spirited into a car and whisked off to Heathrow.

As an air stewardess, Mary was entitled to ten per cent standby flights. As her husband, so was I. We could go anywhere in the world for a few quid. We picked Kashmir; it was an inspired choice.

After our honeymoon in the Himalayas, we got a mortgage on a farmworker's cottage in Binfield Heath, between Reading and Henley. We acquired half a dozen chickens and a hive of bees and grew vegetables in the long strip of garden. In October we planted a walnut tree and started a small orchard with apples, pears and plums. Then we jetted off to Peru.

Mary had worked out her notice with BOAC; we had five weeks' cheap travel before her perks ended. When we got back, she was going to help out at Reading Wholefoods and I was going to quit my secret job.

From Lima we flew on to Cuzco, the old Inca capital high in the mountains. Sachsuaman, the fortress above the city, was made with blocks of dressed stone that weighed up to two hundred and fifty tons. The builders used no mortar; the stones simply fit together, like a three-dimensional jigsaw. I could hardly find a place to slide a cigarette paper between the giant blocks, so perfectly were they made. The unbelievable thing about Sachsuaman, and all the other extraordinary constructs in and around Cuzco, was that they had been built by the Quecha, a people who hadn't discovered the wheel.

Crossing Lake Titicaca, we landed in dirt-poor Bolivia and took the highest train ride in the world to its capital. La Paz sits in a bowl in the Altiplano, the high plain. The local people, stocky Indians with great barrel chests, live on the rim of the bowl, at fifteen thousand feet. There's barely enough air to breathe. The wealthy live right in the centre of the city, at the bottom of the bowl, where the the air is thickest. When it comes down to the nitty-gritty, there's only one thing more important in life than water, and that's air.

There were tanks and troops on the streets of La Paz. The air might have been thin but the atmosphere was heavy. Another general had taken over the government, the latest switch in the Bolivian game of presidential chairs. Every time the brassy music stops, someone has a coup. This one was led by General Hugo Banzer. It was the second time he'd seized power. The country had had almost two hundred different governments in its hundred and fifty years as an independent state. A café owner pointed out a curiosity: a lamp-post permanently guarded by two soldiers. A plaque explained that this was the impromptu gallows from which one of the country's many tyrants had been hung.

We left the city of tanks and headed back to Peru. On the return journey to the lake, the train broke down at midnight in the middle of the Altiplano. A guard eventually came round to say that another engine would be along in five hours. Mary and I walked away from the lights of the train, over a ridge and into the darkness. I spread a poncho on the ground. We lay down and looked up.

In the southern hemisphere, many of the stars are different. At fourteen thousand feet the air is very thin and in the moonless night, far from any city, those stars were shining with unparalleled brightness. I've never seen such a display, never had such a physical encounter with our galaxy as that night spent wrapped in a poncho, high in the Andes.

In the mountains, I'd felt my secret-life tension ebb away. A change of location is the simplest way to get a fresh perspective on your situation. I knew that I felt so wonderful because I wasn't playing my double game.

'What were you thinking, living under the sword of Damocles?' I asked myself. 'It's not as though you're working for the great breakthrough for the acid revolution.'

Why had the hippies' high hopes for a transformation of consciousness not been realised? I thought about this a lot in the Andes. I'd been a very green eighteen-year-old when I first took LSD and the experience had been overwhelming, transformational. The feedback from my new life was almost entirely positive, which reinforced my belief that I was on the right track. At the start, as the hippy movement grew and grew, everything seemed to be working out beautifully. But taking a drug that expands your consciousness doesn't, in itself, change your life. You come back to your everyday reality. You're changed because you've seen what life could be like, but after the drug wears off, you're back in your own consciousness again, in all its pettiness.

One minute you're astride the world, young lords and ladies of creation, able to see the very processes of life unfolding. Then you're in your clammy bedsit, wondering how you're going to pay the rent. A glimpse of heaven can be inspiring, but when it contrasts so strongly with your life it can also be dispiriting. And it's no good taking more mind-expanding stuff to lift you above the fray, because acid operates on the law of diminishing marginal utility: the more you take, the less it does.

Nearly all the benefit of psychedelics comes in the first few trips, after that it's mostly variations on a theme and underneath it all there's a nagging feeling that your life isn't measuring up to the marvellous visions you've had. And this is the crux: the chemicals can let you see the possibilities, but it's up to you to realise them. Transforming your consciousness is a demanding process that takes a lifetime of work. There are no short cuts to enlightenment.

We boarded a small plane and flew through a fearsome electrical storm to the upper reaches of the Amazon. I was met by the warm earthy smell of the jungle that I'd first encountered in Kuala Lumpur. Once smelt, never forgotten. At the decaying rubber town of Iquitos, two thousand miles from the ocean, the river is a mile wide. We battled our way upstream in a rusty steamboat and, for a week, hung out in a lodge perched between rainforest and river.

The jungle reverberated with the screeching of insects, parrots and monkeys. Buttressed trees, festooned with lianas, reached right up to the sky. We were constantly pointing out to each other fresh examples of the amazing variety of life-forms. Giant butterflies flapped languidly through small clearings. Insects crawled over everything, some of them as big as my hand.

In a small Indian village, where everyone was lounging around in hammocks, I acquired a seven-foot blowpipe from a stone-age man with a Beatle-mop haircut. He gave me a quiver full of darts and a piranha jaw for sharpening them. We had a training session where he showed me how to launch the darts with a lung-emptying cough. The weapon was deadly accurate over short distances. I played with the idea of lying in wait and sending darts into the plump buttocks of the fox hunters who occasionally careered through Binfield Heath – see how the jolly hunters like the sensation of being the quarry.

Sitting on the bank of the mighty river, I watched an iridescent butterfly, the size of a plate, set off for the other side, a mile away across the water. It started out with strong purposeful beats of its wings. I'd been like that butterfly, I thought. Brightly coloured, optimistic, ignorant of the length and the dangers of the journey, I'd tried to fly the stream of life.

Coming out of my reverie, I scanned the river for the

butterfly. It was gone from sight. The paranoia was the killer, I realised. My consciousness was diminished by all the negative energy that flowed from my illicit life.

I wondered where my psychedelic experiences would have taken me, if they'd occurred in a tribal society that regarded them as a valid undertaking. I'd never know, but I knew I didn't have to deal acid any more. I was living with a marvellous woman in a happy home. I had a satisfying means of earning a living with interesting challenges ahead. What more could I possibly want?

Back in the British winter, I called Brian and arranged a meet.

'I want to pull out,' I told him and Henry. 'I've been getting more and more wound up about it and it's time for me to stop.'

'I understand what you're saying.' Brian was sympathetic. 'I've been feeling the strain too.'

'We're all feeling it, for Christ's sake,' Henry put in, 'only we're sitting on a couple of million tabs. The distribution chain is working beautifully and if we stop it we may never get it moving so smoothly again. At the rate we're shifting them, those tabs will be gone in a few months and then we can stop. Surely we can keep our act together that long.'

I was persuaded to put off my retirement for a while.

Why do we do what we do? Mostly because of the momentum in our lives. Our decisions are influenced by the things we've done before and the loyalties we feel to those close to us. After the initial impulse which sets us on a course of action, we run on momentum. Normally we need a big jolt to make a major change of direction.

'You've never let yourself be ruled by your cowardice,' I told myself sternly. 'Don't start now.'

My renewed resolve lasted until the first time I had to visit the stash. It was awful. Each subsequent handover was worse. I battled with my loss of nerve until one frozen February morning. In the middle of gluing shut a box of dog biscuits, I heard a noise in the undergrowth and lost the ability to move. Helpless, crouching in the sour stench of my own fear, I waited for the bushes to burst apart and for hordes of uniformed men to pin me to the ground. Nothing happened. I was alone, save for my paranoia.

After this miserable experience, I spoke again to Brian and Henry about my state of mind. We were all feeling the strain and agreed to call a halt soon. In the meantime, we could halve the number of handovers by doubling the quantities: Russ and Eric would have a hundred thousand a time.

At the end of February, I took a break with my sister Judy. We didn't see a lot of each other, so it was great to have some time together. Reminiscing all the way, we drove to Germany for the christening of our brother Roger's daughter, the first of the next generation of Fieldings.

On the way home, racing to catch the ferry, Judy and I were hurtling down the autobahn at eighty miles an hour, going flat out in my Mini. It was five in the morning, still dark. I made out something in the distance that appeared to be sideways across the motorway. It was a juggernaut, I realised with horror. Immediately I braked and slid on a patch of ice, possibly the same one that had undone the truck. Totally out of control, we started spinning round and round, still travelling forwards. In a disconnected moment,

I remembered our mother had died in a car crash.

We juddered to a halt two feet short of the juggernaut, facing the way we'd come. I fumbled with my seat belt, stumbled out of the car, sank to my knees and threw up.

In March, Henry came down to Binfield Heath with a little over three hundred thousand trips, all that was left in one of his stashes. A road crew was digging up the road not far from my house.

'What are those workmen doing?' Henry asked, bristling with suspicion.

'Oh, they're fixing the drains or something.'

'Are they for real? What if they're a police surveillance team? Let's go and check them out. Can't be too cautious.'

We went to see what they were doing and to talk to them. They seemed OK. How could you tell?

I was in the middle of racking one of my demijohns of home-made wine when Eric rang. 'Hey, how's it going?'

'Fine. How are you?'

'Great. Hey, guess who I had in last night? Johnny Rotten. He was out of his brains, screaming his head off, ready to fight with anyone. Good publicity for the Last Resort though. Got to move with the times. We don't want to be stuck with an old hippy image…'

Eric rattled on a while. The simple fact that he'd rung meant he wanted to make his next pick-up the following day. I drove off to the M3, parked in my lay-by and walked into the woods. There were two hundred thousand volcanoes left. I took them all and split them between two boxes of dog biscuits. One I put in the lunchbox in his pick-up point. Some minutes later, Eric wandered by with his dog Sugar and collected his trips. When he'd gone I returned to his cache and stashed the other biscuit box in it. It saved me a bit of work. Next time I wouldn't have to handle any acid at all. I wouldn't have to do anything but observe Eric pick up his final batch.

The following day Russ rang to say he was recovering a broken-down car in High Wickham and asked if he could stay over. That meant he wanted to collect too. In the early morning I dug up and packaged the hundred and twelve thousand microdots that remained. I gave them to him before he left.

I rang Russ two days later. I'd just heard a very disturbing rumour. Llandewi Brefi, the small village where his principal customer lived, was supposed to be crawling with plain-clothes police. Not wanting to talk on the phone, I suggested Mary and I drive down to his home in Mid-Wales for the weekend.

'Great,' Russ said. 'I'll make one of my curries. We've got something to celebrate. I'll tell you when you get here.'

We packed a weekend bag, threw it in the back of the car and set off.

I woke with a start. The light of a torch lanced the darkness and settled on my face. I raised my hand to shield my eyes and was pinned to the bed by an octopus, hands everywhere.

'Got him!' a voice yelled triumphantly.

19　The Timex men

I ARRIVED AT LEYHILL open prison with sixteen months of my sentence to run. It could be as little as eight months with parole or as much as four years with total loss of remission. I was uncuffed, admitted into the nick, given my hut and cubicle number and told I could go. I stood by the door, waiting for a warder to unlock it.

'It's open,' the reception screw called out.

For an instant I didn't know what he meant. The only doors that I'd been able to open for the past four years were the half-doors of the toilets. I thought I'd kept myself together through the time in Horfield, but suddenly I saw how I'd been stunted by my confinement. The prisoner's mentality had stealthily covered me, like ivy creeping over a disused shed.

The screw must have watched this scene at the door many times.

'Hold on,' he said. 'Jones will take you up there in a moment.'

Jones, the reception orderly, was amiable and chatty.

'One of the Julie mob, aren't you? Heard you were on your way. First time in an open nick? It's different here. You'll like it once you get used to it. The grub's a lot better for a start. And there's a lot of opportunities in a place like this, if you know what I mean. Only you've got to be careful. Leyhill is full of grasses, see. Keep your business to yourself and you'll be all right.'

I was looking around, taking stock of the first new place I'd been in years.

'See those buildings…' Jones pointed off to the right, 'they're the workshops. That's the governor's office on the left. Straight ahead is the television room.'

As he said the words, three men appeared from behind the building. I saw that the central figure was the giant from my dream of five years before. He was flanked by two scrawny henchmen. It was unquestionably the same trio. The giant had black curly hair, a big black beard and was wearing a coalman's sleeveless leather jerkin. Every detail fitted. The three men from my nightmare waited for us outside the door of the television room. I forced my jelly legs to keep going. As we were passing, Goliath said hi.

He was addressing me. In total contrast to the dream, his voice was friendly.

'You're in the Julie mob, aren't you? Heard you were coming. I've been looking forward to meeting you. Look, I'm a bit busy now but I'd like to have a talk later.'

Unable to speak, I nodded and moved on. There was a swarm of bees inside my head. I had no idea what Jones was telling me as we walked up the corridor between the Nissen huts. I made it to my cubicle and lay down. A big hole had been punched in my reality. What was going on? There was no time to dwell on it because someone outside was saying, 'Hi, Leaf. Can I come in?'

I knew that voice, but couldn't immediately place it. 'Yeah, come in,' I called.

The curtain twitched open. It was Nick, from the poker school at Horfield.

'I thought you'd appreciate the snout,' he said ingratiatingly.

'What snout?'

'Under your pillow.'

I looked. There were three half ounces of Old Holborn.

'I brought you a couple of pots of yogurt as well. Haven't had yogurt for years, have you?'

My alarm system was functioning again. Though time had just run amok, I still had to sink or swim among my fellow cons. And Nick was a shark who had to be played carefully.

I thanked him for the tobacco and let him know that I wouldn't immediately press him for the rest of the debt. I wasn't letting him off, that would have been taken as a sign of weakness, neither was I backing him into a corner. Not prepared to eat food he'd given me, I returned the yogurt.

After Nick, I had a succession of visitors. The prison grapevine spreads news at the speed of sound. Dave Robertson, one of the acid dealers busted with us, dropped by for a chat. Men I'd known in Bristol called in to say hello and neighbours came to introduce themselves.

Dave and I met up again at supper, in the cons' canteen. Over a sumptuous meal of two fried eggs, lots of baked beans, a great mound of freshly made chips, strong tea, a piece of cake and a yogurt, I saw what the veggie diet should really be like. Dave started to fill me in on the advantages and pitfalls of the open-prison regime. Although I knew he was giving me valuable information, I couldn't pay much attention. I was fully occupied in looking around, weighing up all the new faces and looking for familiar ones, checking the exits. My eyes hadn't had so much to look at in years.

That night, in my cubicle, I replayed the events of this extraordinary day. There are certain key moments in life after which things can never be the same again. The death of my mother, my first LSD trip, my arrest... today was one of those life-changing days. It had now sunk in that I'd received a warning five years earlier. How was that possible? Gripping the sides of the fragile coracle of my mind, I was spinning round a whirlpool of questions.

What is time? It's not just a line from the past through the present to the future, apparently it can loop the loop. Is all time always now, as Eliot said? Or is nothing real, as Lennon had it? What is time? How can you see something five years before it happens?

The next day, the giant came to my table at lunchtime and introduced himself.

'Hi. I'm Danny Fellows. Nice to meet a real criminal. This place is full of crazy murderers, bent coppers and corrupt councillors.'

'Well, Danny,' I said, 'I think of myself as a political prisoner rather than a criminal, but there you go.' I stood, picked up my tray and left. I didn't have the helpless feeling I'd had in my nightmare, or on first sight of him in the flesh. It turned out I knew quite a few people in Leyhill and could call on plenty of friends if the need arose.

I later found out that Fellows was working as an informer for an investigation into police corruption called Operation

Countryman. Strangely, no policemen were ever charged as a result of Countryman, but many long-term prisoners were convicted of a number of unsolved crimes, thanks to the work of snitches such as my nightmare man.

On that second day at Leyhill, I very nearly blew it. Cons were counted several times a day and three times at night, to see if anyone had legged it. Exploring the further reaches of the grounds, smelling plants I'd forgotten all about, I didn't hear the roll-call bell and arrived late for the afternoon count. In the doorway of the Nissen hut, I came up behind a red-headed screw as he finished his tally. All the squares by the cubicle numbers on his clipboard had been ticked, except mine.

'Fielding. Number five,' I said, coming up behind him, pointing to the blank square. I walked to my cubicle and stood outside it, like all the other cons.

'You'd better apologise for being late, Fielding,' the screw rasped. 'And you call me sir. Got that?'

Dry-mouthed from the grass I'd been smoking, I remained silent.

'Did you hear me, Fielding?'

'Yes.'

The silence lengthened. Down at the far end of the hut someone began to laugh. Others joined in. The screw went brighter and brighter red. Abruptly, he spun on his heel and strode off. Cheers and jeers followed him.

'Fuck off, screw!'

'On your bike, Ginger.'

'Good for you, mate!'

A congratulatory crowd gathered around me. I was in.

All these tests we have to pass... Had I apologised or said 'sir' I would've been finished.

I was shaking in reaction to the incident. Confrontations leave me feeling weak and angry – a bad combination. What would this temporary popularity end up costing me? I'd publicly humiliated one of the warders. He had all the advantages if he wanted to get his own back.

Leyhill had been built during the Second World War as a field hospital for the Canadian army, with a life expectancy of three years. We were housed in crumbling forty-year-old Nissen huts. There were eight of them and each held forty-odd cons. It was very basic accommodation and if you didn't like it you could leave; Leyhill was an open prison, it didn't have a secure perimeter.

This was a difficult one to deal with. However stupid it would be to go on the run, it was insulting to be seen as tame enough to be trusted to keep yourself in prison. Keep yourself in prison? Something only an insane or broken man would do, surely.

Sometimes cons did a runner, almost invariably because there was trouble at home. Otherwise we stuck it out, knowing we were almost at the end of our sentences – as long as nothing went wrong.

But things could easily go wrong. There were plenty of opportunities to bring contraband into the prison or to slip away for a rendezvous. To men long deprived, these temptations were usually irresistible. The nick was awash with drugs and alcohol. Sex was available a couple of fields away if you could pay, or if your wife, girl or boyfriend would take the trouble to be there at a prearranged time.

A quarter of Leyhill's cons were lifers doing the last year or two of their stretch. The time they'd served was usually well into double figures. Some of them were fine, others were pretty fucked in the head. Few of them had either money or friends outside to help them. Purple and black currents of envy and jealousy coursed through Leyhill. Infringements of the rules abounded and so did informers. The atmosphere was poisonous.

Open prison was startlingly full of choices. There was a pottery where I spent some happy evenings throwing pots and remembering my time in Cornwall twelve years before. I was sent to work in the print shop, but managed to get away from the disgusting smell of ink by going on a six-month City and Guilds course in computer programming. For fun, I played cricket and tennis. With my inclusion, the Leyhill tennis team became a statistical freak: all four of us were left-handed Librans. The odds against that are over two hundred million to one.

Cricket was on everyone's lips that summer, 1981, the year Botham and Willis wrested the ashes from the Aussies. Fielding on the boundary, I heard most of Botham's epic innings in my opening match. Inspired, I found I hadn't forgotten how to use a bat, even though I hadn't played in years. I scored a few runs in that game and went straight into the Leyhill team.

After a six-week probationary period, cons were allowed to leave the open prison under approved circumstances. My first outing was for a cricket match, an away fixture at a village ground on a lovely summer's day. It was a kind of reintroduction to life.

I was patrolling the boundary at third man. The batsman flashed outside the off stump and got an edge. The ball sped past me and splashed into the stream. I went to fish it out. There were kingcups and watercress, dragonflies and nettles, greenfinches in the bushes. I got stung and wet, but I got the ball. The tingle of the nettle rash and the cheers of the crowd made me feel doubly alive. At lunch there was powerful beer for us in the pavilion. In the afternoon, when it was our innings, I didn't care for caution, but cheerfully flung the bat until I missed a straight delivery.

I joined the small group of cons who spent Sunday afternoons helping at the Home Farm Trust, a residential centre where mentally handicapped adults assisted with many of the simpler tasks of farming. There were professionals in charge of the home and the farm livestock. The job of the three or four visiting cons was to help with preparing and clearing food, and entertaining the residents. I spent my time washing up, playing ping-pong or having tea parties. Sometimes there were tantrums and salty tears, but mostly it was jelly and laughter, uncomplicated fun, a chance for us all to relax and play. It was hard having to put my armour back on before returning to the charged atmosphere of the nick.

Summer detumesced into autumn. It was time for my annual parole application. I thought about not making my third and final submission, but serving out my time without asking any favours from anyone. Of course I applied in the end. You can't ignore an opportunity of freedom.

~ ~ ~ ~ ~

I knew immediately from the tiny writing that it was
a letter from my dad. Letters never came easy to him.
Sometimes they only amounted to three or four lines. This
one he'd stretched to a page:

> *Hello boy,*
> *We're well, hope that you are too.*
> *I'm told that if I want to see you I must get you to*
> *issue me with a thing called a visiting order. Well, time's*
> *moving on and Roger tells me that you'll be back with us*
> *before too long, so I thought it would be a good time for*
> *me to come and see you – if you want to, that is.*
> *Fantastic apple harvest this year, but the soft fruit*
> *was a complete washout. Anyway I'll tell you all our*
> *news when you send me the visiting order.*
> *Much love*
> *Pa*

Amazing, that admission of doubt – if you want to, that
is. Unprecedented in our gruff relationship. How could he
think that I wouldn't want to see him? I'd always loved him
and I knew he loved me – even if we never said it, even in
the years when we infuriated each other beyond belief. I
sent him a visiting order straight away.

We cons were all sitting at tables when the visitors were
allowed in. I stood when I saw him and waved. He looked
smaller, ill at ease. I knew he must feel totally out of place
in the prison visiting room. He wouldn't take a seat at first
but held my hand, looked me in the eye and said, 'Well,
you've been a right bloody fool, haven't you?'

'I know. I have. Come on, Dad. Sit down. Thanks for
coming. Good to see you.'

'Your mother sends her best – said to make sure to visit us when you're – you know, when you're…'

'When I'm out. I will, Dad. Just a sec – let's have some tea here, Jacko,' I called to the visits orderly. 'So how's Susi?'

'Well, she's getting excited about seeing you. She doesn't understand the uncertainty about quite when that will be. Er, we haven't completely explained your circumstances to her. Do you know any more?'

'Not yet. It will either be four months or a year, depending on my parole result.'

'Well, I'm sure you're behaving yourself…'

I was about to assure him I was when I saw the twinkle in his eye.

'Oh, Dad, I can't tell you how good it is to see you.'

At the beginning of 1982, after my fifth Christmas in prison, it got cold and snowed and then carried on getting colder and colder. The big freeze took us in its giant grip and squeezed. The central heating fuel turned solid. Ice was inches thick on the inside of the ancient Nissen huts. I wore all of my clothes in bed and still couldn't stop shivering. The screws had gloves; we cons left layers of skin on any metal surface we touched. Small birds fell out of the trees and lay frozen on the ground. Vehicles were unable to negotiate the hill to the prison. We were cut off.

The kitchen continued to operate, churning out hot food that froze if you didn't immediately shovel it into your mouth. We were about to be evacuated by helicopter, so the rumour went, when the thaw arrived. With it came my parole envelope. I opened it with trembling fingers. At first I thought they'd muddled the paperwork, then I realised that the reason I didn't have the familiar short slip was because I hadn't been knocked back. I read the key sentence again and again. Parole granted. Parole granted. I reread the release date: the first of March.

The succeeding weeks slow-motioned by. February was the longest month in the history of the world. I held back, not allowing myself to think of my release as a given fact. I'd seen it all foul up for other people close to their date. So many things could cost you parole. An enemy might plant something in your cubicle and then grass you up, you could get into a fight, fall foul of a screw... a lot of things could go wrong.

The countdown of the days got into single figures. My jabbering excitement was threatening to break out, but every now and then I'd remember the red-headed screw I'd scored off at the start of my time in Leyhill and worry that he'd get his revenge at the last moment. Then I was smacked from behind and fell to my knees, unmanned by an acute spasm of fear at the enormity of being released. 'You won't be able to deal with it,' the panicking coward within me wailed. 'You've forgotten what it's like on the out. It'll all have changed anyway. You'll have to start everything all over again.'

Institutionalisation is the longest word many cons know. I was aware of the nature of the fears I was dealing with. I also knew I had a lot of back-up out in the world. I had a place to stay and a job: Reading Wholefoods was still going strong. 'You'll be all right,' I told my quivering self, 'you'll pick up the pace.'

I went to see my last movie. Next Sunday I'll be out,

I thought, then slapped myself for tempting fate. But I couldn't stop the thoughts rolling round my mind: last day in the prison workshops, last shower, last breakfast, lunch and tea, last roll-call, last night.

I didn't even try to sleep on that final night, but sat talking with a couple of friends until three. Then I lay, fully clothed on the bed, and savoured the moment. I caught myself having yet another internal conversation and laughed aloud. Imaginary dialogues are strewn along the erratic track of my life. Planning the moves ahead is a useful habit in prison when, at any moment, you may be called upon to justify or explain. Would I be able to leave off this verbal war-gaming after I walked out of the gate? Probably not. Dr Johnson said: 'The chains of habit are too weak to be felt until they're too strong to be broken.' What a man he was.

Every thought sequence shortened my remaining time by a few seconds or minutes. Now there were only a couple of hours to go. I'd done it. I'd swallowed one thousand, seven hundred and forty-eight prison hedgehogs and not only survived but grown strong.

At 5 a.m. I strode down the dark corridor to reception. I took off my convict's uniform and threw it on the floor. My old clothes were wrinkled and musty, but they still fitted and they felt good – they were mine, not prison issue. I emptied the property box of the oddments I'd had on me when I was busted, five years before: a little money, a watch with a mouldy strap and a wallet containing a driving licence and a photo of Mary that brought back a flood of memories and the pricking sensation in my eyes that used to herald tears. I didn't cry so easily now. I put the coins in my pocket. The weight of them, tugging my trousers down, felt odd yet so familiar. After signing for my gear, I joined the small group of Timex men on the bench opposite the wall clock.

We sat waiting for seven o'clock. The strained silence was interrupted by little sprays of nervous chatter and a few stifled laughs. None of us wanted to call down the wrath of the gods by saying anything too definitive. We waited for the vital phone call to come through, knowing that if anyone had escaped in the night, our release would be put on hold. The phone rang.

'Gatehouse. Yeah, OK. Right, got it.' The gate screw gently placed the phone in its cradle.

'All right lads, you can go,' he said.

We seven time-expired men got to our feet. We were all smiling now. All tension gone, we shook hands and walked out of the open gate.

Epilogue

ON A LOVELY MARCH morning in 1982, I zig-zagged roughly northwards through Somerset country lanes. There were clumps of daffodils on village greens. A passing spring shower threw a rainbow across the sky. I drove past Chew Magna and the Nortons, parked as close as I could to the knoll and walked to the stand of trees on the crest. Sunshine made the rain-wet leaves sparkle like diamonds. The light had a hallucinogenic clarity. So did my thoughts. I was free, charged with stored energies, imbued with a force only available to people who've survived long confinement. It was a wonderful sustained high. I had my life back and I would never take it for granted again. Never. Every moment is the time of my life.

'Here I am, at last,' I called out to the trees that had given me such solace in my Bristol cell. After a glance at the city on the northern skyline, I turned to face south and sat between two large roots. I closed my eyes and let the sun warm my face. An extraordinary opportunity had opened before me, I realised. Right now – at the tender age of thirty-three, I was beginning my life again.

Whatever happened to...?

I'VE LOST TRACK OF the friends I made in my wanderings. I've no idea where the Electric Eel is, or John Amati, Tyrrell and Myla, American Pete... Our paths crossed, we walked together a while and our ways parted. My old friends, I wish you all well.

My father and Katie died a few years ago. These days I have a closer relationship with my brother and sisters than at any time since childhood. We still share something special with the Ballards and we always will.

Mary married her childhood sweetheart, the boy next door. Of my friends, Dave Solomon and Billy Bolitho are dead. Jack set up an eco-energy business in Ireland, where he has been for nearly forty years. Rob and Duncan both live deep in the West Country. Viking John teaches and studies Buddhism in Thailand. Martin is a gardener in Oxfordshire.

Smiles grows organic vegetables in his rural retreat, Richard lives in Spain, Andy is looking after his mother in Ireland. I'm not in touch with any others in the Julie mob – not through any fallings out, it's just the drift of time.

I have changed some names. Scooter and Chip, for example, are a number of friends rolled into two for the simple purpose of concealing their identities.

After my release from prison, I travelled for a year in India, then retrained and worked for thirteen years as an English teacher in Barcelona. Following a trip to Malawi, my travelling companion and I determined to build a home for street children. After three years fundraising and building, we opened our home for orphaned girls in 2003. That's a long story which will be at the heart of the second part of my memoirs.

I now live with my partner Sue in the French Pyrenees where I am writing and selling organic food.

I did my best to write my story in the moment – how I felt at the time. Not easy, because as the sun moves across the sky of your life, the light changes. As my shadow began to lengthen, my perspective inevitably altered. Looking back, I can scarcely credit the psychedelic lightning strike that illuminated my existence as it vaporised my horizons. For years I was as careless with myself as I was with the acid that flowed through my hands and into the heads of others.

None of us can escape the past. We are responsible for everything we've done and the repercussions of our actions flow through the rest of our lives.

One of the consequences of the way I lived (the subordinate clause at the end of my long sentence) is that I still get prison dreams, one or two a month. I had another last night. Banged up again. No idea why... I woke sick at heart and filmed with sweat.

Reprieved, I flung back the damp sheet and thanked the sweet universe that I wasn't really locked up in a cell but safe at home, in bed with Sue.

Glossary of prison slang

(circa 1981)

A RICH ARGOT is in use in prison. The terms below are by no means exhaustive, merely a list of words that appear in the memoir.

Bang-up	Lock-up time
Banged up	Confined to cell
Bird/Porridge/Time	Prison sentence
The block	Punishment cells
Burglar	Security screw
Con	Prisoner
Do a runner	Escape
GBH	Grievous bodily harm
Hooch	Prison-brewed alcohol
Knockback	Refusal – of an application, a petition, parole…
Nick	Prison
Nit-o	Watch out!
Nonce	Sex offender
On the out	Outside prison, at liberty

Peter	Cell
A result	A positive reply
Screw	Warder
Slop out	Emptying of night waste
Snout	Tobacco
Stretch	Long prison sentence
Swooper	Collector of dog-ends
Weighed off	Sentenced

Acknowledgements

I WOULD LIKE TO THANK Pete Ayrton, Sam Humphreys, John Williams, Rebecca Gray, Penny Daniel, Ruthie Petrie, Ruth Killick, Niamh Murray, Tina Mories and all the wonderful team at Serpent's Tail. My grateful thanks also to my amazing agent, David Smith, and The Literary Consultancy: Becky Swift for her unflagging support, Alan Wilkinson for his trenchant comments and keen insight and Karl French for his valuable suggestions and encouragement.

Friends who have helped in one way or another with this book include Rosemary Bailey, Peter Ballard, Michelle Beresford, Christine Bott, Kat Brittenden, Hassanah Burton, Sarah Catliff, John and Ghyslaine Cloke, Judy Colman, Mark Cowling, Min Cowling, Dave and Pilar Dukes, Gill Farrer-Halls, Roger Fielding, Susi Fielding, Janet Hulse, Jane Jones, Richard Kemp, Lewe, Barry and Catherine Lovering, Jessie MacIver, Jane Jeanneteau, Barry Miles, Simon Pleasance, Andy Roberts, Johan Van

Rooyen, Norman and Kathy Sigrist, Smiles, Andy Stewart, Paul and Polly Timberlake, Dave Tomory, Keith and Glenys Weymer, Caroline Whittle, John Wickenden, Martin Wise, Mike and Karyn Willey, Fronza Woods and Geoff Young.

Special thanks to Carol Meaden, confectioner extraordinaire, who made the cake of the book.

Last and foremost, my heartfelt thanks to Sue Whatmough.